R E V I S E D & E X P A N D E D

FEATURES UPDATED EXCHANGE VALUES

CONVENIENCE FOOD FACTS

Help for Planning Quick, Healthy, and Convenient Meals

R E V I S E D & E X P A N D E D

FEATURES UPDATED EXCHANGE VALUES

CONVENIENCE FOOD FACTS

Help for Planning Quick, Healthy, and Convenient Meals

Arlene Monk, R.D., C.D.E.,
with introduction by
Marion J. Franz, R.D., M.S.

 DCI/CHRONIMED Publishing

International Diabetes Center
Park Nicollet Medical Foundation
5000 West 39th Street
Minneapolis, Minnesota 55416

Library of Congress Cataloging-in-Publication Data
Monk, Arlene.
    Convenience food facts : help for planning quick, healthy, and convenient meals / Arlene Monk : introduction by Marion J. Franz. — Rev. & expanded, 3rd ed.
        p.   cm. — (Wellness & nutrition library)
    ISBN 0-937721-77-8 : $10.95
    1. Food—Composition—Tables. 2. Convenience foods—Composition—Tables. 3. Brand name products—Composition—Tables. 4. Diabetes—Nutritional aspects. I. Title. II. Series.
TX551.M56   1991
641.1—dc20   91-40471
                                                                                CIP

Editor: Peggy Linrud
Cover and Text Design and Production: MacLean & Tuminelly
Cover Photography: Paul Lundquist
Production Manager: David Wexler
Printed in the United States of America

10 9 8 7 6 5 4 3 2 1

Published by:
DCI/CHRONIMED Publishing
PO Box 47945
Minneapolis, MN 55447-9727

Table of Contents

Acknowledgements

We would "conveniently" like to thank the following for adding to the "easy performance" in the writing and publishing of this book:

The **food companies**, who so willingly and quickly sent information on their food products.

A special thanks to **Jennifer Hadley**, who so willingly and capably assisted in collecting food company data.

The entire **International Diabetes Center staff** for its support, especially Helen Bowlin, administrator; Donnell D. Etzwiler, medical director; Mary Ann Roeder, who so capably typed the tables; and Peggy Linrud, editor.

The **production people** who made this book possible, including David Wexler and the staff at DCI; Nancy Tuminelly, art and production director at MacLean & Tuminelly; and Lana Harris, for accurately typesetting the tables.

And thanks to the readers and buyers of this book. Here's to quick, easy, and convenient-to-prepare meals that still contribute to good health!

Convenient Nutrition for Everyone

Convenience \kən-ˈven-yən(t)s\. Webster's Dictionary defines convenience as "being suited to personal comfort or to easy performance." In our busy, hustle-and-bustle society, "easy performance" and "personal comfort" are some things many of us are looking for, especially when it comes to food preparation. If we're not grabbing a bite at a fast-food restaurant, we're looking for a meal that is quick, easy, and "convenient" to prepare at home.

Convenience foods are the fastest growing processed food group for just that reason—they offer quick, easy to prepare, good tasting, and relatively inexpensive meals. But consumers are also interested in nutrition.

So how can you combine both—convenience and good nutrition? That's what this book is designed to help you do. By knowing what nutrients are in the foods you buy, you can plan a healthy diet which also offers the convenience you desire. *Convenience Food Facts* will give you this information.

Are you one of the 80 percent of consumers who read product labels when you shop for groceries? A survey by the National Food Processor Association, Washington DC, reported this percentage of shoppers read food labels and half of them, or 40 percent, reported being influenced by what they read. Although consumers may read and be influenced by what's on the label, many are not sure exactly what all the information means, and many are not sure how to use the information.

This book is designed to help you know what the information on labels means, but more importantly, how to use the information on labels, and how to make the best possible choice available to you.

What Information Is on Food Labels?

To assist in making food purchasing decisions, three types of information are found on food labels. First, and most useful is nutrition labeling. Currently nutrition labeling is not required on all food products, but in the very near future it will be required on nearly all food products.

Second is the ingredient listing. This is required for all Food and Drug Administration (FDA) regulated foods except for a few with a "standard of identity" (standardized ingredients). However, it is proposed that all foods, including FDA-standardized foods, be required to list ingredients.

The third type of information to look for on labels are label claims or health claims or messages. Some label claims, such as those related to sodium and calories, are well-defined and regulated, others such as "low fat," "high fiber," "high calcium," "light," and "natural" have no regulations covering their use. Health claims or messages have not been well regulated either, and a proposal on health messages is also being planned.

Who Regulates Information on Labels?

The overseeing of labeling of most foods is done through two agencies, the Food and Drug Administration (FDA) and the United States Department of Agriculture (USDA). Both have their own areas of supervision and labeling requirements.

The FDA regulates foods labels on the following foods: dairy products, fresh and processed seafood, fresh produce, and most other food products, including "processed foods." "Processed foods" means foods treated to extend shelf life, or to improve taste, nutrition, color, or texture. "Processing" can include adding preservatives, coloring or flavoring agents; fortifying foods; enriching foods; dehydrating, smoking, deboning, drying, freezing foods; and a number of other treatments. FDA labeling requirements are called "regulations." The FDA is proposing new labeling regulations that will go into effect during the 1990s.

USDA labeling requirements are called "policies." The USDA oversees the inspection and labeling of most meat products, most poultry products, and eggs. The USDA also oversees the grading for fresh and processed fruits and vegetables, eggs, dairy products, meat and poultry products, catsup, peanut butter, honey, and similar products. Examples of grade names are "Prime," "Choice," "Fancy," "No. 1," and "Grade A." The FDA does not grade products.

Sometimes both the USDA and the FDA will have a definition for similar terms, but the definitions may not be the same. Examples are their definitions for low fat, lean, and extra lean.

And to further confuse the issue, the Federal Trade Commission (FTC) regulates food advertising. It is their role to protect consumers from false and misleading advertising. However, often advertising claims are allowed that would not be allowed on labels. The Nutrition Advertising Coordination Act of 1991 has proposed that the FTC be required to adopt the FDA's rules and guidelines. This would mean that uniform standards would apply to health and nutrition claims in food advertising and labeling.

To Know What You Are Buying Use the Nutrition Labeling Information

A nutrition label regulated by the FDA has a standard format that includes:

- serving size
- servings per container
- calories per serving

- grams (g) protein, carbohydrate, and fat per serving
- milligrams (mg) of sodium per serving
- percentages of the US Recommended Daily Allowances (USRDA) per serving for these nutrients: protein, vitamin A, thiamine (B1), riboflavin (B2), niacin, calcium, and iron. (The USRDA is a list of amounts for the daily intakes of various nutrients)
- milligrams (mg) of cholesterol, grams (g) of saturated and unsaturated fats, grams (g) of dietary fiber are optional

The USDA allows a shortened nutrition label listing serving size, servings per container, calories per serving, and grams (g) of protein, carbohydrate, and fat per serving. Milligrams of sodium and percentages of the USRDA need not be listed.

A gram, incidentally, is a metric unit of weight. There are about 28 (often rounded up to 30) grams in one ounce. A teaspoon of most dry powders, such as salt or sugar, weighs about five grams. A milligram is also a metric unit of weight and is equal to one thousandth of a gram. For example, a teaspoon of salt is about five grams or 5,000 milligrams. Because salt is 40 percent sodium and 60 percent chloride, a teaspoon of salt contains about 2,300 milligrams of sodium.

A serving size is determined by the food manufacturer. It is to mean a reasonable quantity eaten by an adult. In addition, it should be listed in common units, such as ounces, teaspoons, cups, or slices. However, always check the serving size on the label against the amount you eat. You may find the nutrition information is based on a serving size different from your own, and frequently, it may be much smaller than the serving size you choose or wish to choose!

Calories

Most adults require about 1,800 to 2,400 calories per day for weight maintenance, or about 600 to 800 calories at each meal. Caloric values of convenience foods can help you decide on your portion size.

A weight control program that is nutritionally sound, as well as low in calories, should provide 1,200 to 1,500 calories per day, or 400 to 500 calories at each meal.

Knowing the number of calories per serving will help you decide if and how a product might fit into your meal plan. In the nutrition tables the first column next to the product name contains the portion sizes on which the nutritional information is based. The next column indicates the number of calories contained in that portion of the product.

Products	SERVING SIZE	CALORIES	CARBO-HYDRATE (gm)	PROTEIN (gm)	FAT (gm)	SAT. FAT (gm)	CHOLES-TEROL (mg)	SODIUM (mg)	EXCHANGES

Carbohydrate, Protein, and Fat

There are no specific recommendations for the number of grams of carbohydrate that should be eaten each day. It is generally recommended that about half or 50 to 60 percent of your calories be from carbohydrate food sources.

The 1989 Recommended Dietary Allowances of the National Research Council for protein is 63 grams per day for males after age 25 and 50 grams per day for females after the age of 25. During pregnancy, protein intake is to be increased by an additional 10 grams per day and during lactation, from 12 to 15 grams per day.

The National Cholesterol Education Program for Adults and for Children, the Dietary Guidelines for Americans, and the American Heart Association are three organizations that have recommended that Americans consume about 30 percent of their calories from fat.

In the nutrition tables to the right of the calorie column are three columns that list the carbohydrate, protein, and fat content in grams per serving size. Twenty one grams of protein for men and 17 grams for women per meal will supply one third of the day's requirements for protein.

The column listing grams of fat can help you judge the amount of fat in the product. To achieve the goal of 30 percent

of your calories from fat, on a weight maintenance intake of 1,800 to 2,400 calories, the amount of fat should be 60 to 80 grams per day or 20 to 28 grams of fat per meal. On a weight loss diet of 1,200 to 1,500 calories, it is about 40 to 50 grams of fat per day or about 14 to 18 grams of fat per meal.

Products	SERVING SIZE	CALORIES	CARBO-HYDRATE (gm)	PROTEIN (gm)	FAT (gm)	SAT. FAT (gm)	CHOLES-TEROL (mg)	SODIUM (mg)	EXCHANGES

Saturated Fat and Cholesterol

Although it is recommended that total fat intake during the day be about 30 percent of your calories, it is really the saturated fats that health professionals are the most concerned about. The saturated fats have the greatest effect on blood cholesterol level.

The column to the right of fat lists the saturated fat content of the food in grams per serving. It is recommended that saturated fat intake be limited to 10 percent of the calories per day—about 13 to 20 grams or about 5 to 7 grams per meal.

Dietary cholesterol is a secondary concern. The recommendation is to eat 300 milligrams or less per day of dietary or food cholesterol. The column to the right of the saturated fat content will provide information on cholesterol in milligrams per serving.

Products	SERVING SIZE	CALORIES	CARBO-HYDRATE (gm)	PROTEIN (gm)	FAT (gm)	SAT. FAT (gm)	CHOLES-TEROL (mg)	SODIUM (mg)	EXCHANGES

Sodium/Salt

Salt which is 40 percent sodium has been linked to high blood pressure (hypertension). The average American eats 30 to 60 times the 200 milligrams of sodium the body needs in a day. The American Heart Association's current recommendation is to limit sodium to about 3,000 milligrams (about one and a half teaspoons of salt). Persons with high blood pressure may see a better blood pressure response from a sodium intake of about 2,000 to 2,300 milligrams per day. You can see that when evaluating sodium content of foods in terms of milligrams, we are looking at relatively large numbers.

Sodium content in milligrams per serving is listed in the column second from the left. At one meal, sodium intake should not exceed 1,000 milligrams; people on sodium restricted diets should consume less than 700 milligrams per meal.

In addition, look for single servings of foods that have less than 400 milligrams of sodium or main meal entrees with less than 800 milligrams of sodium.

Products	SERVING SIZE	CALORIES	CARBO-HYDRATE (gm)	PROTEIN (gm)	FAT (gm)	SAT. FAT (gm)	CHOLES-TEROL (mg)	SODIUM (mg)	EXCHANGES

Exchanges

The column labeled "exchanges" is intended for individuals who use the exchange system of meal planning. This system was designed to take the guesswork and calorie counting out of meal planning. The exchanges are based on the grams of carbohydrate, protein, and fat, as well as the calories in a serving of food. (Later in the introduction we will show you how you can also use this information to determine exchanges).

This is a commonly used meal planning system for people who have diabetes as well as for people on weight loss or maintenance diets. To use this system you need an individualized meal plan that tells you how many servings (exchanges) you should select for meals or snacks. If you do not have a meal plan or do not know how to use the exchange system of meal planning, we encourage you to see a registered dietitian (a health professional with the letters RD after the name) who can help you. Ask your doctor for a referral.

Products	SERVING SIZE	CALORIES	CARBO-HYDRATE (gm)	PROTEIN (gm)	FAT (gm)	SAT. FAT (gm)	CHOLES-TEROL (mg)	SODIUM (mg)	EXCHANGES

Guidelines for Choosing Convenience

To summarize, look for meals that meet these guidelines:

Calories per meal for weight maintenance	**600 to 800**
Calories per meal for weight loss	**400 to 500**
Fat, grams per meal for weight maintenance	**20 to 28**
Fat, grams per meal for weight loss	**14 to 18**
Saturated fat, grams per meal	**5 to 7**
Cholesterol, milligrams per meal	**100**
Sodium, milligrams per meal	**less than 1,000**

In addition, look for frozen entrees or dinners with:

* about 300 calories per serving
* no more than 3 grams of fat per 100 calories
* less than 800 milligrams of sodium
* less than 100 milligrams of cholesterol

To Know What You Are Buying Look at the Ingredient Listing

The ingredient listing will provide the information to tell you what the main ingredients are in a food product. Ingredients must be listed in descending order by weight. For example, when the amount of each ingredient is weighed, the ingredient that weighs the most is listed first. The ingredient that weighs the least is listed last. However, ingredients that make up two percent or less of a food are listed at the end of the ingredient listing in no particular order.

If a fat or sugar is listed first on a label it is a main ingredient of the food. Currently you may see several ingredients that are sweeteners, and similar to sugar, listed throughout the ingredient listing. If all these sweeteners were grouped together they may well have been the first ingredient listed on the label. (Incidentally, the FDA's proposed regulations recommend that the term "sweeteners" be used on the ingredient listing and all the sweeteners in the food be listed in descending order by weight in parenthesis after the term "sweeteners").

If you see a sugar or a caloric sweetener as the first ingredient, evaluate carefully the use of this food. However, also look at the number of ingredients. If there are only three or four ingredients, such as with some cereals, even though sugar or a caloric sweetener is the second ingredient there may not be much of it in the product. (Less than five grams of sugar or sweetener would be considered small and an acceptable amount).

Ingredient listing is required for all FDA- and USDA-regulated foods, except for FDA-regulated foods that have a "standard of identity," or food standard. These are categories of foods that must contain specified ingredients. There are about 300 foods whose ingredients are fixed by law. An example of an FDA standard of identity is catsup, which must contain tomato liquid or tomato concentrate and at least one ingredient from each of these categories: vinegars, calorie-containing sweeteners, spices, flavorings, onions or garlic. Other examples of foods with standardized ingredients are canned fruit cocktail, peanut butter, margarine, ice cream, frozen breaded shrimp, and spaghetti sauce with meat. The USDA, however, requires an ingredient listing even for products with a standard of identity. Because consumers and health care professionals have expressed concern about these exceptions to ingredient listing, the FDA in their new regulations is proposing that all foods, including FDA-standardized foods, be required to list ingredients.

Regulations for Claims Found on Labels

Two types of claims are found on labels. The first type is usually descriptive in nature and relates to a specific nutrient or food component, a claim such as "low sodium," "no sugar," or "low calorie." Some of these terms are well regulated and some are not. Some are regulated by the FDA and some by the USDA. Some are facing proposed new regulations, and some will probably continue to not be regulated at all.

The FDA has recently become concerned about health claims or messages on labels that can be misleading to the public. It is proposed that health claims be based on scientific evidence. Claims would be considered in the following areas: calcium, fiber, sodium, and fat. Specific messages for claims would be written by the United States Public Health Service and would be the only health claims allowed on packages.

Calorie Information on Labels

Calories are a unit that measures energy. Calories come from four sources: carbohydrate, protein, fat, and alcohol. When nutrition information is listed on packaged foods, calories are listed for one serving. The following list shows the calorie value for each source of energy:

1 gram of carbohydrate (either sugars or starches)	= 4 calories
1 gram of protein	= 4 calories
1 gram of fat	= 9 calories
1 gram of alcohol	= 7 calories

The following example shows how to determine the calorie value of a food product. One granola bar may have 16 grams of carbohydrate, 3 grams of protein, and 4 grams of fat.

Carbohydrate: 16 grams x 4 calories per gram = 64 calories from carbohydrate

Protein: 3 grams x 4 calories per gram = 12 calories from protein

Fat: 4 grams x 9 calories per gram = 36 calories from fat

1 granola bar = 64 + 12 + 36 = 112 calories

Calorie Food Labeling Terms

Several terms are well regulated:

Low Calorie. (FDA regulation and USDA policy) Products with no more than 40 calories per serving and no more than 0.4 calorie per gram may be labeled "low calorie," "low in calories," or "low-calorie food." Foods that are naturally low in calories, such as celery, may be labeled as "[name of food], a low-calorie food." However, foods naturally low in calories cannot be labeled "low calorie" immediately before the name of the food. This would suggest the food has been changed to lower its calories with respect to similar foods.

Reduced Calorie. (FDA regulation) These are products containing at least one-third fewer calories than the one they are replacing. The label must have a statement that describes the comparison. These products may be labeled "reduced calorie," "reduced in calories," or "a reduced-calorie food."

Other terms are not well regulated, or may be regulated by the USDA but not by the FDA, and as a result may be confusing or misleading to consumers:

Diet, Dietetic. These are products that have at least one ingredient changed or restricted. It may have fewer calories or less salt, sugar, or fat. It is necessary to check the label to see which ingredient has been changed. If the product states or implies that the food is useful in maintaining or reducing calorie intake or body weight, it must meet the same requirements as "low calorie" or "reduced calorie" foods. This does not mean they will be low in calories, just lower than the regular products. If the product is not a reduced-calorie food, it must carry this additional statement: "This food is not a reduced-calorie food." For example, some "dietetic" candy bars may have less sugar but more fat and calories than a regular candy bar. The label must carry the additional statement.

Lite, Light, Lightly. (USDA policy) These terms usually suggest that a product has fewer calories than a similar product. However, they can also mean that a product has less fat, salt, sodium, breading, or other ingredients than a similar product. According to USDA policy, a reduction of 25 percent is usually enough for manufacturers to use this term. If these terms are used on a product label, the term must be explained, unless the product is unquestionably low in calories, salt, breading, or sodium. The explanation must show a comparison to the government standards, to similar products on the market, or to the average analysis of similar products.

The FDA, however, has no **regulations** related to these terms. It can mean lighter in color, flavor, or reduced in salt, sugar, or calories. But the FDA does have a **policy** for these terms. It states that unless the meaning of the term is obvious (such as "light brown sugar") or is spelled out (such as "light in color"), "light" means "reduced calorie." The FDA considers "lightly salted" a reduced-sodium claim. The FDA is in the process of preparing a definition for "light" and "lite."

Fat Information on Labels

In regard to fat, consumers should look at two important points when reading food labels: the type of fat and the amount of fat. Both play a role in blood cholesterol levels.

There are three types of dietary fat: monounsaturated, polyunsaturated, and saturated. Fats high in saturated fatty acids usually remain solid at room temperature. They include animal fats, such as butter, chicken fat, beef fat, and lard. Tropical oils—palm, palm kernel, and coconut—also contain high amounts of saturated fatty acids. Sometimes monounsaturated and polyunsaturated fats are chemically changed to raise the amount of saturation. This process is called hydrogenation. Examples are solid vegetable shortening, some margarines, and commercially baked products prepared with hydrogenated fats. Saturated fats increase blood cholesterol levels more than anything else you eat—even more than dietary cholesterol.

Eating more unsaturated (monounsaturated and polyunsaturated) and less saturated fat seems to lower blood cholesterol levels. Fats with mostly monounsaturated and polyunsaturated fatty acids are usually liquid at room temperature. Olive, peanut, and canola oils are examples of monounsaturated fat. Examples of oils higher in polyunsaturated fat are corn, safflower, soybean, cottonseed, sunflower, and sesame oil.

The National Cholesterol Education Program recommends limiting total fat to an average of 30 percent of total calories and saturated fats to less than 10 percent of total calories. To convert 30 percent of calories to grams of fat, multiply the calories by 30 percent (0.30). Then divide the answer by 9. For example:

1,500 calories x 0.30 = 450 calories in fat per day

450 divided by 9 calories per gram = 50 grams of fat

Another useful guide is to determine the percent of calories from fat. To convert grams of fat to percentage of calories, multiply the grams of fat by 9. Then divide the answer by the calories. For example, a product contains 4 grams of fat and 112 calories in one serving:

4 grams of fat x 9 = 36 calories from fat per serving

36 divided by 112, the total calories per serving =
32 percent of the calories from fat per serving

Fat Food Labeling Terms

Fat and/or Oil Ingredients. These ingredients are usually listed by their specific common or usual name (for example, beef fat, cottonseed oil) in descending order by weight. An FDA regulation states that fat "and/or" oil ingredients must be listed if the fat is sometimes changed in an FDA product.

Low Fat. (FDA regulation) This applies to milk and milk products that have had some degree of milk-fat removed. A "lowfat" milk, yogurt, or cottage cheese must contain one of the following milk-fat contents by weight: 0.5, 1.0, 1.5, or 2.0 percent.

Leaner, Lower Fat, Less Fat. (USDA policy) These are comparative terms about lean or fat content of meat or poultry products that may be used if there is at least a 25 percent reduction in fat or an increase in lean content in a suitable comparison. An explanation for the claim and the comparison must be included on the label.

Low Fat, Lean, Extra Lean. (USDA policy) Meat or poultry products (except ground beef and hamburger) labeled "low fat" or "lean" contain no more than 10 percent fat by weight; if labeled "extra lean" they contain no more than five percent fat by weight. The actual amount of fat in the product must be shown and the products are not allowed to become "lean" by the addition of water or extenders unless they meet the criteria for "lean" before processing.

The terms "lean" or "extra lean" may be used on ground beef or hamburger that contains no more than 22.5 percent fat by weight. (This is a 25 percent reduction in fat from the regulatory standard of 30 percent fat).

___**Percent Fat Free.** (USDA policy) This description is based on the percent of fat by total weight of the product including water. For example, a processed meat may be labeled "95 percent fat free," but still have 35 percent of its calories from fat. Because the "percent fat-free" statements are based on the percentage of fat by total weight, not calories, the consumer may be confused. (A consumer is unable to determine the "percent fat free" based on label information).

Cholesterol Information on Labels

Cholesterol is a fat-like substance found in body cells of humans and animals. However, unlike fats, cholesterol does not supply energy or calories. Instead the body uses cholesterol to form hormones and cell membranes. The liver and other body cells can make cholesterol, and the foods we eat also supply cholesterol.

Dietary cholesterol is found only in foods of animal origin, such as meat, poultry, seafood, eggs, and fat containing dairy products. It is not found in plant foods or oils.

Blood cholesterol increases over time when foods high in saturated fat are eaten. Excessive calories also tend to increase blood cholesterol. Dietary cholesterol has less effect on raising blood cholesterol levels than saturated fat. Guidelines from the National Cholesterol Education Program recommend that for healthy people over the age of two the daily intake of dietary cholesterol be less than 300 milligrams. Food labels list cholesterol in milligrams per serving.

If manufacturers make claims about cholesterol they must list nutrition information and the amount of cholesterol per serving.

Cholesterol Food Labeling Terms

The FDA has proposed four cholesterol terms to be used on food labels:

Cholesterol Free or No Cholesterol. This proposed FDA regulation would allow these terms on foods that contain fewer than two milligrams of cholesterol per serving. In addition, the food must also contain no more than five grams of fat per serving and no more than two grams of saturated fat per serving to be so labeled. ·

Low Cholesterol. This proposed regulation would allow foods with 20 milligrams or less of cholesterol per serving to use this term. However, these foods must also meet the total fat and saturated fat per serving requirements of "no-cholesterol" or "cholesterol-free" products.

___**Percent Less Cholesterol.** This proposed regulation would allow foods reduced in cholesterol by at least 25 percent to carry the label "___percent less cholesterol than ___." The label must also show the percentage of reduction and to what it is compared. The amount of cholesterol per serving before and after the change must also be shown.

Reduced Cholesterol. This proposed FDA regulation would allow foods containing at least 75 percent less cholesterol per serving than the original product to use this term. The label would show the amounts of cholesterol in milligrams per serving in the original and in the improved products.

Sodium Information on Labels

Sodium is a mineral needed by the body to maintain body fluids and to keep nerves functioning. However, in some persons excess sodium may contribute to high blood pressure, a risk factor for heart disease. High blood pressure affects almost 58 million Americans. Reducing sodium intake also helps to lessen side effects from certain medications.

Sodium is found naturally in foods and is also often added during food processing. Dietary sodium is measured in milligrams. This is the amount seen on food labels. Table salt, the most common form of sodium, is about 40 percent sodium.

Some sodium is necessary for the body to function. But the average person in the United States consumes far more than needed—about 11 grams of 11,000 milligrams of salt (two teaspoons) or about 4,600 milligrams of sodium per day. Americans get about 10 percent of their sodium from the natural sodium content of food. An additional 15 percent comes from salt added during cooking and at the table. The final 75 percent comes from sodium added during processing and manufacturing.

Sodium Food Labeling Terms

The FDA and USDA require listing of sodium in milligrams per serving when a claim appears about the sodium or about the salt content of a product. However, if nutrition information is provided on a product, sodium is also included (except in the USDA abbreviated nutrition information).

There are a variety of terms on food labels that describe sodium content. The following are terms regulated by the FDA or USDA:

Sodium Free. These are products that contain fewer than five milligrams of sodium per serving.

Very Low Sodium. (FDA regulation, USDA policy) These are products that contain no more than 35 milligrams of sodium in a serving.

Low Sodium. (FDA regulation, USDA policy) These are products that contain no more than 140 milligrams of sodium in a serving.

Reduced Sodium. (FDA regulation, USDA policy) The sodium in a food product has been reduced by at least 75 percent. The product label must also include a comparison to the original product.

Unsalted, No Salt Added, Without Added Salt, Low Salt. (FDA regulation, USDA policy) Any of these terms may be used on foods processed without salt that usually are processed with salt. Since salt is not the only ingredient that contains sodium, a food that is low in salt is not necessarily low in sodium. The food could still contain significant levels of sodium, either naturally or from substances added for preservation, leavening, palatability, or other purposes.

Fiber Information on Labels

Dietary fiber is a form of complex carbohydrate found in plants that cannot be digested by humans. Because it cannot be absorbed it has no calories. Dietary fiber supplies bulk in the diet and gives a feeling of fullness.

There are two forms of dietary fiber: insoluble and soluble. Insoluble fibers, such as wheat bran, whole grains, and seeds, keep bowels regular and prevent constipation. Soluble fibers, such as that found in oats, barley, dried beans and legumes, rye, some fruits and vegetables, may help to lower blood cholesterol levels.

The average American now eats 10 to 15 grams of fiber per day. However, an intake of 20 to 35 grams of fiber a day is often recommended.

When the amount of fiber is listed on the food label, it is listed in grams per serving. "Dietary fiber" includes both soluble and insoluble fibers, unless they are listed separately. Grams of fiber, although included in the total grams of carbohydrate, are not included in the calorie count because the fiber does not provide calories.

Listing grams of fiber per serving is now voluntary. New FDA proposals would require the amount of dietary fiber in grams per serving on nutrition information labels. The amount of soluble and insoluble fiber in grams per serving could be listed voluntarily by the manufacturer.

Claims about soluble and insoluble fiber would require listing amounts of total dietary fiber, soluble fiber, and insoluble fiber in grams per serving. Health claims about fiber would be considered. However, claims must be based on scientific evidence.

Fiber Food Labeling Terms

There are no FDA regulations or USDA policies for fiber labeling terms. The FDA is considering new standards based on a daily recommendation of 25 grams of fiber. The following proposals were made based on this recommendation. It is not yet decided what the daily fiber recommendation will be or if the proposed changes will take effect.

Source of dietary fiber. These are foods that contain 10 percent of the daily recommendation or 2.5 grams of dietary fiber.

Good source of dietary fiber. These are foods that contain 25 percent of the daily recommendation or 6 grams of dietary fiber.

Excellent source of dietary fiber. These are foods that contain 40 percent of the daily recommendation or 10 grams of dietary fiber.

Sugar and Sweetener Information on Labels

Sugar is a simple carbohydrate that provides four calories per gram or about 16 calories per teaspoon. Examples of sugars include corn syrup, high fructose corn syrup, fructose, dextrose, honey, and fruit juice concentrates.

Sugar terminology can be confusing because there are so many kinds of sugars. Terms such as "sugar free," "reduced sugar," and " no sugar added" do not tell you how much sugar, if any, is in a food product. Some sugars are easily recognized by their "ose" endings, such as glucose, dextrose, fructose, maltose, lactose, or sucrose (common table sugar). There are also sugar alcohols, such as sorbitol, mannitol or xylitol, that have about the same number of calories as table sugar. Many products for people with diabetes contain fructose or sugar alcohols as sweeteners because they appear to have a lower blood glucose response after being consumed, compared to other sugars. Generally, sugar alcohols are less sweet than other sugars, so a larger amount is required for the same degree of sweetness. Fructose may be an exception, as fructose in some products has a greater sweetening power so less may be needed.

Artificial sweeteners are calorie free or are used in such small quantities that their caloric content is very low. Examples are saccharin; aspartame, which you may know by the brand name Equal® or NutraSweet®; acesulfame K, also known by brand names Sunette™ or Sweet One™; or sucralose, which is marketed as SPLENDA® Brand Sweetener. Alitame and cyclamates are also up for approval. Before any of these sweeteners are approved for market they must meet rigorous guidelines from the FDA and have undergone years of safety testing.

Food products labeled "sugar free," "sugarless," and "no sugar" may still be sweetened with a sugar alcohol, hydrogenated starch hydrolysates (HSH), or fruit juice concentrates. These products may contain the same amount of calories as products sweetened with other forms of sugar. Labels on these products must include a disclaimer, such as "not for weight control" or "not non-caloric."

It is the position of the American Diabetes Association that the terms "sugar free," "sugarless," "no sugar added," "no sugar," "made without sugar," or "unsweetened" are confusing to consumers and can be misleading. They should not be used for foods that contain 1) any added caloric sweetener (for example, sucrose, dextrose, fructose, lactose, maltose, honey, corn syrup, molasses, fruit juices or fruit juice concentrate), or 2) a sugar alcohol (for example, mannitol, sorbitol, or hydrogenated starch hydrolysate) unless the food also meets the FDA's definition of low or reduced calorie.

The ingredient listing on food labels will list which sugar (for example, dextrose, fructose, honey) or artificial sweeteners are in a product. Sugar is included as part of the carbohydrate content on the nutrition label.

The FDA's new regulations propose that 1) manufacturers voluntarily list sugar content in grams per serving; 2) if a claim about sugar appears on a label, the listing of sugar in grams per serving be required; 3) manufacturers voluntarily list sugar alcohols; and 4) if a claim about sugar appears on a product containing sugar alcohols, the total sugar content in grams per serving be listed. Also, a listing of the amounts of sugar alcohols in grams per serving would be required.

Sugar Food Labeling Terms

Low In Sugar. There is no FDA regulation for this term. It is necessary to study the product label carefully to understand its meaning. It does not always mean "low in calories."

No Sugar Added, No Added Sugar. These terms usually describe a product sweetened with a naturally occurring sweetener such as raisins, dates, or fruit juices. Products sweetened with fruit, fruit juices, or sugar may all have similar calorie counts.

Sugar Free, Sugarless, No Sugar. (FDA regulation) This is a low-calorie food or one reduced in calories. If the product is not low calorie or reduced in calories, its label must state that the food is useful for a purpose other than weight control. For example, a "dietetic" candy bar may be labeled "sugar free" but because it is sweetened with sorbitol, it is not lower in calories. Therefore, the label must also state it is not a low calorie food.

Food Additive Information on Labels

Today the list of food additives has grown to over 3,000 substances, but sugar, salt, and vinegar—the first common food additives, continue to head the list.

A food additive is a substance that becomes part of a food product when added directly (intentionally) or indirectly (incidentally) during production or processing. These additives are present at very low levels in the finished food. They are added intentionally to maintain or improve nutritional quality, to maintain freshness, to help process or prepare food, or to make food more appealing. Examples of intentional additives are vitamins, minerals, flavorings, colorings, antioxidants (such as BHA and BHT) used to preserve freshness, sweeteners, and emulsifiers. Intentional additives account for only one percent of the weight of the foods we eat, and incidental additives account for even less. Examples of incidental additives are drugs used in livestock production and processing aids.

Most additives are safe in the amounts usually consumed by humans. Some substances found to be harmful to animals or people may be allowed at levels of 1/100 of the amount thought to be harmful. This margin of safety protects the consumers by greatly limiting the quantity consumed. However, other good advice to remember is that by eating a variety of foods you also avoid eating too much of a certain additive.

Some people have allergic reactions—from mild to severe—to some food additives. Such individuals need to read labels carefully.

The FDA and USDA each regulate the use of additives in products they regulate. On a food label, food and color additives must be listed in the ingredient listing in order of predominance. A special rule exists for ingredients that make up two percent or less of an FDA regulated product. They may be grouped at the end of the ingredient listing in no particular order. FDA standardized products may not have a full ingredient listing; therefore, additives may not be listed.

Food Additive Food Labeling Terms

Natural. (USDA policy) The USDA policy for the term "natural" generally means a product has no artificial flavor, coloring ingredient, chemical preservative, or any other artificial or synthetic ingredient. In addition, ingredients cannot be more than minimally processed.

The FDA, however, has no regulation for the term "natural." Manufacturers may use the term on FDA labels without a legal definition. Therefore, "natural" often means anything the manufacturer wishes it to mean.

No Preservatives. (USDA definition) This term can be used only on USDA foods that would be expected to contain preservatives, but do not. This label cannot be used on foods that normally do not contain preservatives. "No preservatives" does not mean "no food additives."

There is no FDA definition for "no preservatives." It may be used on FDA products, but has no special meaning.

Organic. This term has no legal meaning and can be used without any guidelines. The USDA, however, does not allow its use on meat or poultry products.

Enriched or Fortified. These products contain added vitamins, minerals, or protein. The label must include full nutritional disclosure; "per serving" amounts of nutrients must be given.

Imitation. These products are nutritionally inferior—that is, lower in protein, vitamins, or minerals—to the standard product. Foods that are lower in calories, fat, or cholesterol are the exception; they are not considered imitation.

What Changes in Labeling Can You Expect to See in the Future?

In 1990, Congress passed and the President signed into law landmark legislation entitled the Nutrition Labeling Education Act of 1990. This legislation mandates major reforms in all FDA-regulated food and nutrition labeling. These new policies are to be presented to consumers in 1993. The reforms are intended to provide consumers with accurate and useful information about the foods we eat.

Although nutrition information is currently required by the FDA only if nutrients are added to foods or if a claim is made, many food companies provide labeling. In the new regulations, the FDA is proposing that nutrition information be required on most foods regulated by the FDA. Exceptions would be spices, restaurant foods, and foods prepared in retail stores.

Today fresh meats, poultry, seafood, fruits, and vegetables are not required to carry nutrition information. However, the new FDA regulations would require that nutrition information for fresh fruits and vegetables and fresh fish and shellfish be provided. This could be on a shelf, in booklets placed nearby, on cards, tear-off pads, posters, brochures, or other materials and would not necessarily be on individual packages.

It is also proposed that the amount of saturated fat, fiber, cholesterol, and calories from total fat be required on nutrition information labels. The listing of thiamine, riboflavin, and niacin would be optional. It has been suggested that carbohydrate be divided into grams of sugars and grams of starches. However, because most food tables today do not have this information available this probably will not be required.

Health care professionals and the public have been concerned about the inconsistencies in serving sizes, so it is proposed that serving sizes of FDA regulated foods be standardized for 159 food categories. This would make serving size information uniform and, hopefully, reasonable for foods in these categories.

Nutrition information is also required by the USDA on the food products it regulates if a nutrition claim or a dietary guideline appears on the label. An interesting exception relates to the "percent fat-free" claim. The USDA does not require nutrition information on these products. However, concern about "fat-free" claims or descriptions has also been expressed. Many companies describe fat content by weight, a common method for meat, rather than by percentage of calories from fat. For instance, a lean type of meat might be described as "96 percent fat-free" by weight, but 28 percent of its calories are from fat. Incidentally, this is still an excellent choice. Companies could still advertise the merits of their products by the low percentage of calories from fat, rather than trying to mislead the consumer into thinking the product is almost fat free.

The U.S. Recommended Daily Allowances (USRDA), which are what FDA percentages are based on, are also being updated. They are to reflect the National Academy of Sciences latest Recommended Dietary Allowances.

Alternative nutrition label formats will also be tested. Below you see examples of a present label and a proposed form for labels.

To be omitted	-	To be added	+
PRESENT LABEL		PROPOSED LABEL	
Nutrition information		Nutrition information	
Serving size	1/4 pizza	Serving size	1/4 pizza
Servings per		Servings per Container	4
Container	4	Calories	240
Calories	240	Calories from fat	63 +
Protein	9g	Protein	9g
Carbohydrate	35g	Carbohydrate	35g
Fat	7g	Dietary Fiber	2g +
Sodium	640mg	Fat	7g
		Saturated Fat	4g +
Percent of U.S. Recommended		Cholesterol	15mg +
Daily Allowances		Sodium	640mg
Protein	20 -		
Vitamin A	15	Percent of U.S. Recommended	
Thiamine	8 -	Daily Allowances	
Riboflavin	10 -	Vitamin A	15
Niacin	10 -	Vitamin C	8
Vitamin C	8	Calcium	10
Calcium	10		
Iron	6		

How To Use Nutritional Labeling To Determine Exchanges

Nutritional labeling is especially valuable if you use the exchange system for meal planning. If you understand the basis for grouping foods into exchange lists, you can effectively use the information on product labels. Each exchange list is comprised of a group of foods in amounts that contain approximately the same number of calories and grams of carbohydrate, protein, and fat per serving.

Amounts of Nutrients in Food Exchanges

Exchange	Calories	Carbohydrate	Protein	Fat
1 starch/bread	80	15 gm	3 gm	trace
1 lean meat	55	—	7 gm	3 gm
1 medium-fat meat	75	—	7 gm	5 gm
1 high-fat meat	100	—	7 gm	8 gm
1 vegetable	25	5 gm	2 gm	—
1 fruit	60	15 gm	—	—
1 milk (skim)	90	12 gm	8 gm	trace
1 fat	45	—	—	5 gm

By looking at the nutritional information on the label, you can estimate how many exchanges are in a serving of food. This will help you decide if and how you can include it in your meal plan. Exchange conversions have already been done for all of the convenience foods in the tables starting on page 36. But for other foods, you can use the food exchanges table and example to convert information from a label to the exchange system. Pay particular attention to the grams of carbohydrate, protein, and fat, although the grams do not need to be exactly equal to the grams listed for the exchange lists. In most meal plans, variations of a few calories or grams of protein, carbohydrate, or fat are not significant.

Steps For Converting
Nutritional Labeling to Exchanges

The following label is from a 10-ounce box of frozen pizza.

Nutritional Information Per Serving

Serving size ....1/2 pizza (5 oz)
Servings per container 2
Calories 350
Protein..17 gm
Carbohydrate ....33 gm
Fat ....16 gm

To make it easier to convert label information to the exchange system, follow these steps:

1. Check the label for the information you need to convert to the exchange system. You need:

Serving size ....1/2 pizza (5 oz)
Calories 350
Protein...17 gm
Carbohydrate...33 gm
Fat...16 gm

2. Check the serving size. Is this a reasonable size for your use?

3. Compare the label information with the carbohydrate, protein, fat, and calories on the exchange table. First, look at the amount and source of carbohydrate in the food product. In this case, you'll be converting the carbohydrate to starch/bread exchanges. Note in the exchange table that 15 gm of carbohydrate and 3 gm of protein equal 1 starch/bread exchange. This means that the 30 gm of carbohydrate plus 6 gm of the protein in your pizza serving equal 2 starch/bread exchanges.

	Carbohydrate	Protein	Fat
1/2 pizza	33 gm	17 gm	16 gm
2 starch/bread exchanges	30 gm	6 gm	—

4. Next, subtract the grams of protein you used in figuring the starch/bread exchanges from the total amount of protein in the serving size. Then convert the remaining grams of protein to meat exchanges. Use the medium-fat meat exchange values from the exchange table.

	Carbohydrate	Protein	Fat
1/2 pizza	33 gm	17 gm	16 gm
2 starch/bread exchanges	30 gm	- 6 gm	—
		11 gm	16gm
2 medium-fat meat exchanges		14gm	10gm

5. Next, subtract the grams of fat in the meat exchanges from the fat contained in the serving size. Then convert the remaining grams of fat to fat exchanges.

	Carbohydrate	Protein	Fat
1/2 pizza	33 gm	17 gm	16 gm
2 starch/bread exchanges	30 gm	- 6 gm	—
		11 gm	16gm
2 medium-fat meat exchanges		14gm	- 10gm
			6 gm
1 fat exchange			5 gm

6. If you eat half of this 10-ounce pizza, you use the following exchanges from your meal plan:

2 starch/bread, 2 medium fat meat, 1 fat

7. Final check:

	Carbohydrate	Protein	Fat	Calories
1/2 pizza	33 gm	17 gm	16 gm	350
Exchanges:				
2 starch/bread	30 gm	6 gm		160
2 medium-fat meat		+14 gm	10 gm	150
1 fat			+5 gm	45
	30 gm	20 gm	15 gm	355

8. If the difference between the grams per serving and the grams accounted for by the exchange system is less than half of an exchange, you do not need to count those extra grams.

How To Use the Convenience Foods Nutrition Tables

The nutrition information contained in the tables was solicited and received in 1991 from a wide variety of food processing companies. The convenience food products are grouped according to major food categories that represent the way you would most likely use the product. Within each food category, brand names are in alphabetical order, with the parent company shown in parentheses after the brand name. Products are then listed alphabetically under the brand name.

In the tables themselves, each product is listed in a suggested serving size along with the number of calories and grams of carbohydrate, protein, fat and saturated fat. Milligrams of cholesterol and sodium per serving are listed next.

The exchange value column is for people who use the exchange system of meal planning and is based on the 1986 revision of the exchange lists.(See table page 30). Product formulations will change from time to time. It is a good idea to check the information in the tables with current data on food labels. The nutrition information on the actual product label will be the most current. The exchanges listed are only suggested exchanges. You may decide to use the calories and grams of carbohydrate, protein, and fat as other exchanges. Exchange values are largely a matter of personal preference, used for fitting foods into most meal plans as conveniently as possible. You may find that many of the foods in the tables do not fit into your meal plan. They may contain too many calories or be too high in fat. As a result, the exchange values may be greater than the number of exchanges you have available in your meal plan. Because of this, not all of the food items in the tables are recommended for your use. Check YOUR allowance.

Foods listed with a † have a moderate amount of sugar (between one teaspoon to one tablespoon per serving) and foods with a ** have more than one tablespoon of sugar per serving. This information is intended for people who have diabetes, but it may be useful to anyone who wants to cut back on the amount of sucrose in the diet. For people with diabetes, foods with a † are recommended for occasional use. Foods marked ** do not have suggested exchange values listed because of the higher sugar content. A 🛒 symbol in the left margin is another indicator that a product contains more than one teaspoon of sugar per serving. A 🗎 symbol in the left margin indicates that the product contains more than two fat exchanges per serving. You may want to limit products which contain large amounts of fat.

This information will help you fit convenience foods into a nutritious, well-balanced diet. You cannot rely on these foods for all your meals, just as you cannot rely on any single type of food. It is true that the best consumer is an informed consumer, and we hope you will also act on this information to meet the nutrition goals that can mean a healthier life. And best of all, you can enjoy added variety and flexibility in the planning of your meals and snacks.

To a convenient, but health-enhancing lifestyle!

Marion J. Franz MS, RD, CDE
Nutrition and Publications
International Diabetes Center

Convenience Food Nutrition Tables

Products	SERVING SIZE	CALORIES	CARBO-HYDRATE (gm)

APPETIZERS AND DIPS

BANQUET® HOT BITES® (ConAgra® Frozen Foods Co.)

Mozzarella Cheese Nuggets	¼ pkg. (2.63 oz.)	240	16

CHUN KING® (ConAGra® Frozen Foods Co.)

Chicken Egg Rolls	2 rolls (3.6 oz.)	220	32
Meat & Shrimp Egg Rolls	2 rolls (3.6 oz.)	220	31
Pork Egg Rolls, restaurant style	2 rolls (3 oz.)	180	23
Shrimp Egg Rolls	2 rolls (3.6 oz.)	200	31

DIPS

BLUE BUNNY® (Wells' Dairy Inc.)

Onion Snack Dip, lite, all varieties (average)	1 oz.	30	2

FRITO-LAY'S® (Frito-Lay, Inc.)

Cheese Dips	1 oz.	45	3
Jalapeno Bean Dip	1 oz.	30	4
Onion Dip	1 oz.	60	3
Picante Sauce	1 oz.	10	3

HAIN® (PET, Inc.)

Dips, canned Bean, all varieties (average)	¼ cup	65	10
Taco	¼ cup	25	5
Salsa, all varieties (average)	¼ cup	22	4

KRAFT® (Kraft, Inc.)

Premium Dips, all varieties (average)	2 Tbsp. (1 oz.)	45	2
Other Dips, all varieties (average)	2 Tbsp. (1 oz.)	55	3

PROTEIN (gm)	FAT (gm)	SAT. FAT (gm)	CHOLES-TEROL (mg)	SODIUM (mg)	EXCHANGES
14	13	—	—	530	1 starch, 1½ meat, 1 fat
5	8	—	—	600	2 starch, 1½ fat
6	8	—	—	680	2 starch, 1½ fat
6	6	—	—	450	1½ starch, 1 fat
4	6	—	—	480	2 starch, 1 fat
2	2	—	—	50	½ fat
1	3	—	5	310	1 fat
1	1	—	0	180	1 vegetable
1	5	—	10	270	1 fat
0	0	—	0	160	Free
4	1	—	5	250-270	1 starch
1	1	—	5	350	1 vegetable
1	0	—	0	410-480	1 vegetable
1	4	2-3	10-20	125-250	1 fat
1	4	2-3	0-30	160-240	1 fat

* Not available　　▤ More than 2 fat exchanges　　🛒 Moderate to high sugar content

Products	SERVING SIZE	CALORIES	CARBO-HYDRATE (gm)
LAND O'LAKES® (Land O'Lakes)			
Dips, flavored (average)	¼ cup (2 oz.)	80	4
Lean Cream™ Dip, all varieties (average)	1 Tbsp.	20	2
RESER® (Reser's Fine Foods, Inc.)			
Lite Dips			
Clam	2 Tbsp. (1 oz.)	20	2
French Onion	2 Tbsp. (1 oz.)	20	2
Ranch	2 Tbsp. (1 oz.)	40	2
Regular Dips			
Clam	2 Tbsp. (1 oz.)	97	2
French Onion	2 Tbsp. (1 oz.)	89	2
Vegetable Ranch	2 Tbsp. (1 oz.)	93	2

BEANS/BEAN COMBINATIONS

B & M® (PET, Inc.)

Baked Beans

Baked Pea	8 oz.	270	50
Barbeque	8 oz.	280	56
Honey	8 oz.	240	50
Hot N Spicy	8 oz.	240	50
Maple	8 oz.	240	52
Red Kidney	8 oz.	240	48
Small Red	8 oz.	223	36
Tomato	8 oz.	230	48

† For occasional use   ** Not recommended for use

PROTEIN (gm)	FAT (gm)	SAT. FAT (gm)	CHOLES- TEROL (mg)	SODIUM (mg)	EXCHANGES
2	6	—	—	280	1 veg., 1 fat
1	1	—	—	82-117	Free
1	2	—	<5	110	Free
<1	2	—	<1	140	Free
<1	4	—	<5	130	1 fat
1	10	—	6	104	2 fat
<1	9	—	4	17	2 fat
1	9	—	6	117	2 fat
14	6	—	5	750	2½ starch, 1 meat
13	4	—	5	850	3 starch, ½ meat
15	2	—	0	940	2½ starch, 1 lean meat
14	3	1	3	990	2½ starch, 1 lean meat
14	2	1	<5	890	2½ starch, 1 lean meat
12	4	—	5	680	2½ starch, 1 lean meat
9	5	1	5	725	2 starch, 1 lean meat
12	3	1	1	1010	2½ starch, 1 lean meat

* Not available   ▯ More than 2 fat exchanges   🛒 Moderate to high sugar content

Products	SERVING SIZE	CALORIES	CARBO-HYDRATE (gm)
Vegetarian	8 oz.	280	50
Yellow Eyed	8 oz.	326	50
CAMPBELL'S® (Campbell Soup Co.)			
Barbecue Beans	7⅞ oz.	210	43
Home Style Beans	8 oz.	230	48
Old Fashioned Beans in Molasses & Brown Sugar Sauce	8 oz.	230	49
Pork and Beans in Tomato Sauce	8 oz.	190	43
Ranchero Beans	7 ¾ oz.	180	36
HEALTH VALLEY® (Health Valley Foods)			
Boston Baked Beans, fat free	7½ oz.	190	41
Vegetarian Beans with Miso	7½ oz.	180	38
LIPTON® (Thomas J. Lipton, Inc.)			
Beans and Sauce, all varieties (as prepared) (average)	½ cup	126	27
OLD EL PASO® (PET, Inc.)			
Garbanzo	½ cup	90	16
Pinto	½ cup	100	19
Refried Beans, all varieties (average)	½ cup	110	16
Vegetarian Refried Beans	½ cup	140	30
S & W® (S & W Fine Foods, Inc.)			
Baked Beans	½ cup	160	28
Chili Beans	½ cup	130	23
Kidney Beans, dark red	½ cup	120	22
Kidney Beans, "Lite" (50% less salt)	½ cup	120	22
Pork 'N Beans	½ cup	130	22

† For occasional use   ** Not recommended for use

PROTEIN (gm)	FAT (gm)	SAT. FAT (gm)	CHOLES- TEROL (mg)	SODIUM (mg)	EXCHANGES
15	2	—	0	750	3 starch, 1 lean meat
15	7	—	4	770	3 starch, 1 lean meat, ½ fat
10	4	—	—	900	2½ starch, ½ lean meat
11	4	—	—	900	2½ starch, ½ lean meat
11	3	—	—	730	2½ starch, ½ lean meat
9	3	—	—	730	2½ starch
9	4	—	—	860	2 starch, ½ lean meat
8	0	—	—	290	2½ starch
8	1	—	—	60	2 starch, ½ lean meat
6	1	—	—	408-567	1½ starch
5	<1	—	—	250	1 starch
6	0	0	0	320	1 starch, ½ lean meat
6	<1	—	1	380-530	1 starch, ½ lean meat
12	2	—	0	1180	1 starch, 1 lean meat
7	2	—	—	560	2 starch
7	1	—	—	520	1½ starch
6	1	—	—	596	1½ starch
7	1	—	—	355	1½ starch
5	2	—	—	135	1½ starch

* Not available   ▤ More than 2 fat exchanges   🛒 Moderate to high sugar content

Products	SERVING SIZE	CALORIES	CARBO-HYDRATE (gm)
VAN CAMP'S® (Quaker Oats Co.)			
Baked Beans, all varieties (average)	1 cup	270	55
Beanee Weenee®	1 cup	330	32
Butter Beans	1 cup	160	30
Kidney Beans, all varieties (average)	1 cup	180	35
Pork and Beans	1 cup	220	41
Vegetarian Style Beans	1 cup	210	42

BEVERAGES

Author's Note: Some of these products contain large amounts of sugars and fats. If you decide to use them occasionally, make them part of your meal plan and use them with a meal or before exercise.

COFFEE, TEA

	SERVING SIZE	CALORIES	CARBO-HYDRATE (gm)
INTERNATIONAL COFFEES® (General Foods Corp.)			
🛒 International Coffees, all flavors (average)	6 oz.	50	8
Sugar Free International Coffees, all flavors (average)	6 oz.	30	3
LIPTON® (Thomas J. Lipton, Inc.)			
🛒 Canned Tea, lemon flavored (average)	8½ oz.	96	24
Canned Tea, lemon flavored, sugar free	8 oz.	2	0
🛒 Chilled Tea, lemon flavored, pre sweetened	8 oz.	83	20
Chilled Tea, lemon flavored, sugar free	8 oz.	0	0
🛒 Iced Tea Mix, lemon flavored, all varieties (average)	6 oz.	55	14

PROTEIN (gm)	FAT (gm)	SAT. FAT (gm)	CHOLES-TEROL (mg)	SODIUM (mg)	EXCHANGES
12	4	—	—	640-1020	3 starch, 1 lean meat
15	15	5	15	990	2 starch, 1½ high fat meat, ½ fat
11	1	—	—	710	1½ starch, 1 lean meat
12	1	—	—	830-940	1½ starch, 1 lean meat
11	2	1	0	1000	2 starch, 1 lean meat
11	1	—	—	950	2 starch, 1 lean meat
0	2	—	0	15-110	½ fruit, ½ fat†
0	2	—	0	15-80	½ fat
2	0	—	—	20	**
0	0	—	—	25	Free
0	0	—	—	11	**
0	0	—	—	10	Free
0	0	—	—	1	**

* Not available   ▤ More than 2 fat exchanges   🛒 Moderate to high sugar content

Products	SERVING SIZE	CALORIES	CARBO-HYDRATE (gm)
Iced Tea Mix, with Nutrasweet, all varieties (as prepared)	8 oz.	5	1
Iced Tea Mix, sugar free, all varieties (as prepared)	8 oz.	1	0
Instant Tea, regular or lemon flavored, all varieties	8 oz.	2	0

NON ALCOHOLIC BEERS
CARLING BLACK LABEL® (Heilman Brewing Co.)

Non Alcoholic Malt Beverage	12 oz.	60	13

KINGSBURY® (Heilman Brewing Co.)

Non Alcoholic Malt Beverage	12 oz.	60	13

SHARP'S (Miller Brewing Co.)

Non Alcoholic Brew Premium Malt Beverage	12 oz.	74	16

BREAD, BREAD PRODUCTS

BISCUITS
1869® (The Pillsbury Co.)

Baking Powder or Buttermilk Biscuits	2	200	24

BALLARD® (The Pillsbury Co.)

Oven Ready® Biscuits	2	100	20

HUNGRY JACK® (The Pillsbury Co.)

Biscuits, all varieties except Extra Rich Buttermilk (average)	2	175	24
Extra Rich Buttermilk Biscuits	2	100	18

PILLSBURY® (The Pillsbury Co.)

Big Country® Biscuits, all varieties (average)	1	100	14
Buttermilk, Country and Butter Biscuits (average)	2	100	20
Good 'N Buttery Fluffy	2	180	22

† For occasional use   ** Not recommended for use

PROTEIN (gm)	FAT (gm)	SAT. FAT (gm)	CHOLES-TEROL (mg)	SODIUM (mg)	EXCHANGES
0	0	0	0	2	Free
0	0	0	0	5	Free
0	0	0	0	0	Free
1	0	—	—	27	1 starch
1	0	—	—	5	1 starch
<1	0	—	—	3	1 starch
4	10	1	0	600	1½ starch, 2 fat
2	2	0	0	360	1 starch, ½ fat
4	8	1	0	560-600	1½ starch, 1 fat
2	2	1	0	340	1 starch, ½ fat
2	4	1	0	320	1 starch, ½ fat
2	2	0	0	360	1 starch, ½ fat
2	10	2	0	540	1½ starch, 1½ fat

Products	SERVING SIZE	CALORIES	CARBO-HYDRATE (gm)
Heat 'n Eat Buttermilk Biscuits	2	170	27
Heat 'n Eat Big Premium Biscuits	1	140	16
ROBIN HOOD® (General Mills, Inc.)			
Biscuit Mix (as prepared)	⅛ mix	90	14

BREADS, DINNER ROLLS
PEPPERIDGE FARM® (Campbell Soup Co.)

Products	SERVING SIZE	CALORIES	CARBO-HYDRATE (gm)
Bread, verithin sliced, all varieties (average)	2 slices	70	13
Brown and Serve Rolls			
Club Enriched	1 roll	100	20
French Enriched (3/pkg)	½ roll	120	24
French Enriched (2/pkg)	½ roll	180	36
Hearty Enriched	2 rolls	100	20
Croissants			
All Butter	1	240	25
Petite All Butter	1	140	14
Dinner Rolls			
Dinner Enriched	1	60	10
Finger Rolls, all varieties (average)	1	60	9
Old Fashioned	1	50	7
Parker House	1	60	9
Party	3	90	15
English Muffins			
Cinnamon Apple	1	140	27
Cinnamon Chip	1	160	28
Cinnamon Raisin	1	150	28
Plain	1	140	27
Sourdough	1	140	27
Stone Ground Wheat	1	130	26
Fancy Rolls			
Butter Crescents	1 roll	110	13
Golden Twist	1 roll	110	13

PROTEIN (gm)	FAT (gm)	SAT. FAT (gm)	CHOLES- TEROL (mg)	SODIUM (mg)	EXCHANGES
4	5	1	0	530	1½ starch, 1 fat
3	8	3	0	305	1 starch, 1½ fat
2	3	1	0	270	1 starch, ½ fat
3	1	—	—	150-180	1 starch
3	1	—	—	200	1 starch
4	1	—	—	250	1½ starch
6	2	—	—	400	2 starch
4	2	—	—	200	1 starch
4	14	—	—	290	1½ starch, 2½ fat
3	8	—	—	160	1 starch, 1½ fat
2	2	—	—	90	½ starch, ½ fat
2	2	—	—	80-90	½ starch, ½ fat
1	2	—	—	90	½ starch, ½ fat
2	1	—	—	80	1 starch
3	3	—	—	150	1 starch, ½ fat
4	1	—	—	190	2 starch
4	3	—	—	210	2 starch
5	2	—	—	180	2 starch
5	1	—	—	200	2 starch
5	1	—	—	240	2 starch
5	1	—	—	190	1½ starch
2	6	—	—	150	1 starch, 1 fat
2	6	—	—	150	1 starch, 1 fat

* Not available   ▉ More than 2 fat exchanges   ♛ Moderate to high sugar content

Products	SERVING SIZE	CALORIES	CARBO-HYDRATE (gm)
Five Star Fibre Breads			
Apple Spice Swirl	1 slice	70	11
Harvest Wheat	1 slice	70	10
Orchard Fruit & Nut	1 slice	70	11
White	1 slice	60	9
Hard Rolls			
French Style (9/pkg)	1 roll	110	20
French Style (4/pkg)	½ roll	120	22
Sourdough French Style	1 roll	100	19
Party Breads			
Dijon Slices	4 slices	70	12
Pumpernickel Slice	4 slices	70	12
Rye Slices	4 slices	60	12
Sandwich Rolls			
Dijon Frankfurter Rolls	1	130	23
Frankfurter Rolls	1	140	23
Hamburger Buns	1	130	22
Onion Sandwich Buns with Poppy Seeds	1	150	26
Sandwich Buns with Sesame Seeds	1	160	28
Soft Family Rolls	1	110	18
PILLSBURY® (The Pillsbury Co.)			
Butterflake Rolls	1	140	20
Cornbread Twists	1	70	8
Crescent Rolls	2	200	22
Crusty French Loaf	one 1" slice	60	11
Hot Roll Mix (as prepared)	1 roll	120	21
Pipin' Hot® Loaf	one 1" slice	80	13
Soft Bread Sticks	1	100	17
SARA LEE® (Kitchens of Sara Lee)			
Bagels, all varieties (average)	1	190	38

PROTEIN (gm)	FAT (gm)	SAT. FAT (gm)	CHOLES-TEROL (mg)	SODIUM (mg)	EXCHANGES
3	2	—	—	110	1 starch
3	2	—	—	120	1 starch
3	2	—	—	105	1 starch
2	2	—	—	125	½ starch, ½ fat
4	1	—	—	230	1½ strach
4	2	—	—	250	1½ starch
4	1	—	—	240	1 starch
3	1	—	—	170	1 starch
2	1	—	—	180	1 starch
2	1	—	—	280	1 starch
6	3	—	—	230	1½ starch, ½ fat
5	3	—	—	320	1½ starch, ½ fat
4	2	—	—	240	1½ starch
5	3	—	—	260	2 starch
5	3	—	—	220	2 starch
3	2	—	—	200	1 starch, ½ fat
3	5	2	5	520	1 starch, 1 fat
2	4	1	5	140	½ starch, ½ fat
4	12	4	10	460	1½ starch, 2 fat
2	1	0	0	120	1 starch
4	2	—	—	215	1½ starch
2	2	<1	0	170	1 starch
3	2	<1	0	230	1 starch, ½ fat
8	1	—	—	230-460	2½ starch

* Not available　　**⊟** More than 2 fat exchanges　　🛒 Moderate to high sugar content

Products	SERVING SIZE	CALORIES	CARBO-HYDRATE (gm)
Croissants			
Butter Original	1 (1½ oz.)	170	19
Butter Petite	1 (1 oz.)	120	13

BREAD AND CRACKER CRUMBS
KEEBLER® (Keebler Co.)

Graham Crumbs	1 cup	520	90
Zesta Meal	1 cup	370	61

KELLOGG'S® (Kellogg Co.)

Corn Flake Crumbs	⅓ cup (1 oz.)	110	25

PROGRESSO® (PET, Inc.)

Bread Crumbs, all varieties (average)	3 Tbsp.	90	17

MUFFINS, CORNBREAD
AUNT JEMIMA® (Quaker Oats Co.)

Easy Mix Corn Bread (as prepared)	⅙ recipe	210	34

BALLARD® (The Pillsbury Co.)

Corn Bread Mix (as prepared)	⅛ recipe	140	26

BETTY CROCKER® (General Mills, Inc.)

Light Muffin Mix: Wild Blueberry (as prepared, standard recipe)	1 muffin	70	16
Muffin Mix: Banana Nut, Wild Blueberry, Apple Cinnamon (as prepared) (average)	1 muffin	120	18
Muffin Mix: Carrot Nut, Chocolate Chip, Oatmeal Raisin, Strawberry Crown (as prepared) (average)	1 muffin	150	22
Muffin Mix: Oat Bran, Streusel Varieties (as prepared) (average)	1 muffin	200	27

PROTEIN (gm)	FAT (gm)	SAT. FAT (gm)	CHOLES-TEROL (mg)	SODIUM (mg)	EXCHANGES
4	9	—	—	240	1 starch, 2 fat
3	6	—	—	160	1 starch, 1 fat
8	14	—	0	630	6 starch, 1 fat
8	10	2	0	100	4 starch, 1 fat
2	0	—	—	278	1½ starch
3	0	—	0	165-480	1 starch
4	7	1	—	600	2 starch, 1 fat
3	3	—	—	570	1½ starch, ½ fat
1	<1	—	20	140	1 starch
2	4	1	25	140-150	1 starch, 1 fat
3	5	1	25	125-180	1½ starch, 1 fat
3	8	2	35	240	1½ starch, 1½ fat

* Not available   ᗺ More than 2 fat exchanges   ☕ Moderate to high sugar content

Products	SERVING SIZE	CALORIES	CARBO-HYDRATE (gm)
DUNCAN HINES® (Proctor & Gamble)			
Muffin Mixes (as prepared)			
Bakery Style, all varieties (average)	1 muffin	200	30
Hearty Style, all varieties (average)	1 muffin	210	30
Regular (Blueberry, Oat Bran Blueberry, Oat Bran Honey) (average)	1 muffin	120	18
ESTEE® (Estee Corporation)			
Oat Bran Muffin Mix (as prepared)	1 muffin	100	15
FLAKO® (Quaker Oats Co.)			
Corn Muffin Mix (as prepared)	1 muffin	120	20
HAIN® (PET, Inc.)			
Oat Bran Muffin Mix, all varieties (as prepared) (average)	1 muffin	140	27
HEALTHY CHOICE® Breakfast (ConAgra® Frozen Foods Co.)			
Blueberry Muffins	1 muffin	190	39
HEALTH VALLEY® (Health Valley Foods, Inc.)			
Fat Free Fruit Muffins, all varieties (average)	1	135	30
Oat Bran Fancy Fruit Muffins, all varieties (average)	1	180	31
Rice Bran Fancy Fruit Muffins	1	210	35
MIRACLE MAIZE® (Little Crow Foods)			
Corn Bread Mix, all varieties (as prepared) (average)	2" x 2" square	105	24
PEPPERIDGE FARM® (Campbell Soup Co.)			
Old Fashioned Muffins, all varieties (average)	1 muffin	180	28

PROTEIN (gm)	FAT (gm)	SAT. FAT (gm)	CHOLES- TEROL (mg)	SODIUM (mg)	EXCHANGES
3	8	—	—	215-250	2 starch, 1 fat
3	9	—	—	295	2 starch, 1½ fat
2	5	—	—	185-220	1 starch, 1 fat
2	4	<1	0	65	1 starch, ½ fat
2	4	1	—	360	1½ starch, ½ fat
4	3	—	0	190-200	1½ starch, ½ fat
3	4	<1	0	110	1 starch, 1 fruit, ½ fat
4	0	—	0	100-	1 starch, 1 fruit
4	4	—	0	80-100	1 starch, 1 fruit, 1 fat
5	7	—	0	125	1 starch, 1 fruit, 1½ fat
3	2	—	—	193-389	1½ starch
2	6	—	—	170-300	2 starch, 1 fat

* Not available   ⯀ More than 2 fat exchanges   🛒 Moderate to high sugar content

Products	SERVING SIZE	CALORIES	CARBO-HYDRATE (gm)
PILLSBURY® (The Pillsbury Co.)			
Lovin Lites™ Blueberry Muffin Mix (as prepared with water and egg white)	1 muffim (1⁄12 mix)	100	21
ROBIN HOOD® (General Mills, Inc.)			
Cornbread Mix, white or yellow (as prepared) (average)	1⁄6 mix	150	23
Muffin Mixes, all varieties (as prepared) (average)	1⁄6 mix	150	25
SARA LEE® (Kitchens of Sara Lee)			
Free and Light Blueberry Muffin	1	120	28
Golden Corn Muffin	1	240	31
Muffins, all varieties (average)	1	210	34
WEIGHT WATCHERS® Microwave Breakfast (H. J. Heinz Co., Inc.)			
Banana Nut Muffins	2.5 oz. (1⁄2 pkg.)	170	32
Blueberry Muffins	2.5 oz. (1⁄2 pkg.)	170	32

MISCELLANEOUS

BISQUICK® (General Mills, Inc.)			
Bisquick® Mix, dry	2 oz. (1⁄2 cup)	240	37
FEATHERWEIGHT® Healthy Recipes® (Sandoz Nutrition)			
Seasoned Coating Mix for Chicken/Fish (average)	1⁄4 pkg.	18	8
HAIN® (PET, Inc.)			
Whole Wheat Baking Mix, dry	1 1⁄2 oz.	150	30
KEEBLER® (Keebler Co.)			
Breadstix, all varieties (average)	6	90	18
KELLOGG'S® CROUTETTES® (Kellogg Co.)			
Croutons			
Dry Mix	2⁄3 cup	70	15
As Prepared	2⁄3 cup	130	15

† For occasional use ** Not recommended for use

PROTEIN (gm)	FAT (gm)	SAT. FAT (gm)	CHOLES- TEROL (mg)	SODIUM (mg)	EXCHANGES
3	1	0	0	160	1½ starch
4	5	—	—	500	1½ starch, ½ fat
3	6	—	—	220-250	1½ starch, 1 fat
3	0	—	0	90	1 starch, 1 fruit, **or** 1½ starch
5	13	—	0	310	2 starch, 2 fat
4	8	—	—	170-320	2 starch, 1 fat
3	5	1	10	360	1 starch, 1 fruit, 1 fat
3	5	1	10	330	1 starch, 1 fruit, 1 fat
4	8	2	0	700	2½ starch, 1 fat
1	0	—	0	10-30	Free
6	1	—	—	680	2 starch
3	2	—	—	60-90	1 starch
3	0	—	—	270	1 starch
3	7	—	—	—	1 starch, 1 fat

* Not available   More than 2 fat exchanges   Moderate to high sugar content

Products	SERVING SIZE	CALORIES	CARBO-HYDRATE (gm)
MRS. PAUL'S® (Campbell Soup Co.)			
☕ Apple Fritters	2 fritters	270	36
Corn Fritters	2 fritters	250	33
PEPPERIDGE FARM® (Campbell Soup Co.)			
Croutons, all varieties (average)	½ oz.	70	9
PILLSBURY® (The Pillsbury Co.)			
All Ready Pizza Crust	⅛ of pizza crust	90	16
SALAD CRISPINS® (The Clorox Company)			
Salad Crispins®, all varieties (average)	2 heaping Tbsp.	60	8
SHAKE 'N BAKE® (General Foods, Corp.)			
Seasoning Mixture, all varieties (average)	¼ pouch	80	15
Oven Fry® Coating Homestyle	¼ pouch	80	15
Extra Crispy Recipe (average)	¼ pouch	120	20

TORTILLAS

LA CAMPANA PARADISO™ (La Campana Paradiso)			
100% Whole Wheat Tortillas	1 tortilla	75	14
Flour Tortillas	1 8" tortilla	90	18
Flour Tortillas	1 10" tortilla	120	25
OLD EL PASO® (PET, Inc.)			
Corn Tortillas	1	60	10
Flour Tortillas	1	150	27
Mexican Crisps	5	150	16
Taco Shells	1	55	6
Taco Shells, Mini	3	70	7
Tostaco Shells	1	100	11
Tostada Shells	1	55	6

† For occasional use   ** Not recommended for use

PROTEIN (gm)	FAT (gm)	SAT. FAT (gm)	CHOLES- TEROL (mg)	SODIUM (mg)	EXCHANGES
3	13	—	—	610	1½ starch, 1 fruit, 2 fat†
4	12	—	—	630	2 starch, 2 fat
2	3	—	—	160-220	½ starch, ½ fat
3	1	<1	0	170	1 starch
2	2	—	—	—	½ starch, ½ fat
1	1	—	0	410-700	1 starch
1	2	—	0	970	1 starch
3	3	—	0	690-810	1 starch, ½ fat
3	1	—	—	150	1 starch
3	3	—	—	160	1 starch
5	3	—	—	200	1½ starch
1	1	—	—	170	1 starch
4	3	—	—	360	2 starch
1	9	—	0	75	1 starch, 1½ fat
0	3	—	—	50	½ starch, ½ fat
1	4	—	0	60	½ starch, ½ fat
1	5	—	0	10	½ starch, 1 fat
<1	3	—	—	65	½ starch, ½ fat

* Not available   ▯ More than 2 fat exchanges   🛒 Moderate to high sugar content

Products	SERVING SIZE	CALORIES	CARBO-HYDRATE (gm)
RESER'S® (Reser's Fine Foods, Inc.)			
Corn Tortilla	1	63	12
Flour Tortilla			
6 inch	1	79	14
8 inch	1	109	20
10 inch	1	134	25
12 inch	1	158	29
Homestyle Tortilla	1	125	19

BREAKFAST ITEMS

Author's Note: Some of these products contain large amounts of sugars and fats. If you decide to use them occasionally, make them part of your meal plan and use them with a meal or before exercise.

BREAKFAST BARS AND DRINKS
CARNATION® (Carnation Co.)

🛒 Breakfast Bar, all varieties (average)	1 bar	200	20
🛒 Instant Breakfast, all varieties (average)	1 pkg. dry mix only	130	25
	1 pkg. & 8 oz. skim milk	220	36
Instant Breakfast, diet, all varieties (average)	1 pkg. dry mix only	70	10
	1 pkg. & 8 oz. skim milk	160	22
FIGURINES® (The Pillsbury Co.)			
Figurine® Diet Bars, all varieties (average)	1 bar	100	11
KELLOGG'S® (Kellogg Co.)			
Smart Start® Nutri-Grain® Cereal Bars, all varieties (average)	1 bar	150	25

† For occasional use   ** Not recommended for use

PROTEIN (gm)	FAT (gm)	SAT. FAT (gm)	CHOLES-TEROL (mg)	SODIUM (mg)	EXCHANGES
2	1	—	0	50	1 starch
2	1	—	0	74	1 starch
3	2	—	0	103	1 starch, ½ fat
4	2	—	0	126	1½ starch
4	3	—	0	149	2 starch
3	4	—	0	289	1 starch, 1 fat
6	11	—	—	150-180	1 starch, ½ skim milk, 2 fat **or** 1 meat, 1 fruit, 1 fat†
6	1	—	—	135	1 fruit, 1 skim milk **or** 1½ starch†
14	1	—	—	260	1½ starch, 1 skim milk **or** 1 fruit, 2 skim milk†
6	1	—	<5	115	1 skim milk **or** ½ starch, 1 lean meat
14	1	—	—	240	2 skim milk **or** ½ starch, 1 lean meat, 1 skim milk
2	5	—	—	45-55	1 starch, 1 fat
11	5	—	—	60	1½ starch, 1 fat

* Not available   ⊟ More than 2 fat exchanges   🛒 Moderate to high sugar content

Products	SERVING SIZE	CALORIES	CARBO-HYDRATE (gm)
PILLSBURY (The Pillsbury Co.)			
Instant Breakfast, all flavors (as prepared) (average)	1 pouch & 8 oz. skim milk	210	39

BREAKFAST ENTREES
DOWNYFLAKE® (PET, Inc.)

Breakfast Entrees			
Pancakes and Sausage	5.5 oz.	430	47
Scrambled Eggs with Ham and Hash Browns	6.25 oz.	270	18
Scrambled Eggs with Ham and Pecan Twirl	6.25 oz.	400	37
Scrambled Eggs with Hash Browns and Sausage	6.25 oz.	420	17
Scrambled Eggs with Sausage and Pecan Twirl	6.25 oz.	510	39
Texas Style French Toast & Sausage	4.25 oz.	400	37

HEALTHY CHOICE® Breakfast (ConAgra® Frozen Foods Co.)

English Muffin Sandwich	1 (4.25 oz.)	200	30

MORNINGSTAR FARMS® Country Breakfast (Worthington Foods, Inc.

Vegetarian			
French Toast and Breakfast Patties	6.5 oz.	380	37
Scramblers®, Breakfast Links and Hash Browns	7 oz.	360	22
Scramblers®, Breakfast Links and Pancakes	6.8 oz.	380	33

SWANSON® (Campbell Soup Co.)

Great Starts Breakfast Entrees, frozen			
French Toast with Sausages	6½ oz.	450	42
French Toast (Cinnamon Swirl) with Sausages	6½ oz.	470	42
Omelet with Cheese Sauce & Ham	7 oz.	380	12

† For occasional use   ** Not recommended for use

PROTEIN (gm)	FAT (gm)	SAT. FAT (gm)	CHOLES-TEROL (mg)	SODIUM (mg)	EXCHANGES
14	2	—	—	300-330	2 starch, 1 skim milk†
11	23	—	—	1170	3 starch, 1 high fat meat, 2½ fat
16	15	—	—	610	1 starch, 2 meat, 1 fat
19	19	—	—	600	2½ starch, 1½ meat, 2 fat
12	34	—	—	790	1 starch, 1½ meat, 5 fat
16	33	—	—	710	2½ starch, 1½ meat, 4½ fat
10	24	—	—	550	2½ starch, ½ high fat meat, 3½ fat
16	3	1	20	510	2 starch, 1 lean meat
24	15	—	0	1220	2½ starch, 2½ meat
16	23	—	0	660	1½ starch, 2 meat, 2 fat
18	19	—	0	900	2 starch, 2 meat, 1½ fat
15	25	—	—	640	3 starch, 1 high fat meat, 3 fat
16	26	—	—	660	3 starch, 1 high fat meat, 3 fat
18	29	—	—	1200	1 starch, 2 high fat meat, 3½ fat

* Not available   ▤ More than 2 fat exchanges   🛒 Moderate to high sugar content

Products	SERVING SIZE	CALORIES	CARBO-HYDRATE (gm)
♥ Pancakes and Blueberries in Sauce	7 oz.	410	72
Pancakes and Sausage	6 oz.	470	53
♥ Pancakes and Strawberries in Sauce	7 oz.	430	74
▤ Scrambled Eggs and Sausage with Hash Brown Potatoes	6¼ oz.	430	18
▤ Scrambled Eggs, Home Fries	4 ⅜ oz.	280	15
▤ Scrambled Eggs & Bacon with Home Fries	5¼ oz.	360	18
Spanish Style Omelet	7 ¾ oz.	240	15
Great Starts Breakfast on a Biscuit, frozen ▤ Egg, Canadian Bacon & Cheese	5¼ oz.	420	37
Egg, Sausage & Cheese	5½ oz.	460	34
Sausage	4 ¾ oz.	410	36
Great Starts Breakfast on a Muffin, frozen Egg, Beefsteak & Cheese	4.9 oz.	380	27
Egg, Canadian Bacon & Cheese	4.1 oz.	300	25
WEIGHT WATCHERS® Microwave Breakfast (H. J. Heinz Co.)			
Egg, Candian Style Bacon and Cheese Muffin	4 oz.	230	26
French Toast: with Cinnamon	3 oz.	170	24
with Links	4.5 oz.	260	25

† For occasional use   ** Not recommended for use

PROTEIN (gm)	FAT (gm)	SAT. FAT (gm)	CHOLES-TEROL (mg)	SODIUM (mg)	EXCHANGES
8	10	—	—	800	3 starch, 2 fruit, 2 fat†
14	22	—	—	900	3½ starch, 1 high fat meat, 2 fat
8	11	—	—	860	3 starch, 2 fruit, 2 fat†
12	35	—	—	780	1 starch, 1 high fat meat, 5½ fat
7	21	—	—	500	1 starch, 1 high fat meat, 3 fat
10	28	—	—	690	1 starch, 1 meat, 4½ fat
8	16	—	—	840	1 starch, 1 meat, 2 fat
16	22	—	—	1850	2½ starch, 1½ meat, 2½ fat
17	29	—	—	1400	2 starch, 2 high fat meat, 2 fat
14	22	—	—	1180	2½ starch, 1½ high fat meat, 1 fat
18	22	—	—	770	2 starch, 2 meat, 2 fat
14	16	—	—	780	1½ starch, 1½ meat, 1½ fat
13	8	1	170	610	2 starch, 1 meat
7	4	1	10	350	1½ starch, 1 fat
14	12	2	20	600	1½ starch, 1½ meat, ½ fat

* Not available   ▮ More than 2 fat exchanges   ☕ Moderate to high sugar content

Products	SERVING SIZE	CALORIES	CARBO-HYDRATE (gm)
Pancakes			
Buttermilk	2.5 oz. (½ pkg.)	150	24
☕ with Blueberry Topping	4.75 oz.	260	49
with Links	4 oz.	240	26
☕ with Strawberry Topping	4.75 oz.	230	44
Sausage Biscuit	3 oz.	220	19

COFFEE CAKES

Author's Note: Some of these products contain large amounts of sugars and fats. If you decide to use them occasionally, make them part of your meal plan and use them with a meal or before exercise.

AUNT JEMIMA® (Quaker Oats Co.)

☕ Easy Mix Coffee Cake (as prepared)	⅙ recipe	160	28

ENTENMANN'S® (Entenmann's, Inc.)

Fat Free, Cholesterol Free			
☕ Blueberry Crunch Cake	1 oz. slice (15 serv/pkg)	70	16
☕ Cherry Cheese Pastry	1.3 oz. slice (13 serv/pkg)	90	20
☕ Cinnamon Apple Coffee	1.3 oz. slice (13 serv/pkg)	90	20

KEEBLER® (Keebler Co.)

Elfin Loaves™, all varieties except carrot (average)	1	180	30
Carrot	1	210	27

KELLOGG'S® (Kellogg Co.)

☕ Pop-Tarts® Toaster Pastries, frosted or unfrosted, all varieties (average)	1 pastry	205	37

† For occasional use   ** Not recommended for use

PROTEIN (gm)	FAT (gm)	SAT. FAT (gm)	CHOLES- TEROL (mg)	SODIUM (mg)	EXCHANGES
5	3	1	10	330	1½ starch, ½ fat
6	4	1	15	430	2 starch, 1 fruit, ½ fat†
12	10	1	15	610	1½ starch, 1 meat, 1 fat
6	4	1	15	420	2 starch, 1 fruit, ½ fat†
11	11	2	70	560	1 starch, 1 meat, 1 fat
3	5	1	—	290	2 starch, ½ fat†
1	0	—	0	85	1 starch†
2	0	—	0	85	1 starch, ½ fruit†
2	0	—	0	90	1 starch, ½ fruit†
3	6	1-2	0-20	160-260	1 starch, 1 fruit† 1 fat
3	10	1	25	170	1 starch, 1 fruit, 1½ fat
3	6	—	—	190-230	1 starch, 1½ fruit, 1 fat†

* Not available   ▯ More than 2 fat exchanges   ♣ Moderate to high sugar content

Products	SERVING SIZE	CALORIES	CARBO-HYDRATE (gm)
NATURE'S WAREHOUSE™ (Natures Warehouse, Inc.)			
Pastry Poppers®, all varieties (average)	1 pastry (2 oz.)	212	38
PILLSBURY® (The Pillsbury Co.)			
Best Quick Cinnamon Rolls	1	210	29
Cinnamon Rolls with Icing	1	110	17
Coffee Cake Mix (as prepared)	⅛ cake	240	40
Danish with Icing, all varieties (average)	1	140	19
Fruit Turnovers, all varieties (average)	1	170	23
Quick Bread Mixes, all varieties (as prepared) (average)	1/16 loaf	120	20
SARA LEE® (Kitchens of Sara Lee)			
Cinnamon Rolls, all butter			
without icing	1 roll (¼ pkg)	230	31
with icing	1 roll & ¼ icing pkt.	280	43
Coffee Cakes, all butter, all varieties (average)	⅛ cake	160	20
Coffee Cakes, individually wrapped			
Apple Cinnamon	1	290	40
Butter Streusel	1	230	27
Pecan	1	280	30
Free & Light Apple Danish	1 slice (⅛ pkg)	130	30
Individual Danish, all varieties (average)	1 (⅙ pkg)	130	15
WEIGHT WATCHERS® Microwave Breakfast (H. J. Heinz Co.)			
Coffee Cakes with Cinnamon Streusel	2.25 oz. (½ pkg)	190	28
Sweet Rolls, Apple, Strawberry or Cheese (average)	2.25 oz. (½ pkg)	175	29

† For occasional use ** Not recommended for use

PROTEIN (gm)	FAT (gm)	SAT. FAT (gm)	CHOLES-TEROL (mg)	SODIUM (mg)	EXCHANGES
3	5	—	—	55-56	1½ starch, 1 fruit, ½ fat
2	9	3	10	260	2 starch, 1½ fat†
1	5	1	0	260	1 starch, 1 fat†
3	7	—	—	150	1 starch, 1½ fruit, 1½ fat†
2	8	2	5	230-240	1 starch, 1½ fat†
2	8	3	5	310-320	1 starch, ½ fruit, 1½ fat†
2	4	—	—	113-135	1 starch, 1 fat
3	11	—	—	220	2 starch, 2 fat†
3	11	—	—	220	2 starch, 1 fruit, 2 fat†
3	8	—	—	160-180	1 starch, ½ fruit, 1½ fat†
4	13	—	—	270	2 starch, ½ fruit, 2 fat†
4	12	—	—	270	2 starch, 2 fat†
5	16	—	—	270	2 starch, 3 fat†
2	0	—	0	120	1 starch, 1 fruit†
2	7	—	—	120-140	1 starch, 1 fat†
3	7	1	5	250	1 starch, 1 fruit, 1 fat†
3	5	1	20	90-170	1 starch, 1 fruit, 1 fat†

* Not available   █ More than 2 fat exchanges   ♨ Moderate to high sugar content

Products	SERVING SIZE	CALORIES	CARBO-HYDRATE (gm)

EGG SUBSTITUTES

FEATHERWEIGHT® (Sandoz Nutrition)

Egg Substitute	2 eggs	120	2

FLEISHMANN'S® (Nabisco Brands, Inc.)

Egg Beaters®, cholesterol-free egg product	¼ cup	25	1
Egg Beaters® with Cheez (99% real egg product)	¼ cup	65	2

HEALTHY CHOICE® (ConAgra® Frozen Foods Co.)

Egg Substitute	¼ cup	30	1

MORNINGSTAR FARMS® (Worthington Foods, Inc.)

Scramblers® Egg Substitute	¼ cup	60	3

FRENCH TOAST, PANCAKES, WAFFLES

AUNT JEMIMA® (Quaker Oats Co.)

French Toast, frozen, all varieties (average)	2 slices	170	27
Pancake Batter, frozen, all varieties (as prepared) (average)	three 4" cakes	190	38
Pancakes, microwave, all varieties (average)	three 4" cakes	220	40
Pancake and Waffle Mix (as prepared) Buckwheat	three 4" cakes	230	35
Buttermilk	three 4" cakes	220	30
Buttermilk Complete	three 4" cakes	230	46
Complete	three 4" cakes	250	50
Original	three 4" cakes	200	28
Whole Wheat	three 4" cakes	270	38
Waffles, frozen, all varieties (average)	1 waffle	90	15

† For occasional use   ** Not recommended for use

PROTEIN (gm)	FAT (gm)	SAT. FAT (gm)	CHOLES- TEROL (mg)	SODIUM (mg)	EXCHANGES
9	8	—	15	250	1 meat, 1 fat
5	0	—	0	80	½ lean meat
7	3	—	0	220	1 lean meat
5	<1	—	0	90	½ lean meat
6	3	0	0	130	1 lean meat
7	4	1	41-46	490-550	2 starch, ½ fat
6	3	1	19-27	690-780	2½ starch
6	4	1	19-27	800-860	2½ starch, ½ fat
9	8	—	—	820	2 starch, 1½ fat
8	8	—	95	760	2 starch, 1½ fat
7	3	—	—	950	3 starch
7	4	—	15	1020	3 starch
7	7	—	80	660	2 starch, 1 fat
12	9	—	—	950	2½ starch, 1½ fat
2	3	1	3	295-340	1 starch, ½ fat

* Not available   🖪 More than 2 fat exchanges   🛒 Moderate to high sugar content

Products	SERVING SIZE	CALORIES	CARBO-HYDRATE (gm)
BETTY CROCKER® (General Mills, Inc.)			
Buttermilk Pancake Mix (as prepared)	three 4" cakes	280	39
Complete Buttermilk Pancake Mix (as prepared)	three 4" cakes	210	41
BISQUICK® SHAKE 'N POUR (General Mills, Inc.)			
Pancake & Waffle Mix (as prepared) (average)	three 4" cakes	260	49
DOWNYFLAKE® (PET, Inc.)			
French Toast, frozen			
Regular	2	270	34
Extra Thick Style	1	150	11
Pancakes, frozen			
Blueberry	2	170	22
Buttermilk	3	330	53
Regular	3	330	53
Waffles, frozen			
Blueberry	2	180	32
Buttermilk	2	170	30
Hot-N-Buttery	2	180	27
🗄 Multi Grain	2	250	28
🗄 Oat Bran	2	250	28
Regular	2	120	20
Regular Jumbo	2	170	30
Rice Bran	2	210	25
🗄 Roman Meal	2	280	33
EGGO® (Mrs. Smith's® Frozen Foods, A Kellogg Company)			
Waffles, frozen, all varieties (average)	1	120-130	16
Common Sense™ Oat Bran Waffle, frozen, all varieties (average)	1	130	16
Mini's Homestyle Miniature Waffles	4 mini waffles	90	14

† For occasional use   ** Not recommended for use

PROTEIN (gm)	FAT (gm)	SAT. FAT (gm)	CHOLES- TEROL (mg)	SODIUM (mg)	EXCHANGES
8	10	—	—	810	2½ starch, 2 fat
5	3	—	—	500	2½ starch
7	5	—	0	580-930	3 starch, ½ fat
6	12	—	73	380	2 starch, 2 fat
5	9	—	—	340	1 starch, 1½ fat
3	7	—	—	500	1½ starch, 1 fat
6	9	—	—	1030	3½ starch, 1 fat
6	9	—	—	1030	3½ starch, 1 fat
4	4	—	0	570	2 starch, ½ fat
4	4	—	0	630	2 starch, ½ fat
4	6	—	0	620	2 starch, 1 fat
6	14	—	0	500	2 starch, 2½ fat
6	14	—	0	600	2 starch, 2½ fat
3	3	—	0	420	1 starch, ½ fat
4	4	—	0	570	2 starch, ½ fat
5	11	—	0	230	1½ starch, 2 fat
5	14	—	4	680	2 starch, 2½ fat
3	5	1	—	250	1 starch, 1 fat
3	5	1	—	220	1 starch, 1 fat
2	3	1	10	190	1 starch, ½ fat

* Not available   ▤ More than 2 fat exchanges   ♛ Moderate to high sugar content

Products	SERVING SIZE	CALORIES	CARBO-HYDRATE (gm)
Nutri-Grain™ Waffles, frozen, all varieties (average)	1	130	17
ESTEE® (Estee Corp.)			
Pancake Mix, Dietetic (as prepared)	three 3" cakes	100	21
FAST SHAKE® (Little Crow Foods)			
Pancake Mix, all varieties (as prepared) (average)	½ container	260	51
FEATHERWEIGHT® (Sandoz Nutrition)			
Pancake Mix, Low Sodium (as prepared)	three 4" cakes	140	24
HEALTH VALLEY® (Health Valley Foods)			
Buttermilk Biscuit and Pancake Mix, all varieties (average)	1 oz.	100	20
HUNGRY JACK® (The Pillsbury Co.)			
Pancake and Waffle Mix (as prepared)			
Blueberry	three 4" cakes	320	41
Buttermilk	three 4" cakes	240	29
Buttermilk Complete	three 4" cakes	180	39
Extra Lights®	three 4" cakes	210	30
Extra Lights® Complete	three 4" cakes	190	37
Panshakes	three 4" cakes	250	43
PILLSBURY® (The Pillsbury Co.)			
Microwave Pancakes, frozen, all varieties (average)	2 cakes	170	33
ROBIN HOOD® (General Mills, Inc.)			
Buttermilk Pancake Mix (as prepared)	⅛ mix	100	17

PROTEIN (gm)	FAT (gm)	SAT. FAT (gm)	CHOLES- TEROL (mg)	SODIUM (mg)	EXCHANGES
3	5	1	—	220-250	1 starch, 1 fat
3	0	0	0	130	1½ starch
6	4	—	—	709-823	3 starch
6	2	—	—	90	1½ starch, ½ fat
4	1	—	—	170	1 starch
6	15	—	—	820	2½ starch, 2½ fat
7	11	—	—	570	2 starch, 2 fat
4	1	—	—	710	2 starch
6	7	—	—	490	2 starch, 1 fat
4	2	—	—	700	2½ starch
7	6	—	—	80	2½ starch, 1 fat
4	3	—	—	280-395	2 starch
3	2	—	—	280	1 starch, ½ fat

* Not available   ▌ More than 2 fat exchanges   🛒 Moderate to high sugar content

Products	SERVING SIZE	CALORIES	CARBO-HYDRATE (gm)

CANDY, FROSTINGS, SYRUP

Author's Note: Many of these products contain large amounts of refined sugars. If you decide to use them, work the specific product into your meal plan, using the nutrition information supplied here. And if you have diabetes, remember that when you decide to eat a high sugar food, do so with a meal, when it will be more slowly absorbed; or before exercise, so that it will be readily used for energy.

CANDY
ESTEE® (Estee Corp.)

Products	SERVING SIZE	CALORIES	CARBO-HYDRATE (gm)
Candy, Dietetic			
Chocolate Bars	3 squares	90	7
Chocolate Coated Raisins	20 pieces	60	10
Crunch Chocolate Bar	4 squares	90	8
Fruit and Nut Mix	10 pieces	88	8
Peanut Butter Cups	2	80	6
Hard Candy, Dietetic			
Estee-ets	10 pieces	70	8
Gum Drops	10 pieces	60	15
Gummy Bears	2	13	3
Hard Candy	5 pieces	63	15
Lollipops	2	50	12

FEATHERWEIGHT® (Sandoz Nutrition)

Products	SERVING SIZE	CALORIES	CARBO-HYDRATE (gm)
Sweet Pretenders®			
Butterscotch Candy, Cool Blue Mints, Peppermint Swirls (average)	3	60	15
Caramels	3	90	15
Chocolate Bars, assorted (average)	1 section	80	7
Fruit Drops, all flavors (average)	⅓ oz.	30	8
Hard Candy, assorted flavors	1 piece	12	3

NATURAL TOUCH® (Worthington Foods, Inc.)

Products	SERVING SIZE	CALORIES	CARBO-HYDRATE (gm)
Caroby® Milk Bar	4 sections (⅓ bar or 1 oz.)	150	13

† For occasional use   ** Not recommended for use

PROTEIN (gm)	FAT (gm)	SAT. FAT (gm)	CHOLES- TEROL (mg)	SODIUM (mg)	EXCHANGES
2	7	3	3	15	½ starch, 1 fat†
2	2	2	2	20	1 fruit†
2	6	4	4	20	½ starch, 1 fat†
3	5	5	<3	25	½ starch, 1 fat†
2	6	6	<2	40	½ starch, 1 fat†
2	4	2	<2	20	½ starch, ½ fat†
0	0	0	0	0	1 fruit†
1	0	0	0	0	Free
0	0	0	0	0	1 fruit†
0	0	0	0	0	1 fruit†
0	0	—	0	0-25	1 fruit†
0	3	—	0	30	1 fruit, ½ fat†
1	6	—	0	20	½ fruit, 1 fat†
0	0	—	0	15	½ fruit†
0	0	—	0	0	Free
4	9	—	0	35	1 starch, 1½ fat†

* Not available   ▯ More than 2 fat exchanges   ♥ Moderate to high sugar content

Products	SERVING SIZE	CALORIES	CARBO-HYDRATE (gm)
NATURES WAREHOUSE™ (Natures Warehouse, Inc.)			
Fruit Juice Sweetened			
Candy Bars			
A•OK	1 oz.	130	17
My O My	1 oz.	103	21
No How	1 oz.	140	11
Non Stop	1 oz.	122	18
Nut Wit	1 oz.	135	17

FROSTINGS

BETTY CROCKER® (General Mills, Inc.)

Products	SERVING SIZE	CALORIES	CARBO-HYDRATE (gm)
🛒 Creamy Deluxe® Ready-To-Spread Frostings, all varieties (average)	½ tub	160	25
🛒 Creamy Frosting Mix, all varieties (as prepared) (average)	½ mix	170	30
🛒 Fluffy Frosting Mix	½ mix	70	16
DUNCAN HINES® (Proctor & Gamble)			
🛒 Ready-To-Spread Frostings, all varieties except lemon (average)	½ container	160	24
🛒 Lemon	½ container	120	18
ESTEE® (Estee Corporation)			
Frosting Mix (as prepared)	2 Tbsp.	67	13
PILLSBURY® (The Pillsbury Co.)			
🛒 Cake and Cookie Decorator, all colors (average)	1 Tbsp.	70	12
🛒 Fluffy White Frosting Mix (as prepared) (average)	½ mix	60	15
🛒 Ready-To-Spread Supreme Frosting (average)	½ tub	160	25

PROTEIN (gm)	FAT (gm)	SAT. FAT (gm)	CHOLES-TEROL (mg)	SODIUM (mg)	EXCHANGES
3	6	—	—	32	1 starch, 1 fat†
2	1	—	—	42	½ starch, 1 fruit†
6	10	—	—	48	½ fruit, 1 meat, 1 fat†
2	5	—	—	48	1 starch, 1 fat†
3	6	—	—	32	1 starch, 1 fat†
<1	7	2	0	30-100	**
<1	6	1	0	40-100	**
<1	0	—	0	40	1 fruit†
0	8	2	—	75-120	**
0	6	2	—	60	1 fruit, 1 fat†
1	1	<1	0	0	1 fruit†
0	2	—	—	0	1 fruit†
0	0	—	—	65	1 fruit†
0	7	—	—	45-115	**

* Not available   ▤ More than 2 fat exchanges   ♐ Moderate to high sugar content

Products	SERVING SIZE	CALORIES	CARBO-HYDRATE (gm)

SYRUP

AUNT JEMIMA® (Quaker Oats Corp.)

Syrup

☕ Butter Lite	2 Tbsp. (1 fl. oz.)	50	13
☕ Lite	2 Tbsp. (1 fl. oz.)	50	13
☕ Regular	2 Tbsp. (1 fl. oz.)	110	27

CARY'S® (Borden, Inc.)

Reduced Calorie Syrup (sweetened with sorbitol)	2 Tbsp. (1 fl. oz.)	20	4

ESTEE® (Estee Corp.)

Syrup, Dietetic

Blueberry	1 Tbsp.	8	1
Chocolate	1 Tbsp.	20	5
Pancake	1 Tbsp.	8	1

FEATHERWEIGHT® (Sandoz Nutrition)

Reduced Calorie Syrups, all flavors (average)	1 Tbsp.	16	4

GOLDEN GRIDDLE® (Best Foods, CPC International, Inc.)

☕ Syrup	1 Tbsp.	50	14

KARO® (Best Foods, CPC International, Inc.)

☕ Corn Syrup, dark or light	1 Tbsp.	60	15
☕ Pancake Syrup	1 Tbsp.	60	15

HERSHEY'S® (Hershey Foods Corp.)

☕ Chocolate Flavored Syrup	1 oz. (2 Tbsp.)	80	17

LOG CABIN® (General Foods Corp.)

Syrup

☕ Regular	2 Tbsp. (1 fl. oz.)	100	26
☕ Lite	2 Tbsp. (1 fl. oz.)	50	13

NUTRADIET® (S and W Fine Foods)

Flavored Pancake Syrups	1 Tbsp.	12	3

† For occasional use   ** Not recommended for use

PROTEIN (gm)	FAT (gm)	SAT. FAT (gm)	CHOLES-TEROL (mg)	SODIUM (mg)	EXCHANGES
0	0	0	0	90	1 fruit†
0	0	0	0	90	1 fruit†
0	0	0	0	30	**
0	0	—	—	20	Free
0	0	0	0	25	Free
<1	<1	<1	0	5	Free
0	0	0	0	35	Free
0	0	0	0	25	Free
0	0	0	0	15	1 fruit†
0	0	0	0	30-40	1 fruit†
0	0	0	0	35	1 fruit†
1	1	—	0	20	1 fruit†
0	0	—	—	35	**
0	0	—	—	90	1 fruit†
0	0	—	—	75	Free

* Not available   ▌ More than 2 fat exchanges   ♥ Moderate to high sugar content

Products	SERVING SIZE	CALORIES	CARBO-HYDRATE (gm)
WEIGHT WATCHERS® (H.J. Heniz Co.)			
Naturally Sweetened Syrup	2 Tbsp.	50	12

CEREALS

Author's Note: Some of these products contain large amounts of refined sugars. If you decide to use them occasionally, make them part of your meal plan and use them with a meal or before exercise.

COCO WHEATS® (Little Crow Foods)			
Coco Wheats, traditional, dry	3 Tbsp.	121	27
Coco Wheats, instant	1 packet (1.4 oz.)	148	32
FEATHERWEIGHT® (Sandoz Nutrition)			
Corn Flakes, Low Sodium	1 cup	88	20
Crisp Rice, Low Sodium	¾ cup	83	20
GENERAL MILLS® (General Mills, Inc.)			
Hot Cereals			
Oatmeal Swirlers®, all varieties (average)	1 pkt.	160	34
Total® Oatmeal Instant, all flavored varieties (average)	1 pkt.	160	34
Quick	1 oz.	90	18
Regular	1 pkt.	110	22
Wheat Hearts	1 oz. (3⅓ Tbsp.)	110	21
Ready-to-Eat Cereals			
Basic 4®	½ cup	86	19
Body Buddies®-Natural Fruit	¾ cup	83	18
☕ BooBerry®	¾ cup	83	18
Cheerios®	1 cup	88	16
Cheerios®, Apple Cinnamon	½ cup	75	15
Cheerios®, Honey Nut	½ cup	74	15
☕ Cinnamon Toast Crunch™	½ cup	80	15
☕ Clusters™	½ cup	110	20

† For occasional use   ** Not recommended for use

PROTEIN (gm)	FAT (gm)	SAT. FAT (gm)	CHOLES- TEROL (mg)	SODIUM (mg)	EXCHANGES
0	0	—	—	50	1 fruit†
5	1	—	—	12	2 starch
4	0	—	—	114	2 starch
2	0	—	0	<10	1 starch
2	0	—	0	<10	1 starch
3	2	—	0	100-130	2 starch
4	2	—	0	105-150	2 starch
4	2	—	0	0	1 starch
4	2	—	0	220	1½ starch
4	1	—	0	0	1½ starch
2	1	—	0	152	1 starch
2	1	—	0	210	1 starch
1	1	—	0	158	1 starch†
3	2	—	0	232	1 starch
2	1	—	0	120	1 starch
2	1	—	0	168	1 starch
1	2	—	0	147	1 starch†
3	3	—	0	140	1 starch, ½ fat†

* Not available   ▯ More than 2 fat exchanges   ♥ Moderate to high sugar content

Products	SERVING SIZE	CALORIES	CARBO-HYDRATE (gm)
☕ Cocoa Puffs®	¾ cup	83	19
☕ Count Chocula®	¾ cup	83	18
Country® Corn Flakes	¾ cup	83	18
Crispy Wheats 'N Raisins	¾ cup	100	23
Fiber One®	¾ cup	90	35
☕ Frankenberry®	¾ cup	83	18
☕ Fruity Yummy Mummy®	¾ cup	83	18
☕ Golden Grahams®	½ cup	73	18
Kaboom®	¾ cup	83	17
Kix®	1 cup	73	16
☕ Lucky Charms®	¾ cup	83	18
Oatmeal Crisp	¾ cup	83	17
Oatmeal Raisin Crisp	⅓ cup	75	14
Raisin Nut Bran®	½ cup	110	20
Raisin Oat Bran	¾ cup	150	31
Total®	¾ cup	75	17
Total® Corn Flakes	¾ cup	83	18
Total Raisin Bran®	1 cup	140	33
Triples®	½ cup	73	16
☕ Trix®	¾ cup	83	19
Wheaties®	¾ cup	75	17
HEALTH VALLEY® (Health Valley Foods, Inc.)			
Hot Cereals Oat Bran Natural, all varieties (average)	¼ cup	100	19
Ready-to-Eat Cereals Amaranth Cereal with Bananas	½ cup	110	20
Amaranth Crunch™ with Raisins	¼ cup	110	20
Amaranth Flakes™, 100% Organic	½ cup	90	21
Blue Corn Flakes, 100% Organic	½ cup	90	19
Bran Cereal, 100% Organic, all varieties (average)	¼ cup	100	21

† For occasional use   ** Not recommended for use

PROTEIN (gm)	FAT (gm)	SAT. FAT (gm)	CHOLES-TEROL (mg)	SODIUM (mg)	EXCHANGES
1	1	—	0	128	1 starch†
2	1	—	0	158	1 starch†
2	<1	—	0	210	1 starch
2	1	—	0	140	1 starch, ½ fruit
3	2	—	0	210	1 starch
1	1	—	0	158	1 starch†
1	1	—	0	120	1 starch†
1	1	—	0	210	1 starch†
2	1	—	0	218	1 starch
1	<1	—	0	172	1 starch
2	1	—	0	135	1 starch†
2	2	—	0	135	1 starch
1	1	—	0	95	1 starch
3	3	—	0	140	1 starch, ½ fat
4	2	—	0	130	1 starch, 1 fruit
2	1	—	0	105	1 starch
2	1	—	0	210	1 starch
3	1	—	0	190	1 starch, 1 fruit
1	1	—	0	165	1 starch
1	1	—	0	105	1 starch†
2	1	—	0	150	1 starch
3	0	—	0	10	1 starch
4	2	—	0	5	1 starch, ½ fat
3	3	—	0	10	1 starch, ½ fat
3	0	—	0	5	1 starch
3	0	—	0	10	1 starch
4	1	—	0	5-10	1 starch

* Not available   ▤ More than 2 fat exchanges   � Moderate to high sugar content

Products	SERVING SIZE	CALORIES	CARBO-HYDRATE (gm)
Fiber 7 Flakes™, 100% Organic, all varieties (average)	½ cup	90	20
Fruit and Fitness®	½ cup	110	19
Fruit Lites™, all varieties (average)	1 cup	90	21
Healthy Crunch™, No Fat Added, all varieties (average)	¼ cup	90	18
Healthy O's™, 100% Organic	¾ cup	90	18
Lites™, Puffed Cereal, all varieties (average)	¾ cup	75	18
Oat Bran Flakes, 100% Organic, all varieties (average)	½ cup	100	20
Oat Bran O's™, all varieties (average)	½ cup	110	19
Orangeola®, No Fat Added, all varieties (average)	¼ cup	90	20
Raisin Bran Flakes, 100% Organic	⅓ cup	70	14
Real® Oat Bran Cereal, all varieties (average)	¼ cup	120	20
Rice Bran Cereal with Almonds and Dates	½ cup	110	19
Rice Bran O's™	⅓ cup	75	15
Sprouts 7®, all varieties (average)	¼ cup	90	16
Swiss Breakfast™, No Fat Added, all varieties (average)	¼ cup	80	20
10 Bran Cereal, Fat Free, all varieties (average)	1 oz.	90	19
HEARTLAND® (PET, Inc.)			
Ready-to-Eat Cereals			
Coconut	1 oz.	130	18
Plain	1 oz.	130	18
Raisin	1 oz.	130	18

PROTEIN (gm)	FAT (gm)	SAT. FAT (gm)	CHOLES- TEROL (mg)	SODIUM (mg)	EXCHANGES
3	0	—	0	0	1 starch
5	2	—	0	3	1 starch, ½ fat
3	0	—	0	4	1 starch
4	1	—	0	10	1 starch
3	1	—	0	1	1 starch
3	0	—	0	0	1 starch
3	1	—	0	0-5	1 starch
3	2	—	0	0	1 starch, ½ fat
3	1	—	0	2	1 starch
2	<1	—	0	3	1 starch
5	3	—	0	2	1 starch, ½ fat
2	3	—	0	2	1 starch, ½ fat
1	1	—	0	3	1 starch
4	1	—	0	5	1 starch
3	1	—	0	5	1 starch
3	0	—	0	5	1 starch
3	5	—	0	80	1 starch, 1 fat
3	4	—	0	80	1 starch, 1 fat
3	4	—	0	80	1 starch, 1 fat

Products	SERVING SIZE	CALORIES	CARBO-HYDRATE (gm)
KELLOGG'S® (Kellogg Company)			
Ready-to-Eat Cereals			
All Bran®	⅓ cup	70	22
All Bran® with Extra Fiber	¾ cup	75	33
♥ Apple Jacks®	¾ cup	83	19
Apple Raisin Crisp®	⅔ cup	130	32
♥ Bigg Mixx™	⅓ cup	74	16
♥ Bigg Mixx™ with Raisins	½ cup	140	31
Bran Buds®	⅓ cup	70	22
Bran Flakes	⅔ cup	90	23
♥ Cocoa Krispies®	½ cup	73	17
Common Sense™ Oat Bran	½ cup	100	22
Common Sense™ Oat Bran with Raisins	½ cup	120	29
Corn Flakes®	¾ cup	75	18
♥ Corn Pops®	¾ cup	83	20
♥ Cracklin' Oat Bran®	½ cup	110	20
Crispix®	¾ cup	83	19
♥ Froot Loops®	¾ cup	83	19
♥ Frosted Flakes®	½ cup	73	17
♥ Frosted Krispies®	½ cup	73	17
Frosted Mini-Wheats®	3 biscuits	75	18
Frosted Mini-Wheats®, bite size	⅓ cup	67	16
Fruitful Bran™	⅔ cup	110	29
♥ Fruity Marshmallow Krispies®	¾ cup	84	19
Heartwise	⅔ cup	90	23
♥ Honey Smacks®	½ cup	74	17
Just Right™ with Fiber Nuggets	½ cup	70	16
Just Right™ with Fruit & Nuts	¾ cup	140	30
Kenmei™ Rice Bran	½ cup	74	18
Kenmei™ Rice Bran, Almond and Raisin	¾ cup	150	31

† For occasional use   ** Not recommended for use

PROTEIN (gm)	FAT (gm)	SAT. FAT (gm)	CHOLES- TEROL (mg)	SODIUM (mg)	EXCHANGES
4	1	—	0	260	1 starch
6	0	—	0	210	1 starch
2	0	—	0	94	1 starch†
2	0	—	0	230	1 starch, 1 fruit
1	1	—	0	127	1 starch†
2	2	—	0	190	1 starch, 1 fruit†
3	1	—	0	170	1 starch
3	0	—	0	220	1 starch
1	0	—	0	127	1 starch†
4	1	—	0	270	1 starch
4	1	—	0	250	1 starch, ½ fruit
2	0	—	0	218	1 starch
1	0	—	0	68	1 starch†
3	4	—	0	150	1 starch, ½ fat†
2	0	—	0	165	1 starch
2	1	—	0	94	1 starch†
1	0	—	0	134	1 starch†
1	0	—	0	147	1 starch†
2	0	—	0	0	1 starch
2	0	—	0	0	1 starch
3	0	—	0	230	1 starch, ½ fruit
1	0	—	0	126	1 starch†
3	1	—	0	140	1 starch
1	0	—	0	47	1 starch†
1	1	—	0	134	1 starch
3	1	—	0	190	1 starch, 1 fruit
2	1	—	0	188	1 starch
3	2	—	0	240	1 starch, 1 fruit, ½ fat

* Not available   ᛒ More than 2 fat exchanges   ♥ Moderate to high sugar content

Products	SERVING SIZE	CALORIES	CARBO-HYDRATE (gm)
🛒 Mini Buns, Cinnamon	½ cup	73	17
Mueslix® Crispy Blend	⅔ cup	160	33
Mueslix® Golden Crunch™	½ cup	120	25
🛒 Nut & Honey Crunch®	½ cup	74	16
🛒 Nut & Honey Crunch O's™	½ cup	74	16
Nutri Grain® Almond Raisin	⅔ cup	140	31
Nutri Grain® Raisin Bran	1 cup	130	31
Nutri Grain® Wheat	½ cup	67	16
🛒 Oatbake™ Honey Bran	⅓ cup	110	21
🛒 Oatbake™ Raisin Nut	⅓ cup	110	21
Product 19®	¾ cup	75	18
Raisin Bran	½ cup	80	21
Rice Krispies®	¾ cup	83	19
Shredded Wheat Squares™, all varieties (average)	½ cup	90	23
Special K®	¾ cup	83	15

NABISCO® Brand Cereals (Nabisco, Inc.)

Hot Cereals

Cream of Wheat® Mix 'n Eat, all varieties (as prepared) (average)	1 packet	130	30
Wholesome 'N Hearty Oat Bran®, Instant all flavored varieties, (as prepared) (average)	1 packet (1⅜ oz.)	120	28
Regular	1 packet (1 oz.)	80	20

Ready-to-Eat Cereals

Frosted Wheat Squares®	¾ oz.	75	18
Fruit Wheats®	1 oz.	90	23
100% Bran	1 oz.	80	22
Shredded Wheat®	1 biscuit	80	19
Shredded Wheat 'n Bran®	1 oz.	90	23
Shredded Wheat with Oat Bran®	¾ oz.	75	17

PROTEIN (gm)	FAT (gm)	SAT. FAT (gm)	CHOLES-TEROL (mg)	SODIUM (mg)	EXCHANGES
1	1	0	0	145	1 starch†
3	2	—	0	150	1 starch, 1 fruit, ½ fat
3	2	—	0	170	1 starch, ½ fruit
1	1	—	0	133	1 starch†
1	1	—	0	127	1 starch†
3	2	—	0	220	1 starch, 1 fruit
4	1	—	0	200	1 starch, 1 fruit
2	0	—	0	113	1 starch
2	3	—	0	180	1 starch, ½ fat†
2	3	—	0	190	1 starch, ½ fat†
2	0	—	0	240	1 starch
2	1	—	0	155	1 starch
2	0	—	0	218	1 starch
2	0	—	0	0-5	1 starch
5	0	—	0	173	1 starch
—	—	—	—	—	1 starch, 1 fruit
—	—	—	—	—	1½ starch†
—	—	—	—	—	1 starch
—	—	—	—	—	1 starch
—	—	—	—	—	1 starch
—	—	—	—	—	1 starch
—	—	—	—	—	1 starch
—	—	—	—	—	1 starch
—	—	—	—	—	1 starch

* Not available   ▇ More than 2 fat exchanges   ♥ Moderate to high sugar content

Products	SERVING SIZE	CALORIES	CARBO-HYDRATE (gm)
Spoon Size® Shredded Wheat	1 oz.	90	23
Team® Flakes	¾ oz.	83	18
POST® (General Foods Corp.)			
🛒 Alpha-Bits®	¾ oz.	83	18
C.W. Post® Hearty Granola Cereal, all varieties (average)	¾ oz.	98	16
🛒 Cocoa Pebbles®	¾ oz.	83	19
Fruit and Fibre®, all varieties (average)	1 oz.	96	21
🛒 Fruity Pebbles®	¾ oz.	83	19
Grape-Nuts®	¾ oz.	83	17
Grape-Nuts® Flakes	¾ oz.	75	17
Honey Bunches of Oats®, all varieties (average)	¾ oz.	85	17
🛒 Honeycomb®	¾ oz.	83	19
Natural Bran Flakes	1 oz.	90	23
Natural Raisin Bran	1 oz.	80	21
Oat Flakes	¾ oz.	83	16
Post Toasties® Corn Flakes	¾ oz.	83	18
Raisin Grape Nuts®	¾ oz.	75	17
🛒 Smurf-Magic Berries®	¾ oz.	90	20
🛒 Super Golden Crisp®	¾ oz.	83	20
QUAKER® (Quaker Oats Co.)			
Hot Cereals Enriched Corn Meal, White or Yellow (uncooked)	3 Tbsp. (1 oz.)	100	22
Grits Instant Grits, plain	1 packet (0.8 oz.)	80	18
Instant Grits, all flavors (average)	1 packet (1 oz.)	100	22
Oat Bran Cereal	⅓ cup, uncooked (⅔ cup, cooked)	90	17
Oatmeal, Quick and Old Fashioned	⅓ cup, uncooked (⅔ cup, cooked)	100	19

† For occasional use   ** Not recommended for use

PROTEIN (gm)	FAT (gm)	SAT. FAT (gm)	CHOLES-TEROL (mg)	SODIUM (mg)	EXCHANGES
—	—	—	—	—	1 starch
—	—	—	—	—	1 starch
2	1	—	0	143	1 starch†
2	3	—	0	60	1 starch, ½ fat
1	1	—	0	120	1 starch†
2	2	—	0	136	1 starch
1	1	—	0	120	1 starch†
2	0	—	0	136	1 starch
2	1	—	0	120	1 starch
2	2	—	0	120-135	1 starch
2	0	—	0	128	1 starch†
3	0	—	0	240	1 starch
2	1	—	0	134	1 starch
3	1	—	0	98	1 starch
2	0	—	0	232	1 starch
2	0	—	0	105	1 starch
2	1	—	0	45	1 starch†
2	0	—	0	34	1 starch†
2	1	—	0	0	1½ starch
2	0	0	0	440	1 starch
3	1	0-1	0	590-800	1½ starch
6	2	0	0	0	1 starch
4	2	0	0	0	1 starch

* Not available   ▤ More than 2 fat exchanges   ♛ Moderate to high sugar content

Products	SERVING SIZE	CALORIES	CARBO-HYDRATE (gm)
Oatmeal, Instant			
Regular Flavor	1 packet	90	18
☕ Apple and Cinnamon	1 packet	120	26
☕ Cinnamon and Spice	1 packet	160	35
☕ Maple and Brown Sugar	1 packet	150	32
☕ Peaches and Cream	1 packet	130	26
Raisins and Spice	1 packet	150	31
Raisins, Dates, and Walnuts	1 packet	140	25
☕ Strawberries and Cream	1 packet	130	27
Quaker Extra™ Instant Oatmeal			
Regular	1 packet	100	18
☕ Flavors (average)	1 packet	130	27
Ready-to-Eat Cereals			
☕ Cap'n Crunch®, all varieties (average)	½ cup	80	16
King Vitamin®	1 cup	73	15
Kretschmer® Wheat Germ, all varieties (average)	¼ cup	110	15
Life®, Regular or Cinnamon (average)	⅔ cup	100	19
☕ Oh!s®, all varieties (average)	¾ cup	90	17
☕ Popeye® Sweet Crunch	¾ cup	90	18
Quaker®			
100% Natural Cereal, all varieties (average)	¼ cup	130	18
Crunch Bran™	⅔ cup	90	23
Oat Bran	¾ cup	100	20
Oat Squares™	½ cup	100	21
Puffed Rice	1½ cups	75	20
Puffed Wheat	1½ cups	75	17
Shredded Wheat	1 biscuit	65	16
Unprocessed Bran	2 Tbsp.	8	4
Sun Country® Granola, all varieties (average)	¼ cup	120	19

PROTEIN (gm)	FAT (gm)	SAT. FAT (gm)	CHOLES-TEROL (mg)	SODIUM (mg)	EXCHANGES
4	2	0	0	270	1 starch
3	1	0	0	130	1½ starch†
5	2	0	0	320	2 starch†
4	2	0	0	320	2 starch†
3	2	1	0	180	1½ starch†
4	2	0	0	270	2 starch
4	4	0	0	220	1½ starch ½ fat
3	2	1	0	200	1½ starch†
4	2	0	0	220	1 starch
4	2	0	0	120-190	1½ starch†
1	1	<1	—	160-188	1 starch†
2	1	0	—	187	1 starch
8	3	0	0	270-330	1 starch, 1 lean meat
5	2	—	—	170	1 starch
1	2	1	0	120-165	1 starch†
1	2	1	—	250	1 starch†
3	5	3	—	15	1 starch, 1 fat
2	1	0	0	320	1 starch
5	2	0	0	125	1 starch
4	2	—	0	160	1 starch
2	0	0	0	0	1 starch
3	0	0	0	0	1 starch
2	1	—	—	0	1 starch
1	0	0	—	0	Free
3	5	1	0	10	1 starch, 1 fat

* Not available   ∄ More than 2 fat exchanges   ☕ Moderate to high sugar content

Products	SERVING SIZE	CALORIES	CARBO-HYDRATE (gm)
RALSTON® (Ralston Purina Co.)			
Hot Cereal			
Ralston® High Fiber	⅓ cup, uncooked	90	20
Ready-to-Eat Cereals			
☕ Almond Delight®	½ cup	75	15
☕ Batman®	¾ cup	83	19
☕ Bran News®, Cinnamon	¾ cup	100	23
☕ Breakfast with Barbie®	¾ cup	83	19
Chex® Cereals			
Corn Chex®	¾ cup	83	19
Double Chex®	½ cup	75	8
☕ Honey Graham Chex®	½ cup	83	19
☕ Honey Nut Oat Chex®	⅓ cup	70	15
Multi-Bran Chex®	½ cup	70	19
Rice Chex®	¾ cup	80	18
Wheat Chex®	½ cup	75	17
☕ Cookie Crisp®, chocolate or vanilla flavors (average)	¾ cup	83	19
☕ Dinersaurs®	¾ cup	83	19
Fruit Muesli, all varieties (average)	½ cup	150	30
☕ Hot Wheels®	¾ cup	83	18
☕ Morning Funnies®	¾ cup	83	19
☕ Nintendo®	¾ cup	83	19
Oat Bran Options®	¾ cup	130	32
Rice Bran Options®	½ cup	90	18
☕ Slimer! And the Real Ghostbusters®	¾ cup	83	20
Sunflakes Multi Grain	¾ cup	75	18
☕ Teenage Mutant Ninja Turtles®	¾ cup	83	20

PROTEIN (gm)	FAT (gm)	SAT. FAT (gm)	CHOLES-TEROL (mg)	SODIUM (mg)	EXCHANGES
4	1	—	0	5	1 starch
1	1	—	0	133	1 starch†
1	1	—	0	105	1 starch†
2	0	—	0	160	1 starch†
1	1	—	0	53	1 starch†
2	0	—	0	233	1 starch
2	0	—	0	143	1 starch
1	1	—	0	135	1 starch†
1	0	—	0	107	1 starch†
2	0	—	0	150	1 starch
1	0	—	0	204	1 starch
2	0	—	0	173	1 starch
1	1	—	0	165	1 starch†
1	1	—	—	53	1 starch†
4	2	—	0	95-140	1 starch, 1 fruit
2	1	—	0	120	1 starch†
1	1	—	0	53	1 starch†
1	1	—	0	53	1 starch†
4	1	—	0	150	1 starch, 1 fruit
2	2	—	0	90	1 starch
1	1	—	0	86	1 starch†
2	1	—	0	180	1 starch
1	0	—	0	143	1 starch†

* Not available   ▌ More than 2 fat exchanges   ♕ Moderate to high sugar content

Products	SERVING SIZE	CALORIES	CARBO-HYDRATE (gm)

CHEESE

ALPINE LACE® (First World Cheese, Inc.)

Products	SERVING SIZE	CALORIES	CARBO-HYDRATE (gm)
American Flavor Pasteurized Processed Cheese Product	1 oz.	80	—
Ched-R-Lo™	1 oz.	80	—
Colbi-Lo™	1 oz.	80	—
Low Moisture Part-Skim Mozzarella	1 oz.	70	—
Monti-Jack-Lo™	1 oz.	80	—
Muenster, low sodium	1 oz.	100	—
Provo-Lo™	1 oz.	70	—
Swiss-Lo™	1 oz.	100	—
Free N' Lean Pasteurized Process Skim Milk Cheese, all varieties (average)	1 oz.	35	1

CHURNY® (Churny Company, Inc.)

Products	SERVING SIZE	CALORIES	CARBO-HYDRATE (gm)
Cheddar Cheese (Vermont)	1 oz.	110	1
Delicia - American & Hot Pepper Cheese Substitutes	1 oz.	80	1
Delicia - American & Salami Cheese Substitute	1 oz.	80	1
Natural Feta Cheese made with Cow's Milk	1 oz.	90	1
Parmesan	1 oz.	110	1
Romano	1 oz.	110	1

CHURNY®LITE (Churny Company, Inc.)

Products	SERVING SIZE	CALORIES	CARBO-HYDRATE (gm)
Cheddar, mild, reduced fat	1 oz.	80	1
Cheddar, sharp, reduced fat	1 oz.	90	1
Colby, reduced fat	1 oz.	80	1
Monterey Jack, reduced fat	1 oz.	80	0
Swiss, reduced fat	1 oz.	90	1

DORMAN'S® (N. Dorman and Co., Inc.)

Products	SERVING SIZE	CALORIES	CARBO-HYDRATE (gm)
Low Sodium Reduced Fat Cheeses Cheda-Jack/Monterey Blend	1 oz.	80	1
Cheddar	1 oz.	80	1
Monterey	1 oz.	80	1

† For occasional use   ** Not recommended for use

PROTEIN (gm)	FAT (gm)	SAT. FAT (gm)	CHOLES- TEROL (mg)	SODIUM (mg)	EXCHANGES
—	7	—	20	200	1 meat
—	5	—	20	95	1 meat
—	5	—	20	85	1 meat
—	5	—	15	75	1 meat
—	5	—	15	75	1 meat
—	9	—	25	85	1 high fat meat
—	5	—	15	85	1 meat
—	7	—	20	35	1 high fat meat
8	<1	0	5	290	1 lean meat
7	9	5	30	180	1 high fat meat
6	6	—	—	300	1 meat
6	6	—	0	370	1 meat
6	7	5	22	388	1 high fat meat
10	7	—	20	450	1½ meat
9	8	—	30	340	1 high fat meat
8	5	3	20	210	1 meat
8	5	3	20	200	1 meat
8	5	3	20	160	1 meat
8	5	3	20	180	1 meat
10	5	2	20	45	1 meat
8	5	3	19	140	1 meat
8	5	3	20	140	1 meat
8	5	3	18	140	1 meat

* Not available   ▊ More than 2 fat exchanges   🛒 Moderate to high sugar content

Products	SERVING SIZE	CALORIES	CARBO-HYDRATE (gm)
Mozzarella	1 oz.	80	1
Muenster	1 oz.	80	0
Provolone	1 oz.	80	1
Swiss	1 oz.	90	0
EASY CHEESE® (Nabisco Brands, Inc.)			
Pasteurized Process Cheese Spread, all varieties (average)	1 oz.	80	2
FEATHERWEIGHT® (Sandoz Nutrition)			
Low Sodium Cheese	1 oz.	110	1
HOFFMAN'S® (Churny Company, Inc.)			
Pasteurized Process American Cheese	1 oz.	110	1
Super Sharp Pasteurized Process Cheddar Cheese	1 oz.	110	2
KRAFT® (Kraft, Inc.)			
Grated cheese			
American Cheese Food	1 oz.	130	9
Parmesan, Romano (average)	1 oz.	130	1
Light Naturals, reduced fat			
Cheddar, mild and sharp (average)	1 oz.	85	1
Colby	1 oz.	80	1
Monterey Jack	1 oz.	80	0
Swiss	1 oz.	90	1
Natural Cheese			
Blue	1 oz.	100	1
Brick	1 oz.	110	0
Caraway	1 oz.	100	1
Cheddar	1 oz.	110	1
Colby	1 oz.	110	1
Edam	1 oz.	90	0
Gouda	1 oz.	110	0
Monterey Jack, all varieties (average)	1 oz.	110	0

† For occasional use   ** Not recommended for use

PROTEIN (gm)	FAT (gm)	SAT. FAT (gm)	CHOLES-TEROL (mg)	SODIUM (mg)	EXCHANGES
9	4	3	—	140	1 meat
8	5	3	18	140	1 meat
9	4	3	17	140	1 meat
10	5	3	17	60	1½ lean meat
4	6	—	—	320-370	½ meat, 1 fat
7	9	—	—	5	1 high fat meat
6	9	—	—	400	1 high fat meat
6	8	—	—	390	1 high fat meat
8	7	4	25	740	½ starch, 1 high fat meat
12	9	5-6	30	350-430	2 meat
8	5	3	20	200-210	1 meat
8	5	3	20	160	1 meat
8	5	3	20	180	1 meat
10	5	3	20	45	1½ meat
6	9	5	30	330	1 high fat meat
7	9	5	30	180	1 high fat meat
7	8	5	30	180	1 high fat meat
7	9	5	30	180	1 high fat meat
7	9	5	30	180	1 high fat meat
8	7	4	20	310	1 high fat meat
7	9	5	30	200	1 high fat meat
7	9	5	30	190	1 high fat meat

* Not available   ▤ More than 2 fat exchanges   🛒 Moderate to high sugar content

Products	SERVING SIZE	CALORIES	CARBO-HYDRATE (gm)
Mozzarella, low moisture, part-skim	1 oz.	80	0
Parmesan Cheese, natural	1 oz.	110	1
Provolone	1 oz.	100	1
Romano	1 oz.	110	1
String Cheese (Mozzarella)	1 oz.	80	1
Swiss, all varieties (average)	1 oz.	110	1
Taco, shredded	1 oz.	110	1
Process Cheese, Singles, all varieties (average)	1 oz.	100	1
Process Cheese Food, all varieties (average)	1 oz.	90	2
Process Cheese Spread, all varieties (average)	1 oz.	80	2
Spreads: Jalapeno, Pimento, Pineapple, etc. (average)	1 oz.	70	3
KRAFT® CASINO® (Kraft, Inc.)			
Havarti	1 oz.	120	0
Monterey Jack with Peppers, mild	1 oz.	110	0
Mozzarella, low moisture	1 oz.	90	1
Swiss	1 oz.	110	1
KRAFT® CHEEZ WHIZ® (Kraft, Inc.)			
Process Cheese Spread, all varieties (average)	1 oz.	80	2
KRAFT® CRACKER BARREL® (Kraft, Inc.)			
Cheese Ball or Log, all varieties (average)	1 oz.	90	4
Cold Pack Cheese Food, all varieties (average)	1 oz.	90	3
KRAFT® GOLDEN IMAGE® (Kraft, Inc.)			
Imitation Cheese Natural Cheddar Cheese	1 oz.	110	0
Colby Cheese	1 oz.	110	1
Process Cheese Food, American Flavor	1 oz.	90	2

† For occasional use   ** Not recommended for use

PROTEIN (gm)	FAT (gm)	SAT. FAT (gm)	CHOLES-TEROL (mg)	SODIUM (mg)	EXCHANGES
8	5	3	15	200	1 meat
10	7	4	20	450	1½ meat
7	7	4	25	260	1 high fat meat
9	8	6	30	340	1½ meat
8	5	3	20	230	1 meat
8	8	5	25	40-45	1 high fat meat
7	9	5	30	190	1 high fat meat
6	8	5	25	420-460	1 high fat meat
5	7	4	20	370-450	1 high fat meat
5	6	4	20	470	1 meat
2	5	3	15	75-160	½ meat, ½ fat
6	11	7	35	140	1 meat, 1 fat
7	9	5	30	180	1 high fat meat
6	7	4	25	190	1 high fat meat
8	8	5	30	35	1 high fat meat
4	6	4	20	430-470	½ meat, 1 fat
5	6	3	15	410	1 high fat meat
5	7	4	20	270-280	1 high fat meat
7	9	2	5	150	1 high fat meat
7	9	2	5	170	1 high fat meat
7	6	2	5	360	1 meat

* Not available   ▌ More than 2 fat exchanges   ♥ Moderate to high sugar content

Products	SERVING SIZE	CALORIES	CARBO-HYDRATE (gm)
KRAFT® HARVEST MOON® (Kraft, Inc.)			
Process Cheese Product, all varieties (average)	1 oz.	70	2
KRAFT® LIGHT N' LIVELY® (Kraft, Inc.)			
Singles, all varieties (average)	1 oz.	70	2
KRAFT® LUNCH WAGON® (Kraft, Inc.)			
Pizza Topping, made with vegetable oil	1 oz.	80	1
Sandwich Slices, made with vegetable oil	1 oz.	90	2
KRAFT® MOHAWK VALLEY® (Kraft, Inc.)			
Limburger, little gem size, natural	1 oz.	90	0
Limburger, process cheese spread	1 oz.	70	0
KRAFT® NIPPY® (Kraft, Inc.)			
Process Cheese Food	1 oz.	90	2
KRAFT® OLD ENGLISH® (Kraft, Inc.)			
Process Cheese, all varieties (average)	1 oz.	110	1
Process Cheese Spread	1 oz.	80	1
KRAFT® ROKA® (Kraft, Inc.)			
Blue Process Cheese Spread	1 oz.	70	2
KRAFT® SMOKELLE® (Kraft, Inc.)			
Process Cheese Food	1 oz.	90	2
KRAFT® SQUEEZ-A-SNAK® (Kraft, Inc.)			
Process Cheese Spread, all varieties (average)	1 oz.	80	1
KRAFT® VELVEETA® (Kraft, Inc.)			
Process Cheese Food, all varieties (average)	1 oz.	100	3
Process Cheese Product, light	1 oz.	70	3
Process Cheese Spread, all varieties (average)	1 oz.	80	3
Slices	1 oz.	90	3

† For occasional use   ** Not recommended for use

PROTEIN (gm)	FAT (gm)	SAT. FAT (gm)	CHOLES- TEROL (mg)	SODIUM (mg)	EXCHANGES
6	4	2	15	420	1 meat
6	4	2	15	380- 410	1 meat
6	6	1	0	350	1 meat
5	7	2	5	370	1 high fat meat
6	8	5	25	250	1 high fat meat
4	6	3	20	420	½ meat, 1 fat
5	7	4	20	380	1 high fat meat
6	9	5	30	400- 440	1 high fat meat
5	7	4	20	480	1 high fat meat
3	6	4	20	270	½ meat, 1 fat
5	7	4	20	370	1 high fat meat
5	7	4	20	430- 510	1 high fat meat
6	7	4	25	410- 430	1 high fat meat
5	4	2	15	450	1 meat
5	6	3	20	400- 520	1 high fat meat
5	6	4	20	400	1 high fat meat

* Not available   ▌ More than 2 fat exchanges   ☕ Moderate to high sugar content

Products	SERVING SIZE	CALORIES	CARBO-HYDRATE (gm)
LAND O'LAKES® (Land O'Lakes, Inc.)			
Cottage Cheese	½ cup (4 oz.)	120	4
Cottage Cheese 2%	½ cup (4 oz.)	100	4
Cottage Cheese 1%	½ cup (4 oz.)	90	4
Natural Cheese, except Part-Skim Mozzarella (average)	1 oz.	110	1
Part Skim Mozzarella	1 oz.	80	1
Process Cheese (average)	1 oz.	90	2
Process Cheese Food Slices, individually wrapped	¾ oz.	70	2
LORRAINE® (Cheese Division, Universal Foods Corp.)			
Lites			
Cheddar, reduced fat	1 oz.	90	1
Colby, reduced fat	1 oz.	90	1
Monterey Jack, reduced fat	1 oz.	90	1
Mozzarella, part skim	1 oz.	80	1
Provolone, reduced fat	1 oz.	80	1
Swiss, reduced fat	1 oz.	90	1
MAY-BUD® (Churny Company, Inc.)			
Farmers Cheese (semi-soft, part-skim cheese)	1 oz.	90	1
PARKERS FARM (Parkers Farm, Inc.)			
Cold Pack Cheese Food, all varieties (average)	1 oz.	94	2
PHILADELPHIA BRAND® (Kraft, Inc.)			
Cream Cheese, regular, whipped, or soft, all varieties (average)	1 Tbsp. (½ oz.)	45-50	1
Cream Cheese, light	2 Tbsp. (1 oz.)	60	2
Neufchatel Cheese, light	1 Tbsp. (½ oz.)	40	1

† For occasional use   ** Not recommended for use

PROTEIN (gm)	FAT (gm)	SAT. FAT (gm)	CHOLES- TEROL (mg)	SODIUM (mg)	EXCHANGES
14	5	3	15	480	2 lean meat
14	2	1	10	440	2 lean meat
14	1	1	5	490	2 lean meat
7	8	—	—	75-275	1 high fat meat
8	5	—	—	150	1 meat
6	7	—	—	330-445	1 high fat meat
4	5	3	15	260	½ high fat meat
8	6	4	20	140	1 meat
8	6	4	20	140	1 meat
8	6	4	20	140	1 meat
8	5	3	15	140	1 meat
8	5	3	15	140	1 meat
9	5	3	20	80	1 meat
6	7	—	20	210	1 high fat meat
6	7	4	18	274	1 high fat meat
1	5	3	13-15	38-80	1 fat
3	5	3	15	160	1 fat
2	4	2	13	58	1 fat

* Not available   ▉ More than 2 fat exchanges   ♥ Moderate to high sugar content

Products	SERVING SIZE	CALORIES	CARBO-HYDRATE (gm)
SARGENTO® (Sargento Cheese Co., Inc.)			
Blue Cheese	1 oz.	100	1
Brie	1 oz.	100	<1
Burger Cheese	1 oz.	110	<1
Cajun	1 oz.	110	<1
Camembert	1 oz.	90	<1
Cheddar	1 oz.	110	<1
Colby	1 oz.	110	1
Colby-Jack	1 oz.	110	<1
Cracker Snacks, processed cheese spreads (average)	1 oz.	105	1
Edam	1 oz.	100	<1
Farmer's Cheese	1 oz.	100	1
Feta	1 oz.	80	1
Finland Swiss	1 oz.	110	<1
Fontina	1 oz.	110	<1
Gjetost	1 oz.	130	12
Gouda	1 oz.	100	1
Havarti	1 oz.	120	<1
Hot Pepper Processed American	1 oz.	110	—
Italian Style Grated Cheese	1 oz.	110	1
Imitation Cheese			
Cheddar	1 oz.	90	<1
Mozzarella	1 oz.	80	<1
Limburger	1 oz.	90	—
Jarlsberg	1 oz.	100	1
Monterey Jack	1 oz.	110	<1
Mozzarella			
Low Moisture, part-skim	1 oz.	80	1
Whole Milk	1 oz.	90	1
Muenster, red rind	1 oz.	100	<1
New York Cheddar	1 oz.	110	<1

PROTEIN (gm)	FAT (gm)	SAT. FAT (gm)	CHOLES-TEROL (mg)	SODIUM (mg)	EXCHANGES
6	8	—	21	400	1 high fat meat
6	8	—	28	180	1 high fat meat
6	9	—	27	410	1 high fat meat
7	9	—	28	165	1 high fat meat
6	7	—	20	240	1 high fat meat
7	9	—	30	180	1 high fat meat
7	9	—	27	170	1 high fat meat
7	9	—	27	160	1 high fat meat
6	9	—	25	390-430	1 high fat meat
7	8	—	25	270	1 high fat meat
7	8	—	26	130	1 high fat meat
4	6	—	25	320	½ high fat, ½ fat
8	8	—	26	75	1 high fat meat
7	9	—	33	—	1 high fat meat
3	8	—	—	170	1 starch, 1½ fat
7	8	—	32	230	1 high fat meat
5	11	—	32	200	1 high fat meat, ½ fat
6	9	—	27	410	1 high fat meat
8	8	—	25	105	1 high fat meat
7	6	—	2	350	1 meat
7	6	—	2	310	1 meat
6	8	—	26	230	1 high fat meat
7	7	—	16	130	1 high fat meat
7	9	—	25	150	1 high fat meat
8	5	—	15	150	1 meat
6	7	—	25	120	1 high fat meat
7	9	—	27	180	1 high fat meat
7	9	—	30	180	1 high fat meat

* Not available   ▤ More than 2 fat exchanges   ♥ Moderate to high sugar content

Products	SERVING SIZE	CALORIES	CARBO-HYDRATE (gm)
Nut Logs			
Port Wine	1 oz.	100	3
Sharp Cheddar	1 oz.	100	3
Swiss Almond	1 oz.	90	2
Parmesan, fresh	1 oz.	110	1
Parmesan, grated	1 oz.	130	2
Parmesan & Romano, grated blend	1 oz.	110	1
Pot Cheese	1 oz.	25	1
Provolone	1 oz.	100	1
Queso Blanco	1 oz.	100	<1
Queso de Papa	1 oz.	110	<1
Ricotta			
Lite	1 oz.	23	1
Part Skim	1 oz.	30	1
Romano	1 oz.	110	1
Smokestick	1 oz.	100	1
String Cheese	1 oz.	80	1
Smoked String Cheese	1 oz.	80	1
Swiss	1 oz.	110	1
Taco	1 oz.	110	<1
Tilsiter	1 oz.	100	1
Tybo-Red Wax	1 oz.	100	<1

WEIGHT WATCHERS® (Nutrition Industries Corp.)

Products	SERVING SIZE	CALORIES	CARBO-HYDRATE (gm)
Cup Cheese, process cheese spread, all varieties (average)	1 oz. (2 Tbsp.)	70	7
Creamed Cheese	1 Tbsp.	18	1
Natural Cheese, all varieties (average)	1 oz.	80	1
Natural Cheese, low sodium	1 oz.	80	1
Process Cheese Product, slices, all varieties (average)	1 oz.	50	2
Process Cheese Product, low sodium, slices	1 oz.	50	2

† For occasional use   ** Not recommended for use

PROTEIN (gm)	FAT (gm)	SAT. FAT (gm)	CHOLES-TEROL (mg)	SODIUM (mg)	EXCHANGES
6	7	—	18	250	1 high fat meat
6	7	—	18	250	1 high fat meat
6	7	—	21	350	1 high fat meat
10	7	—	19	450	1½ meat
12	9	—	22	530	2 meat
10	7	—	24	400	1½ meat
5	<1	—	—	1	½ lean meat
7	8	—	20	250	1 high fat meat
7	9	—	27	180	1 high fat meat
7	9	—	30	180	1 high fat meat
3	1	—	4	20	½ lean meat
3	2	—	10	30	½ meat
9	8	—	29	340	1 high fat meat
7	7	—	24	390	1 high fat meat
8	5	—	15	150	1 meat
8	5	—	15	150	1 meat
8	8	—	26	75	1 high fat meat
7	9	—	27	160	1 high fat meat
7	7	—	29	210	1 high fat meat
7	7	—	23	200	1 high fat meat
4	3	2	10	190-260	½ starch, ½ meat
2	1	—	—	20	Free
8	5	3	15	40-150	1 meat
8	5	3	15	70	1 meat
6	2	1	5-10	370-430	1 lean meat
7	2	1	5	120	1 lean meat

* Not available   ▤ More than 2 fat exchanges   ♣ Moderate to high sugar content

Products	SERVING SIZE	CALORIES	CARBO-HYDRATE (gm)
CHILI			
FEATHERWEIGHT® (Sandoz Nutrition)			
Chili with Beans, Low Sodium	7½ oz.	280	29
GOOD TIMES® (Kraft, Inc.)			
Chili Fixin's, Original with Beans	4 oz.	80	16
Chili Fixin's, Original without Beans	4 oz.	50	11
Chili Fixin's, Texas Style with Beans	4 oz.	90	19
Chili Fixin's, Texas Style without Beans	4 oz.	60	13
HAIN® (PET, Inc.)			
Spicy Chili with Chicken	7½ oz.	130	19
Spicy Tempeh	7½ oz.	160	24
Spicy Vegetarian	7½ oz.	160	29
Spicy Vegetarian, reduced sodium	7½ oz.	170	31
HEALTH VALLEY® (Health Valley Foods, Inc.)			
Fat Free Vegetarian Chili with Black Beans, all varieties (average)	5 oz.	140	23
Vegetarian Chili with Beans, all varieties (average)	5 oz.	160	21
Vegetarian Chili with Beans, no salt added, all varieties (average)	5 oz.	160	21
Vegetarian Chili with Lentils	5 oz.	140	15
Vegetarian Chili with Lentils, no salt added	5 oz.	140	15
HORMEL® (George A. Hormel and Co.)			
Chili with Beans	10.5 oz.	370	38
Chili, No Beans	10.5 oz.	380	19

† For occasional use   ** Not recommended for use

PROTEIN (gm)	FAT (gm)	SAT. FAT (gm)	CHOLES- TEROL (mg)	SODIUM (mg)	EXCHANGES
19	10	—	30	440	1½ starch, 2 meat
3	1	—	—	600	1 starch
2	0	—	—	570	1 starch
4	1	—	—	560	1 starch
2	1	—	—	770	1 starch
11	2	—	40	1030	1 starch, 1 lean meat
7	4	—	0	1350	1½ starch, ½ fat
7	1	—	0	1060	2 starch
7	1	—	0	200	2 starch
11	0	—	0	290	1 starch, 1 lean meat
10	4	—	0	280- 290	1½ starch, 1 lean meat
10	4	—	0	30	1½ starch, 1 lean meat
8	4	—	0	290	1 starch, 1 lean meat
8	4	—	0	50	1 starch, 1 lean meat
22	14	—	—	—	2 starch, 2 meat, 1 fat
25	22	—	—	—	1 starch, 3 meat, 1½ fat

* Not available   ▌ More than 2 fat exchanges   ♥ Moderate to high sugar content

Products	SERVING SIZE	CALORIES	CARBO-HYDRATE (gm)
OLD EL PASO® (PET, Inc.)			
Chili Con Carne	1 cup	162	8
Chili with Beans	1 cup	217	17
STOUFFER'S® (Stouffer Foods Corp.)			
Chili Con Carne with Beans	8 ¾ oz.	260	24
STOUFFER'S® RIGHT COURSE™ (Stouffer Foods Corp.)			
Vegetarian Chili	9 ¾ oz.	280	45
VAN CAMP'S® (Quaker Oats Co.)			
Chili Weenee®	1 cup	310	28
目 Chili with Beans	1 cup	350	21
目 Chili without Beans	1 cup	410	12
WOLF'S® (Quaker Oats Company)			
目 Chili with Beans, all varieties (average)	Scant cup	330	21
Chili without Beans, all varieties (average)	Scant cup	360	15
目 Chili-Mac	Scant cup	320	23

COMBINATION DISHES, DINNERS, ENTREES

ARMOUR CLASSICS® (ConAgra® Frozen Foods Co.)

Products	SERVING SIZE	CALORIES	CARBO-HYDRATE (gm)
Boneless Beef Short Ribs	9.75 oz.	380	34
Chicken and Noodles	11 oz.	230	23
Chicken Fettucini	11 oz.	260	28
Chicken Mesquite	9.5 oz.	370	42

PROTEIN (gm)	FAT (gm)	SAT. FAT (gm)	CHOLES-TEROL (mg)	SODIUM (mg)	EXCHANGES
19	7	—	47	510	½ starch, 2½ lean meat
15	10	—	32	480	1 starch, 2 meat
19	10	—	—	1270	1½ starch, 2 meat
9	7	1	0	590	3 starch, 1 fat
14	16	—	—	1060	2 starch, 1 high fat meat, 1 fat
15	23	—	—	1220	1 starch, 1½ high fat meat, 2½ fat
15	34	—	—	1500	1 starch, 2 high fat meat, 3½ fat
14	21	—	—	930-1010	1½ starch, 1 high fat meat, 2½ fat
19	25	—	—	960-1040	1 starch, 2 high fat meat, 2 fat
12	20	—	—	850	1½ starch, 1 meat, 3 fat
24	16	—	90	790	2 starch, 1 veg., 2½ meat
19	7	—	50	660	1 starch, 1 veg., 2 lean meat
17	9	—	50	660	1½ starch, 1 veg., 1½ meat
15	16	—	55	660	2½ starch, 1 veg., 1 lean meat, 2 fat

Products	SERVING SIZE	CALORIES	CARBO-HYDRATE (gm)
Chicken Parmigiana	11.5 oz.	370	27
Chicken with Wine & Mushroom Sauce	10.75 oz.	280	24
Glazed Chicken	10.75 oz.	300	24
Ham Steak	10.75 oz.	270	36
Meat Loaf	11.25 oz.	360	32
Salisbury Parmigiana	11.5 oz.	410	32
Salisbury Steak	11.25 oz.	350	26
Sirloin Roast	10.45 oz.	190	21
Sirloin Tips	10.25 oz.	230	20
Swedish Meatballs	11.25 oz.	330	23
Turkey with Dressing and Gravy	11.5 oz.	320	34
Veal Parmigiana	11.25 oz.	400	34
Yankee Pot Roast	10 oz.	310	26

ARMOUR CLASSICS LITE® (ConAgra® Frozen Foods Co.)

Products	SERVING SIZE	CALORIES	CARBO-HYDRATE (gm)
Baby Bay Shrimp	9.75 oz.	220	31
Beef Pepper Steak	11.25 oz.	220	29
Beef Stroganoff	11.25 oz.	250	33
Chicken Ala King	11.25 oz.	290	38

† For occasional use   ** Not recommended for use

PROTEIN (gm)	FAT (gm)	SAT. FAT (gm)	CHOLES-TEROL (mg)	SODIUM (mg)	EXCHANGES
22	19	—	75	1060	1½ starch, 1 veg., 2 lean meat, 2½ fat
22	11	—	50	900	1½ strach, 2½ lean meat, ½ fat
15	16	—	60	960	1 starch, 1 veg., 1½ lean meat, 2 fat
15	7	—	50	1320	2 starch, 1 veg., 1½ lean meat
20	17	—	65	1170	2 starch, 1 veg., 2 meat, 1½ fat
22	21	—	60	1120	2 starch, 1 veg., 2 meat, 2 fat
22	17	—	55	1430	1½ starch, 1 veg., 2½ meat, ½ fat
19	4	—	55	970	1 starch, 1 veg., 1½ lean meat
22	7	—	70	820	1 starch, 1 veg., 2½ lean meat
19	18	—	80	720	1 starch, 1 veg., 2 meat, 1½ fat
19	12	—	50	1280	2 starch, 1 veg., 2 lean meat, ½ fat
18	22	—	55	1320	2 starch, 1 veg., 2 meat, 1½ fat
25	12	—	85	670	1½ starch, 1 veg., 3 lean meat
12	6	—	105	890	1½ starch, 1 veg., 1 lean meat, ½ fat
17	4	—	35	970	1½ starch, 1 veg., 1½ lean meat
18	6	—	55	510	2 starch, 1 veg., 1½ lean meat
19	7	—	55	630	2 starch, 1 veg., 2 lean meat

* Not available   ▉ More than 2 fat exchanges   ☕ Moderate to high sugar content

Products	SERVING SIZE	CALORIES	CARBO-HYDRATE (gm)
Chicken Burgundy	10 oz.	210	25
Chicken Marsala	10.5 oz.	250	27
Chicken Oriental	10 oz.	180	24
Salisbury Steak	11.5 oz.	300	29
Seafood with Natural Herbs	10 oz.	190	29
Shrimp Creole	11.25 oz.	260	53
Steak Diane	10 oz.	290	25
☗ Sweet and Sour Chicken	11 oz.	240	39
BANQUET® (ConAgra® Frozen Foods Co.) Casseroles Macaroni and Cheese	8 oz.	350	36
Spaghetti with Meat Sauce	8 oz.	270	35
Cookin' Bags Barbecue Sauce and Sliced Beef	4 oz.	100	11
Breaded Veal Parmigiana	4 oz.	230	20
Chicken Ala King	4 oz.	110	9
Chicken and Vegetables Primavera	4 oz.	100	14
Creamed Chipped Beef	4 oz.	100	9
Gravy and Salisbury Steak	5 oz.	190	8
Gravy and Sliced Beef	4 oz.	100	5
Gravy and Sliced Turkey	5 oz.	100	5

† For occasional use   ** Not recommended for use

PROTEIN (gm)	FAT (gm)	SAT. FAT (gm)	CHOLES- TEROL (mg)	SODIUM (mg)	EXCHANGES
23	2	—	45	780	1 starch, 1 veg., 2½ lean meat
20	7	—	80	930	1½ starch, 1 veg., 2 lean meat
18	1	—	35	660	1 starch, 1 veg., 2 lean meat
21	11	—	40	980	1½ starch, 1 veg., 2 meat
13	2	—	35	1020	1½ starch, 1 veg., 1 lean meat
6	2	—	45	900	3 starch, 1 veg.
27	9	—	80	440	1½ starch, 1 veg., 3 lean meat
18	2	—	35	820	1½ starch, 1 veg., ½ fruit, 1½ lean meat†
11	17	—	—	930	2½ starch, ½ high fat meat, 2 fat
14	8	—	—	1250	2 starch, 1 veg., 1 meat, ½ fat
9	2	—	—	—	½ starch, 1 lean meat
10	11	—	—	—	1 starch, 1 meat, 1 fat
8	5	—	—	—	½ starch, 1 meat
6	2	—	—	—	½ starch, 1 veg., ½ lean meat
7	4	—	—	—	½ starch, 1 lean meat
9	14	—	—	—	½ starch, 1 meat, 1½ fat
8	5	—	—	—	½ starch, 1 lean meat
7	6	—	—	—	½ starch, 1 lean meat

* Not available ▤ More than 2 fat exchanges ♥ Moderate to high sugar content

Products	SERVING SIZE	CALORIES	CARBO-HYDRATE (gm)
Meat Loaf	4 oz.	200	8
Mushroom Gravy & Charbroiled Beef Patty	5 oz.	210	8
Dinners			
Beans and Frankfurters	10 oz.	520	57
Beef Enchilada	12 oz.	500	72
Cheese Enchilada	12 oz.	550	71
Chicken & Dumplings	10 oz.	430	34
Chopped Beef	11 oz.	420	14
Fried Chicken	10 oz.	400	45
Macaroni and Cheese	10 oz.	420	46
Meat Loaf	11 oz.	440	27
Mexican Style	12 oz.	490	62
Mexican Style Combination	12 oz.	520	72
Noodles and Chicken	10 oz.	350	42
Salisbury Steak	11 oz.	500	26
Spaghetti and Meatballs	10 oz.	290	44

PROTEIN (gm)	FAT (gm)	SAT. FAT (gm)	CHOLES-TEROL (mg)	SODIUM (mg)	EXCHANGES
10	14	—	—	—	½ starch, 1 meat, 2 fat
9	15	—	—	—	½ starch, 1 meat, 2 fat
17	25	—	35	1230	3½ starch, 1 veg., 1 high fat meat, 2½ fat
19	15	—	—	1810	4½ starch, 1 veg., 1 meat, 1 fat
22	19	-	—	2170	4½ starch, 1 veg., 1½ meat, 1 fat
17	24	—	45	940	2 starch, 1 veg., 1½ meat, 3 fat
21	32	—	80	600	1 starch, 2½ meat, 3½ fat
15	22	—	—	1100	2½ starch, 1 veg., 1½ meat, 2 fat
14	20	—	30	450	2½ starch, 1 veg., 1 meat, 3 fat
26	27	—	85	770	1½ starch, 1 veg., 3 meat, 2 fat
18	18	—	—	2000	3½ starch, 1 veg., 1½ meat, 1½ fat
20	17	—	—	1980	4½ starch, 1 veg., 1½ meat, 1 fat
10	15	—	45	460	2 starch, 1 veg., ½ meat, 1 fat
23	34	—	80	600	1½ starch, 1 veg., 2½ meat, 4 fat
11	10	—	30	580	2½ starch, 1 veg., ½ meat, 1 fat

* Not available   ▤ More than 2 fat exchanges   ☕ Moderate to high sugar content

Products	SERVING SIZE	CALORIES	CARBO-HYDRATE (gm)
Turkey	10.5 oz.	390	35
⊟ Western	11 oz.	630	40
Extra Helping Dinners ⊟ Beef	16 oz.	870	50
⊟ Chicken Nuggets with Barbecue Sauce	10 oz.	640	56
⊟ Chicken Nuggets with Sweet ⛟ and Sour Sauce	10 oz.	650	64
⊟ Fried Chicken	16 oz.	570	70
⊟ Fried Chicken, all white meat	16 oz.	570	70
⊟ Salisbury Steak	18 oz.	910	49
⊟ Turkey	19 oz.	750	68
Family Entrees Beef Stew	¼ pkg. (7 oz.)	140	18
Chicken and Dumplings	¼ pkg. (7 oz.)	280	28
Chicken and Vegetables Primavera	¼ pkg. (7 oz.)	140	18
Chili Gravy and Beef Enchiladas	¼ pkg. (7 oz.)	270	28
⊟ Gravy and Salisbury Steak	¼ pkg. (8 oz.)	300	12
Gravy and Sliced Beef	¼ pkg. (8 oz.)	160	8
Gravy and Sliced Turkey	¼ pkg. (8 oz.)	150	8
Lasagna with Meat Sauce	¼ pkg. (7 oz.)	270	30

† For occasional use   ** Not recommended for use

PROTEIN (gm)	FAT (gm)	SAT. FAT (gm)	CHOLES-TEROL (mg)	SODIUM (mg)	EXCHANGES
18	20	—	40	1110	2 starch, 1 veg., 2 lean meat, 2 fat
28	41	—	90	720	2 starch, 1 veg., 3 meat, 5 fat
34	61	—	120	810	3 starch, 1 veg., 3½ meat, 8 fat
29	36	—	—	1390	3½ starch, 1 veg., 2½ meat, 3½ fat
28	34	—	—	—	3 starch, 1 veg., 1 fruit, 3 meat, 2½ fat†
20	28	—	—	1470	4 starch, 1 veg., 1½ meat, 2½ fat
20	28	—	—	1470	4 starch, 1 veg., 1½ meat, 2½ fat
50	60	—	175	740	3 starch, 1 veg., 6 meat, 4½ fat
29	42	—	65	1980	4 starch, 1 veg., 3 meat, 4 fat
6	5	—	—	—	½ starch, 1 veg., ½ meat, ½ fat
12	14	—	—	—	2 starch, 1 meat, 1 fat
9	3	—	—	—	1 starch, 1 veg., 1 lean meat
10	13	—	—	—	2 starch, 1 meat, 1 fat
13	22	—	—	—	1 starch, 1½ meat, 2½ fat
20	5	—	—	—	½ starch, 2½ lean meat
12	8	—	—	—	½ starch, 1½ lean meat, ½ fat
15	10	—	—	—	2 starch, 1½ meat

* Not available   ▤ More than 2 fat exchanges   🛒 Moderate to high sugar content

Products	SERVING SIZE	CALORIES	CARBO-HYDRATE (gm)
Macaroni and Cheese	¼ pkg. (8 oz.)	290	32
Mostaccioli and Meat Sauce	¼ pkg. (7 oz.)	170	28
▉ Mushroom Gravy and Charbroiled Beef Patties	¼ pkg. (8 oz.)	290	13
Noodles and Beef with Gravy	¼ pkg. (8 oz.)	200	22
▉ Onion Gravy and Beef Patties	¼ pkg. (8 oz.)	300	14
Veal Parmigian Patties	¼ pkg. (8 oz.)	370	33
Meat Pies			
▉ Beef	7 oz.	510	39
▉ Chicken	7 oz.	550	39
▉ Tuna	7 oz.	540	44
▉ Turkey	7 oz.	510	39
Platters			
▉ Beef	10 oz.	460	20
Chicken, all white meat, fried	9 oz.	430	21
Chicken, all white meat, fried, hot n' spicy	9 oz.	430	21
Chicken Drumsnacker, boneless	7 oz.	430	49
Chicken Nuggets, boneless	6.4 oz.	430	46
Chicken Pattie, boneless	7.5 oz.	380	34
Fish	8.75 oz.	450	33
Ham	10 oz.	400	43

† For occasional use   ** Not recommended for use

PROTEIN (gm)	FAT (gm)	SAT. FAT (gm)	CHOLES-TEROL (mg)	SODIUM (mg)	EXCHANGES
12	13	—	—	—	2 starch, 1 high fat meat, ½ fat
7	3	—	—	—	1½ starch, ½ meat
13	21	—	—	—	1 starch, 1 meat, 3 fat
13	7	—	—	—	1½ starch, 1 meat
12	21	—	—	—	1 starch, 1½ meat, 2½ fat
18	18	—	—	—	2 starch, 2 meat, 1½ fat
12	33	—	25	870	2 starch, 1 veg., 1 meat, 5½ fat
15	36	—	35	860	2 starch, 1 veg., 1½ meat, 5½ fat
17	33	—	30	810	2½ starch, 1 veg., 1½ meat, 5 fat
16	31	—	40	860	2 starch, 1 veg., 1½ meat, 5 fat
22	34	—	75	630	1 starch, 1 veg., 2½ meat, 4 fat
38	22	—	105	—	1 starch, 1 veg., 5 lean meat, 1 fat
38	22	—	105	—	1 starch, 1 veg., 5 lean meat, 1 fat
20	19	—	—	690	3 starch, 1 veg., 2 meat, ½ fat
17	21	—	—	630	2½ starch, 1 veg., 1½ meat, 2 fat
15	21	—	—	760	2 starch, 1 veg., 1½ meat, 2 fat
31	22	—	95	—	2 starch, 1 veg., 3½ lean meat, 1½ fat
20	17	—	50	1180	2½ starch, 1 veg., 2 meat, ½ fat

* Not available   ▉ More than 2 fat exchanges   🛒 Moderate to high sugar content

Products	SERVING SIZE	CALORIES	CARBO-HYDRATE (gm)
BUDGET GOURMET® (All American Gourmet Co.)			
Light & Healthy Dinners			
Beef Pot Roast	10.5 oz.	210	19
Chicken Breast Parmigiana	11 oz.	260	29
Herbed Chicken Breast with Fettucini	11 oz.	240	28
Italian Style Meat Loaf	11 oz.	270	30
Sirloin of Beef in Wine Sauce	11 oz.	270	35
Sirloin Salisbury Steak	11 oz.	260	28
Special Recipe Sirloin of Beef	11 oz.	250	29
Stuffed Turkey Breast	11 oz.	230	29
Teriyaki Chicken Breast	11 oz.	270	35
CAJUN COOKIN'® (PET, Inc.)			
Entrees			
Crawfish Etouffee	12 oz.	390	51
Seafood Gumbo	17 oz.	330	51
Shrimp Creole	12 oz.	390	55
Shrimp Etouffee	17 oz.	360	52
Shrimp Jambalaya	12 oz.	450	43
CHEF AMERICA® HOT POCKETS (Chef America®)			
Barbecue	5 oz.	350	42
Beef 'n Cheddar	5 oz.	370	36
Chicken 'n Cheddar	5 oz.	310	38

PROTEIN (gm)	FAT (gm)	SAT. FAT (gm)	CHOLES-TEROL (mg)	SODIUM (mg)	EXCHANGES
23	8	2	65	440	1 starch, 1 veg., 2 lean meat
22	8	3	50	420	1½ starch, 1 veg., 2 lean meat
23	7	3	55	430	1½ starch, 1 veg., 2 lean meat
20	10	4	45	480	1½ starch, 1 veg., 2 meat
20	8	2	30	520	2 starch, 1 veg., 2 lean meat
21	9	4	30	510	1½ starch, 1 veg., 2 lean meat
18	10	4	70	550	1½ starch, 1 veg., 1½ meat
22	6	2	40	520	1½ starch, 1 veg., 2 lean meat
19	6	1	30	460	2 starch, 1 veg., 1½ lean meat
23	10	—	—	1110	3 starch, 1 veg., 2 lean meat, ½ fat
16	7	—	—	1330	3 starch, 1 veg., 1 lean meat, ½ fat
17	11	—	—	1130	3 starch, 2 veg., 1 lean meat, 1 fat
19	9	—	—	1170	3 starch, 1 veg., 1 lean meat, 1 fat
20	20	—	—	800	2½ starch, 1 veg., 1½ lean meat, 3 fat
14	14	—	42	980	3 starch, 1 meat, 1 fat
17	17	—	60	1390	2½ starch, 1½ high fat meat, ½ fat
16	11	—	—	720	2½ starch, 1 high fat meat

* Not available   ▊ More than 2 fat exchanges   ☕ Moderate to high sugar content

Products	SERVING SIZE	CALORIES	CARBO-HYDRATE (gm)
Ham 'n Cheese	5 oz.	360	36
Pepperoni Pizza	5 oz.	380	40
Sausage Pizza	5 oz.	360	40
Turkey, Ham 'n Cheese	5 oz.	320	37
CHEF AMERICA® LEAN POCKETS (Chef America®)			
Beef and Broccoli	1 pocket	250	30
Chicken Oriental	1 pocket	250	35
Chicken Parmesan	1 pocket	270	35
Chicken Supreme	1 pocket	240	33
Pizza Deluxe	1 pocket	280	34
CHEF BOYARDEE® (American Home Foods)			
Microwave Meals			
ABC's & 123's	7.5 oz.	260	32
Beef Ravioli	7.5 oz.	190	32
Beefaroni®	7.5 oz.	220	31
Dinosaurs	7.5 oz.	240	32
Spaghetti & Meat Balls	7.5 oz.	230	29
CHICKEN APPLAUSE!® (Kraft, Inc.)			
Oven Bake Dinners (as prepared)			
Barbecue Chicken and Scalloped Potatoes	⅕ box	380	44
Mushroom Chicken and Rice	⅕ box	380	46
Sweet N Sour Chicken and Rice	⅕ box	360	45

† For occasional use   ** Not recommended for use

PROTEIN (gm)	FAT (gm)	SAT. FAT (gm)	CHOLES- TEROL (mg)	SODIUM (mg)	EXCHANGES
16	19	—	90	1320	2½ starch, 1 high fat meat, 1½ fat
17	17	—	45	1240	2½ starch, 1½ high fat meat, ½ fat
15	16	—	65	590	2½ starch, 1 high fat meat, 1½ fat
17	11	—	—	780	2½ starch, 1½ meat
11	8	—	—	760	2 starch, 1 meat, ½ fat
14	6	—	—	840	2 starch, 1 meat
19	6	—	—	750	2 starch, 2 lean meat
16	5	—	—	810	2 starch, 2 lean meat
14	9	—	—	500	2 starch, 1 meat, ½ fat
7	11	—	—	—	2 starch, ½ meat, 1 fat
6	4	—	—	—	2 starch, ½ meat
7	7	—	—	—	2 starch, ½ meat, ½ fat
8	9	—	—	—	2 starch, ½ meat, 1 fat
7	10	—	—	—	2 starch, ½ meat, 1 fat
36	7	2	105	1050	3 starch, 3 lean meat
35	6	1	100	1130	3 starch, 3 lean meat
34	—	1	100	850	3 starch, 3 lean meat

Products	SERVING SIZE	CALORIES	CARBO-HYDRATE (gm)
Three Cheese Chicken and Rice	⅕ box	430	35

CHUN KING® (ConAgra® Frozen Foods Co.)
Entrees

Beef Pork Oriental	13 oz.	310	53
Beef Teriyaki	13 oz.	380	68
Chicken Chow Mein	13 oz.	370	53
Crunchy Walnut Chicken	13 oz.	310	49
Imperial Chicken	13 oz.	300	54
Sweet and Sour Pork	13 oz.	400	78
Szechuan Beef	13 oz.	340	57

DINING LITE® (ConAgra® Frozen Foods Co.)

Beef Teriyaki	9 oz.	270	36
Cheese Cannelloni	9 oz.	310	38
Cheese Lasagna	9 oz.	260	36
Chicken Ala King	9 oz.	240	30
Chicken Chow Mein	9 oz.	180	31
Chicken with Noodles	9 oz.	240	28
Fettucini with Broccoli	9 oz.	290	33
Glazed Chicken	9 oz.	220	30
Lasagna with Meat Sauce	9 oz.	240	36
Oriental Pepper Steak	9 oz.	260	33

† For occasional use   ** Not recommended for use

PROTEIN (gm)	FAT (gm)	SAT. FAT (gm)	CHOLES-TEROL (mg)	SODIUM (mg)	EXCHANGES
39	15	7	130	1130	2 starch, 4½ lean meat
17	3	—	—	1300	3½ starch, 1 lean meat
22	2	—	—	2200	4½ starch, 1 lean meat
25	6	—	—	1560	3½ starch, 2 lean meat
16	5	—	—	1700	3 starch,1 meat
17	1	—	—	1540	3½ starch, 1 lean meat
11	5	—	—	1460	3 starch, 2 fruit, ½ meat†
20	3	—	—	1810	4 starch, 1 lean meat
20	5	—	45	850	2 starch, 1 veg., 2 lean meat
19	9	—	70	650	2 starch, 1 veg., 2 lean meat, ½ fat
14	6	—	30	800	2 starch, 1 veg., 1 meat
14	7	—	40	780	2 starch, 1½ lean meat
10	2	—	30	650	1½ starch, 1 veg., 1 lean meat
17	7	—	50	570	2 starch, 1½ lean meat
12	12	—	35	1020	2 starch, 1 veg., 1 lean meat, 1 fat
17	4	—	45	680	1½ starch, 1 veg., 1½ lean meat
13	5	—	25	800	2 starch, 1 veg., 1 meat
18	6	—	40	1050	2 starch, 1 veg., 1½ lean meat

* Not available　　⬛ More than 2 fat exchanges　　🛒 Moderate to high sugar content

Products	SERVING SIZE	CALORIES	CARBO-HYDRATE (gm)
Salisbury Steak	9 oz.	200	14
Sauce & Swedish Meatballs	9 oz.	280	34
Spaghetti with Beef	9 oz.	220	25
DINING RIGHT® (ConAgra® Frozen Foods Co.)			
Cheese Cannelloni with Tomato Sauce	9 oz.	310	38
Cheese Lasagna	9 oz.	260	36
Chicken Ala King with Rice	9 oz.	240	30
Chicken Chow Mein with Rice	9 oz.	180	31
Chicken with Noodles	9 oz.	240	28
Fettucini and Broccoli with Alfredo Sauce	9 oz.	290	33
Lasagna with Meat Sauce	9 oz.	240	36
Salisbury Steak and Vegetables in Zesty Italian Sauce	9 oz.	200	14
Spaghetti with Beef and Mushroom Sauce	9 oz.	220	25
EATING RIGHT® (Kraft Inc.)			
Frozen Dinners			
Beef Pepper Steak	10 oz.	290	37
Beef Sirloin Tips & Noodles	9 oz.	250	22
Chicken Breast & Vegetables	9 oz.	200	26
Chicken Breast Parmesan	9 oz.	300	32
Fettucini Alfredo	10 oz.	220	33

† For occasional use   ** Not recommended for use

PROTEIN (gm)	FAT (gm)	SAT. FAT (gm)	CHOLES- TEROL (mg)	SODIUM (mg)	EXCHANGES
18	8	—	55	1000	1 starch, 2 lean meat
14	10	—	55	660	2 starch, 1 veg., 1½ lean meat, ½ fat
12	8	—	20	440	1½ starch, 1½ lean meat, ½ fat
19	9	—	70	650	2 starch, 1 veg., 2 lean meat, ½ fat
14	6	—	30	800	2½ starch, 1 lean meat
14	7	—	40	780	2 starch, 1½ lean meat
10	2	—	30	650	1½ starch, 1 veg., 1 lean meat
17	7	—	50	570	1½ starch, 1 veg., 1½ lean meat
12	12	—	35	1020	2 starch, 1 veg., 1 meat, 1 fat
13	5	—	25	800	2 starch, 1 veg., 1 lean meat
18	8	—	55	1000	½ starch, 1 veg., 2 lean meat, ½ fat
12	8	—	20	440	1½ starch, 1 veg., 1 meat
19	10	1	35	400	2 starch, 1 veg., 2 meat
24	8	3	70	340	1 starch, 1 veg., 2½ lean meat
19	4	1	30	570	1 starch, 1 veg., 2 lean meat
27	10	3	50	540	1½ starch, 1 veg., 3 lean meat
11	7	3	20	410	2 starch, 1 veg., ½ meat

* Not available   ▊ More than 2 fat exchanges   🛒 Moderate to high sugar content

Products	SERVING SIZE	CALORIES	CARBO-HYDRATE (gm)
Glazed Chicken Breast	10 oz.	240	38
Lasagna with Meat Sauce	10 oz.	270	35
Macaroni & Cheese	9 oz.	270	40
Sliced Turkey Breast	10 oz.	250	27
Swedish Meatballs	10 oz.	290	39
EL MONTEREY® (Ruiz™ Food Products, Inc.)			
Burritos, all varieties (average)	4 oz.	290	37
Crispy Fried Burritos	4 oz.	330	36
FEATHERWEIGHT® HEALTHY RECIPES® (Sandoz Nutrition)			
Beef Ravioli, Low Sodium	8 oz.	220	33
Beef Stew	7½ oz.	160	17
Chicken Stew	7½ oz.	140	23
Dumplings and Chicken, Low Sodium	7½ oz.	160	18
Spaghetti with Meatballs, Low Sodium	7½ oz.	160	23
FRANCO-AMERICAN® (Campbell Soup Co.)			
Beef RavioliOs in Meat Sauce	7½ oz.	250	35
Hearty Pasta Beef Ravioli in Meat Sauce	7½ oz.	280	35
Hearty Pasta Macaroni with Beef in Tomato Sauce	7½ oz.	200	30
Hearty Pasta Twists in Pizza Sauce	7½ oz.	220	32
Macaroni and Cheese	7⅜ oz.	170	24
Spaghetti in Tomato Sauce with Cheese	7⅜ oz.	190	36

† For occasional use   ** Not recommended for use

PROTEIN (gm)	FAT (gm)	SAT. FAT (gm)	CHOLES-TEROL (mg)	SODIUM (mg)	EXCHANGES
17	4	1	35	560	2 starch, 1 veg., 1½ lean meat
22	7	3	30	440	2 starch, 2 lean meat
13	8	3	15	590	2½ starch, 1 meat
25	7	2	50	560	1 starch, 1 veg., 2½ lean meat
20	7	2	55	470	2 starch, 1 veg., 2 lean meat
9	11	—	—	420-500	2½ starch, ½ meat, 1 fat
9	16	—	—	480	2½ starch, ½ meat, 2 fat
9	4	—	—	75	2 starch, 1 meat
17	3	—	35	400	1 starch, 2 lean meat
10	1	—	20	400	1 starch, 1 veg., 1 lean meat
12	5	—	—	115	1 starch, 1 meat
12	3	—	20	400	1½ starch, 1 lean meat
9	8	—	—	920	2 starch, 1 veg., ½ meat, ½ fat
9	11	—	—	810	2 starch, 1 veg., ½ meat, 1½ fat
8	5	—	—	790	1½ starch, 1 veg., ½ meat, ½ fat
8	7	—	—	850	1½ starch, 1 veg., ½ meat, ½ fat
6	6	—	—	960	1½ starch, ½ meat, ½ fat
5	2	—	—	810	2 starch, 1 veg.

* Not available   ▤ More than 2 fat exchanges   🛒 Moderate to high sugar content

Products	SERVING SIZE	CALORIES	CARBO-HYDRATE (gm)
Spaghetti with Meatballs in Tomato Sauce	7⅜ oz.	220	28
SpaghettiOs in Tomato and Cheese Sauce	7½ oz.	170	34
SpaghettiOs with Meatballs in Tomato Sauce	7⅜ oz.	210	25
SpaghettiOs with Sliced Franks in Tomato Sauce	7⅜ oz.	220	26

GOLDEN GRAIN® (Golden Grain Macaroni Co.)

Macaroni and Cheddar (as prepared)	½ cup	310	36

HAMBURGER HELPER® (General Mills, Inc.)
Main Dishes (as prepared)

Beef Noodle	1 cup (⅕ pkg.)	320	26
Beef Romanoff	1 cup (⅕ pkg.)	350	31
Cheeseburger Macaroni	1 cup (⅕ pkg.)	370	28
Cheese Italian	1 cup (⅕ pkg.)	360	30
Chili with Beans	1¼ cup (¼ pkg.)	350	25
Chili Tomato	1 cup (⅕ pkg.)	330	31
Creamy Stroganoff	1 cup (⅕ pkg.)	390	30
Hamburger Hash	1 cup (⅕ pkg.)	320	27
Hamburger Stew	1 cup (⅕ pkg.)	300	25
Lasagna	1 cup (⅕ pkg.)	340	33
Meatloaf	5 oz. (⅕ pkg.)	360	14
Pizza Dish	1 cup (⅕ pkg.)	360	37
Pizzabake®	4.5 oz. (⅙ pkg.)	320	29

† For occasional use   ** Not recommended for use

PROTEIN (gm)	FAT (gm)	SAT. FAT (gm)	CHOLES-TEROL (mg)	SODIUM (mg)	EXCHANGES
9	8	—	—	850	2 starch, ½ meat, 1 fat
4	2	—	—	920	2 starch
9	8	—	—	950	1½ starch, ½ meat, 1 fat
7	9	—	—	990	2 starch, ½ meat, ½ fat
8	15	—	—	620	2 starch, ½ meat, 2½ fat
20	15	—	—	1050	2 starch, 2 meat, 1 fat
22	16	—	—	1080	2 starch, 2 meat, 1 fat
21	19	—	—	1030	2 starch, 2 meat, 1 fat
22	17	—	—	1040	2 starch, 2 meat, 1 fat
24	17	—	—	1740	1½ starch, 2½ meat, 1 fat
20	14	—	—	1410	2 starch, 2 meat, ½ fat
22	20	—	—	870	2 starch, 2 meat, 2 fat
18	15	—	—	1020	2 starch, 2 meat, 1 fat
18	14	—	—	1010	1½ starch, 2 meat, ½ fat
21	14	—	—	1050	2 starch, 2 meat, ½ fat
27	22	—	—	710	1 starch, 3½ meat, 1 fat
21	14	—	—	1010	2½ starch, 2 meat, 1 fat
19	14	—	—	840	2 starch, 2 meat, ½ fat

* Not available   ▯ More than 2 fat exchanges   🛒 Moderate to high sugar content

Products	SERVING SIZE	CALORIES	CARBO-HYDRATE (gm)
Potatoes Au Gratin	1 cup (⅕ pkg.)	320	28
Potato Stroganoff	1 cup (⅕ pkg.)	320	28
Rice Oriental	1 cup (⅕ pkg.)	340	38
Sloppy Joe Bake™	5 oz. (⅙ pkg.)	340	33
Spaghetti	1 cup (⅕ pkg.)	340	32
Tacobake®	5.75 oz. (⅙ pkg.)	320	31
Tamale Pie	1 cup (⅕ pkg.)	380	39
Zesty Italian	1 cup (⅕ pkg.)	340	35
HEALTH VALLEY® (Health Valley Foods, Inc.)			
Fast Menu™ Dinners			
Amaranth with Garden Vegetables	7½ oz.	140	16
Hearty Lentil & Garden Vegetables	7½ oz.	150	16
Honey Baked Organic Beans with Tofu Wieners	7½ oz.	140	15
Oat Bran Pilaf with Garden Vegetables	7½ oz.	210	30
Organic Black Beans with Tofu Wieners	7½ oz.	150	20
Organic Lentils with Tofu Wieners	7½ oz.	170	15
Western Black Beans with Garden Vegetables	7½ oz.	160	14
HEALTHY CHOICE® (ConAgra® Frozen Foods Co.)			
Dinners			
Beef Pepper Steak	11 oz.	290	35
Breast of Turkey	10.5 oz.	290	39
Chicken & Pasta Divan	11.5 oz.	310	45

† For occasional use ** Not recommended for use

PROTEIN (gm)	FAT (gm)	SAT. FAT (gm)	CHOLES- TEROL (mg)	SODIUM (mg)	EXCHANGES
19	15	—	—	910	2 starch, 2 meat, 1 fat
18	15	—	—	950	2 starch, 2 meat, 1 fat
19	14	—	—	1120	2 starch, 1 veg., 1½ meat, 1 fat
18	15	—	—	1100	2 starch, 2 meat, 1 fat
20	15	—	—	1110	2 starch, 2 meat, 1 fat
17	15	—	—	940	2 starch, 1½ meat, 1 fat
19	16	—	—	940	2½ starch, 1½ meat, 1½ fat
21	13	—	—	980	2 starch, 2 meat, ½ fat
8	3	—	0	140	½ starch, 1 veg., 1 lean meat
13	4	—	0	200	½ starch, 1 veg., 1½ lean meat
11	4	—	0	140	1 starch, 1 lean meat
7	7	—	0	330	1½ starch, 1 veg., 1½ fat
14	1	—	0	170	1 starch, 1½ lean meat
15	5	—	0	260	1 starch, 2 lean meat
16	5	—	0	250	½ starch, 1 veg., 2 lean meat
24	6	—	65	530	2 starch, 1 veg., 2 lean meat
21	5	—	45	420	2 starch, 1 veg., 2 lean meat
23	4	—	60	510	2½ starch, 1 veg., 2 lean meat

* Not available   🯄 More than 2 fat exchanges   🛒 Moderate to high sugar content

Products	SERVING SIZE	CALORIES	CARBO-HYDRATE (gm)
Chicken Oriental	11.25 oz.	220	31
Chicken Parmigiana	11.5 oz.	280	38
Herb Roasted Chicken	11 oz.	260	38
Mesquite Chicken	10.5 oz.	310	52
Salisbury Steak	11.5 oz.	300	41
Shrimp Creole	11.25 oz.	210	42
Shrimp Marinara	10.5 oz.	220	42
Sirloin Tips	11.75 oz.	290	33
Sole Au Gratin	11 oz.	270	40
Sweet & Sour Chicken	11.5 oz.	280	44
Yankee Pot Roast	11 oz.	260	36
Entrees			
Beef Pepper Steak	9.5 oz.	250	36
Chicken A' L'Orange	9 oz.	260	39
Chicken Chow Mein	8.5 oz.	220	31
Fettucini Alfredo	8 oz.	240	36
Glazed Chicken	8.5 oz.	230	28
Lasagna with Meat Sauce	9 oz.	250	38
Linguini with Shrimp	9.5 oz.	230	40
Seafood Newburg	8 oz.	200	30

† For occasional use   ** Not recommended for use

PROTEIN (gm)	FAT (gm)	SAT. FAT (gm)	CHOLES-TEROL (mg)	SODIUM (mg)	EXCHANGES
21	2	—	55	460	1½ starch, 1 veg., 2 lean meat
23	3	—	60	310	2 starch, 1 veg., 2 lean meat
20	3	—	40	300	2 starch, 1 veg., 2 lean meat
21	2	—	45	270	3 starch, 1 veg., 2 lean meat
19	7	—	50	480	2 starch, 1 veg., 2 lean meat
8	1	—	65	560	2½ starch, 1 veg., ½ lean meat
9	1	—	50	320	2½ starch, 1 veg., ½ lean meat
25	6	—	70	350	2 starch, 1 veg., 3 lean meat
16	5	—	55	470	2 starch, 1 veg., 1½ lean meat
22	2	—	50	260	1½ starch, 1 veg., 1 fruit, 2½ lean meat†
19	4	—	45	310	2 starch, 1 veg., 2 lean meat
18	4	2	40	340	2 starch, 1 veg., 1½ lean meat
22	2	<1	45	90	2 starch, 1 veg., 2 lean meat
18	3	1	45	440	1½ starch, 1 veg., 2 lean meat
10	7	2	45	370	2 starch, 1 meat
22	3	1	50	340	1½ starch, 1 veg., 2 lean meat
16	4	2	20	420	2 starch, 1 veg., 1½ lean meat
12	2	1	55	390	2 starch, 1 veg., 1 lean meat
13	3	1	55	440	2 starch, 1 lean meat

* Not available   ▤ More than 2 fat exchanges   ♥ Moderate to high sugar content

Products	SERVING SIZE	CALORIES	CARBO-HYDRATE (gm)
Sole with Lemon Butter Sauce	8.25 oz.	230	33
Spaghetti with Meat Sauce	10 oz.	280	47

HORMEL® (Geo. A. Hormel & Co.)
Kid's Kitchen® Microcup® Entrees

Beans & Wieners	7 ¾ oz.	290	34
Beefy Mac	7½ oz.	200	25
Cheezy Mac 'N Cheese	7½ oz.	220	34
Mini Beef Ravioli	7½ oz.	270	34
Spaghetti & Mini Meatballs in Tomato Sauce	7½ oz.	220	27

Microcup® Entrees

Chili Mac	7.5 oz.	200	17
Chili No Beans	7⅜ oz.	380	13
Chili with Beans	7⅜ oz.	250	15
Dinty Moore® Beef Stew	7.5 oz.	190	17
Hot Chili with Beans	7⅜ oz.	250	24
Lasagna	7.5 oz.	250	26
Macaroni & Cheese	7.5 oz.	190	26
Noodles & Chicken	7.5 oz.	180	18
Pork & Beans	7.5 oz.	250	41
Ravioli in Tomato Sauce	7.5 oz.	250	28
Scalloped Potatoes and Ham	7.5 oz.	260	21
Spaghetti & Meatballs	7.5 oz.	210	27

PROTEIN (gm)	FAT (gm)	SAT. FAT (gm)	CHOLES-TEROL (mg)	SODIUM (mg)	EXCHANGES
16	4	2	45	390	2 starch, 1½ lean meat
14	4	2	15	260	2½ starch, 1 veg., 1 lean meat
12	12	—	45	720	2 starch, 1 meat, 1 fat
11	6	—	25	780	1½ starch, 1 meat
8	6	—	20	830	2 starch, ½ meat, ½ fat
9	11	—	20	970	2 starch, 1 meat, 1 fat
12	7	—	—	850	2 starch, 1 meat
11	10	—	25	1040	1 starch, 1 meat, 1 fat
18	28	—	70	1030	1 starch, 2 meat, 3½ fat
15	11	—	65	980	1 starch, 2 meat
10	9	—	50	860	1 starch, 1 meat, 1 fat
15	11	—	55	990	1½ starch, 1½ meat, ½ fat
7	13	—	30	1060	2 starch, ½ meat, 1 fat
7	6	—	20	900	2 starch, ½ meat
7	8	—	20	1000	1 starch, 1 meat, ½ fat
11	5	—	30	650	2½ starch, ½ meat
8	11	—	20	950	2 starch, ½ meat, 1½ fat
8	16	—	25	810	1½ starch, 1 meat, 1½ fat
9	7	—	—	—	2 starch, 1 meat, ½ fat

* Not available   ▤ More than 2 fat exchanges   ☕ Moderate to high sugar content

Products	SERVING SIZE	CALORIES	CARBO-HYDRATE (gm)
Top Shelf® Dinners			
Beef Oriental	10.3 oz.	290	25
Beef Stroganoff	10 oz.	300	23
Boneless Beef Ribs	10 oz.	400	29
Breast of Chicken Acapulco	10 oz.	410	43
Cheese Tortellini in Marinara Sauce	10 oz.	210	33
Cheese Tortellini with Shrimp & Seafood	10 oz.	280	36
Chicken Ala King	10 oz.	340	41
Chicken Cacciatore	10 oz.	190	26
Chili Con Carne Suprema	10 oz.	310	30
Glazed Chicken Breast	10 oz.	190	21
Italian Style Lasagna	10 oz.	350	30
Linguini	10 oz.	350	33
Salisbury Steak	10 oz.	340	19
Spaghettini	10 oz.	260	38
Sukiyaki	10.3 oz.	320	37
🛒 Sweet & Sour Chicken	10 oz.	260	41
Tender Roast Beef	10 oz.	250	20
Vegetable Lasagna	10 oz.	280	32

PROTEIN (gm)	FAT (gm)	SAT. FAT (gm)	CHOLES-TEROL (mg)	SODIUM (mg)	EXCHANGES
26	10	—	95	920	1 starch, 1 veg., 3 lean meat
27	11	—	75	860	1 starch, 1 veg., 3 lean meat, ½ fat
29	19	—	100	510	1½ starch, 1 veg., 3 meat, ½ fat
24	16	—	95	950	2½ starch, 1 veg, 2½ lean meat, 1 fat
10	4	—	30	660	2 starch, 1 veg., ½ meat
16	8	—	55	890	2 starch, 1 veg., 1½ lean meat, ½ fat
17	12	—	40	870	2½ starch, 1 veg., 1½ lean meat, 1 fat
17	2	—	45	720	1 starch, 1 veg., 1½ lean meat
22	11	—	45	890	2 starch, 2 meat
21	2	—	40	820	1 starch, 1 veg., 2 lean meat
23	16	—	60	840	1½ starch, 1 veg., 2½ meat
12	19	—	—	1300	2 starch, 1 veg., 1 meat, 2 fat
24	19	—	65	850	1 starch, 1 veg., 3 meat, ½ fat
13	6	—	45	870	2 starch, 1 veg., 1 meat
25	8	—	—	1420	2 starch, 1 veg., 2½ lean meat
20	2	—	55	750	1½ starch, 1 veg., 1 fruit, 1½ lean meat†
27	7	—	55	940	1 starch, 1 veg., 3 lean meat
16	9	—	30	970	2 starch, 1 veg., 1½ meat

* Not available   ▌ More than 2 fat exchanges   ♥ Moderate to high sugar content

Products	SERVING SIZE	CALORIES	CARBO-HYDRATE (gm)
KID CUISINE™ (ConAgra® Frozen Foods Co.)			
Cheese Beef Patty Sandwich	6.25 oz.	400	47
Cheese Pizza	6.5 oz.	246	41
Chicken Nuggets	6.25 oz.	400	46
Fish Nuggets	7 oz.	320	33
Fried Chicken	7.25 oz.	420	41
Macaroni & Cheese with Mini Franks	9 oz.	380	55
Mini-Cheese Ravioli	8.75 oz.	250	52
Spaghetti with Meat Sauce	9.25 oz.	310	43
KRAFT® (Kraft, Inc.)			
* Sodium Values — Prepared without salt/prepared with added salt			
Dinners, Egg Noodles (as prepared)			
Egg Noodles and Cheese	¾ cup	340	37
Egg Noodles with Chicken	¾ cup	240	31
Dinners, Macaroni (as prepared)			
Deluxe Macaroni and Cheese	¾ cup	260	36
Macaroni and Cheese	¾ cup	290	34
Spiral Macaroni and Cheese	¾ cup	330	36
Dinners, Spaghetti (as prepared)			
American Style Spaghetti	1 cup	300	50
Spaghetti with Meat Sauce	1 cup	360	47

PROTEIN (gm)	FAT (gm)	SAT. FAT (gm)	CHOLES-TEROL (mg)	SODIUM (mg)	EXCHANGES
12	19	—	40	550	3 starch, 1 meat, 2 fat
10	4	—	20	390	2½ starch, ½ meat
11	19	—	60	610	3 starch, 1 meat, 2 fat
13	15	—	45	750	2 starch, 1½ meat, 1 fat
15	22	—	—	1050	2½ starch, 1½ meat, 2½ fat
9	14	—	40	1000	3½ starch, ½ meat, 1½ fat
6	2	—	20	730	3 starch
9	12	—	35	690	2½ starch, ½ meat, 1½ fat
10	17	4	50	*630/ 760	2½ starch, 1 meat, 1½ fat
8	9	2	35	*880/ 950	2 starch, ½ meat, 1 fat
11	8	4	20	*590/ 660	2½ starch, 1 meat
9	13	3	5	*530/ 630	2 starch, 1 meat, 1 fat
9	17	4	10	*560/ 670	2 starch, 1 meat, 2 fat
10	7	2	0	*630/ 770	3 starch, 1 meat
12	14	4	16	*880/ 1010	3 starch, 1 meat, 1 fat

* Not available   ▤ More than 2 fat exchanges   ☕ Moderate to high sugar content

Products	SERVING SIZE	CALORIES	CARBO-HYDRATE (gm)
Entrees, Microwave			
Beef Stroganoff with Noodles	9 oz.	330	30
Chicken Cacciatore	10 oz.	260	37
Lasagna with Meat Sauce	10.2 oz.	370	45
Salisbury Steak with Vegetables & Mushroom Gravy	9.5 oz.	300	29
Spaghetti & Meat Balls with Tomato Sauce	10 oz.	360	46

LA CHOY® (Beatrice/Hunt Wesson, Inc.)

Products	SERVING SIZE	CALORIES	CARBO-HYDRATE (gm)
Bi-Pack Dinners			
Beef Pepper	1½ cups	160	20
Chicken Teriyaki	1½ cups	170	16
Chow Mein			
Beef	1½ cups	140	16
Chicken	1½ cups	160	16
Pork	1½ cups	160	14
Shrimp	1½ cups	140	12
☗ Sweet & Sour Chicken	1½ cups	240	36
Dinner Classics (as prepared)			
Egg Foo Young	2 patties & 3 oz. sauce (¼ recipe)	170	20
Pepper Steak	¾ cup (⅙ recipe)	180	9
☗ Sweet & Sour	¾ cup (¼ recipe)	310	30

PROTEIN (gm)	FAT (gm)	SAT. FAT (gm)	CHOLES- TEROL (mg)	SODIUM (mg)	EXCHANGES
24	13	—	—	970	2 starch, 3 lean meat
17	6	2	60	790	2 starch, 1 veg., 1½ lean meat
14	14	7	40	1370	2½ starch, 1 veg., 1 meat, 1½ fat
18	13	5	<10	1120	1½ starch, 1 veg., 2 meat
16	12	5	25	1410	2½ starch, 1 veg., 1½ meat, ½ fat
14	4	1	34	1900	1 starch, 1 veg., 1½ lean meat
16	4	1	40	1700	½ starch, 1 veg., 2 lean meat
14	2	<1	40	1680	½ starch, 1 veg., 1½ lean meat
14	6	2	36	1940	½ starch, 1 veg., 1½ lean meat, ½ fat
10	8	3	28	1900	½ starch, 1 veg., 1 meat, ½ fat
14	2	<1	26	1720	½ starch, 1 veg., 1½ lean meat
14	4	<1	26	880	1 starch, 1 veg., 1 fruit, 1½ lean meat†
8	7	2	275	1390	1 starch, 1 veg., ½ meat, ½ fat
17	9	3	60	760	1 veg., 3 lean meat
32	6	1	50	860	½ starch, 1 veg., 1 fruit, 3½ lean meat†

Not available   ▌ More than 2 fat exchanges   ⛟ Moderate to high sugar content

Products	SERVING SIZE	CALORIES	CARBO-HYDRATE (gm)
LE MENU® (Campbell Soup Co.)			
Dinners, frozen			
Beef Sirloin Tips	11½ oz.	400	29
Beef Stroganoff	10 oz.	450	30
Chicken A La King	10¼ oz.	330	28
▤ Chicken Cordon Bleu	11 oz.	470	49
Chicken Florentine	10 ¾ oz.	340	38
Chicken Parmigiana	11½ oz.	400	29
Chopped Sirloin Beef	12¼ oz.	440	29
Ham Steak	10 oz.	300	33
Pepper Steak	11½ oz.	370	38
Sliced Breast of Turkey with Mushroom Gravy	10½ oz.	270	37
Sole, Filet of	10 oz.	360	40
▤🛒 Sweet and Sour Chicken	11¼ oz.	450	42
Dinners, Light Style, Frozen			
Chicken Cacciatore	10 oz.	270	28
Chicken Cannelloni	10¼ oz.	270	38
Chicken Chow Mein	10 oz.	260	37
Glazed Chicken Breast	10 oz.	270	27
Herb Roasted Chicken	9¼ oz.	220	21
Salisbury Steak	10½ oz.	220	21

† For occasional use   ** Not recommended for use

PROTEIN (gm)	FAT (gm)	SAT. FAT (gm)	CHOLES-TEROL (mg)	SODIUM (mg)	EXCHANGES
29	19	—	—	780	2 starch, 3 meat, ½ fat
25	25	—	—	1000	2 starch, 3 meat, 1½ fat
22	14	—	—	810	2 starch, 2 lean meat, 1½ fat
23	20	—	—	870	3 starch, 2 lean meat, 2½ fat
23	10	—	—	990	2½ starch, 2 lean meat, ½ fat
26	20	—	—	900	2 starch, 3 lean meat, 2 fat
25	25	—	—	1030	2 starch, 3 meat, 1½ fat
18	10	—	—	1490	2 starch, 2 lean meat, ½ fat
25	13	—	—	1030	2½ starch, 2½ meat
17	6	—	—	1020	2½ starch, 1½ lean meat
18	14	—	—	940	2½ starch, 2 lean meat, 1 fat
20	22	—	—	1170	2 starch, 1 fruit, 2 lean meat, 3 fat†
21	8	—	—	230	1½ starch, 1 veg., 2 lean meat
15	5	—	—	200	2 starch, 1 veg., 1½ lean meat
18	4	—	—	290	2 starch, 1 veg., 1½ lean meat
26	6	—	—	270	1½ starch, 1 veg., 2½ lean meat
21	6	—	—	230	1 starch, 1 veg., 2 lean meat
18	7	—	—	280	1 starch, 1 veg., 2 lean meat

* Not available   ▌ More than 2 fat exchanges   🛒 Moderate to high sugar content

Products	SERVING SIZE	CALORIES	CARBO-HYDRATE (gm)
3-Cheese Stuffed Shells	10 oz.	280	35
Turkey Divan	10 oz.	280	26
Veal Marsala	10 oz.	260	31
Entrees, frozen			
Beef Burgundy	7½ oz.	330	5
Chicken Kiev	8 oz.	530	24
Manicotti, Cheese Filled	8½ oz.	410	40
Oriental Chicken	10½ oz.	330	46
LE MENU® HEALTHY (Campbell Soup Co.)			
Frozen Dinners			
Herb-Roasted Chicken Breast	10 oz.	240	18
Sliced Turkey	10 oz.	210	21
Turkey Divan	10 oz.	260	23
LIBBY'S DINER® (Carnation)			
Microwaveable Meals			
Beef Ravioli	7.75 oz.	240	35
Beef Stew	7.75 oz.	240	22
Chili with Beans	7.75 oz.	280	29
Lasagna	7.75 oz.	200	29
Macaroni & Beef	7.75 oz.	230	34
Pasta Spirals & Chicken	7.75 oz.	120	16
Spaghetti & Meatballs	7.75 oz.	190	30

PROTEIN (gm)	FAT (gm)	SAT. FAT (gm)	CHOLES-TEROL (mg)	SODIUM (mg)	EXCHANGES
16	8	—	—	250	2 starch, 1 veg., 1½ lean meat
22	9	—	—	300	1½ starch, 1 veg., 2 lean meat, ½ fat
20	6	—	—	280	1½ starch, 1 veg., 2 lean meat
25	23	—	—	660	3½ meat, 1½ fat
20	39	—	—	780	1½ starch, 2 lean meat, 6½ fat
17	20	—	—	1030	2½ starch, 1½ meat, 2 fat
16	9	—	—	820	3 starch, 1½ meat
27	7	3	70	400	½ starch, 1 veg., 3 lean meat
21	5	1	30	540	1 starch, 1 veg., 2 lean meat
25	7	2	60	420	1 starch, 1 veg., 2½ lean meat
13	5	—	15	890	2 starch, 1 meat
12	12	—	40	790	1½ starch, 1 meat, 1 fat
15	12	—	40	820	2 starch, 1½ meat
9	5	—	15	780	2 starch, ½ meat
10	6	—	20	670	2 starch, 1 meat
8	3	—	15	900	1 starch, 1 lean meat
10	3	—	15	870	2 starch, ½ meat

Products	SERVING SIZE	CALORIES	CARBO-HYDRATE (gm)
LIPTON® (Thomas J. Lipton, Inc.)			
Hearty Ones (as prepared)			
Beef Vegetable	11 oz.	229	40
Homestyle Chicken Noodle	11 oz.	227	37
Italiano	11 oz.	328	63
Minestrone	11 oz.	189	36
Pasta Garden Medley	11 oz.	323	63
Shells and Cheddar	11 oz.	367	60
Microeasy®			
Barbecue Style Chicken	¼ package	108	24
Country Style Chicken	¼ package	78	15
Hearty Beef Stew	¼ package	71	14
Homestyle Meatloaf	¼ package	87	15
LUNCH BUCKET® (The Dial Corporation)			
Microwaveable Meals			
Beef Stew	8.5 oz.	170	19
Chili Mac	8.5 oz.	270	25
Chili with Beans, all varieties (average)	8.5 oz.	330	29
Fettucini Marinara	8.25 oz.	210	44
Lasagna	8.5 oz.	260	43
Macaroni 'n Beef	8.5 oz.	260	43
Pasta Italiano	8.5 oz.	280	41
Pasta 'n Chicken	8.5 oz.	210	25
Ravioli	8.5 oz.	280	48
Scalloped Potatos with Ham Chunks	8.5 oz.	260	25
Spaghetti 'n Meat Sauce	8.5 oz.	260	43

PROTEIN (gm)	FAT (gm)	SAT. FAT (gm)	CHOLES- TEROL (mg)	SODIUM (mg)	EXCHANGES
10	3	—	29	921	2 starch, 1 veg., ½ meat
10	4	—	37	989	2 starch, 1 veg., ½ meat
14	2	—	0	1240	3½ starch, 1 veg., ½ lean meat
8	3	—	6	821	2 starch, 1 veg., ½ fat
15	4	—	6	914	3½ starch, 1 veg., ½ lean meat
15	7	—	14	1406	4 starch, ½ meat
2	1	—	—	981	1½ starch
3	1	—	—	844	1 starch
2	1	—	—	729	1 starch
4	2	—	—	630	1 starch
12	6	—	40	980	1 starch, 1 meat
10	15	—	35	1370	2 starch, ½ meat, 2 fat
19	16	—	45	1210	2 starch, 2 meat, 1 fat
6	2	—	—	870	2½ starch
9	5	—	30	960	3 starch, ½ meat
9	5	—	30	960	3 starch, ½ meat
8	9	—	—	910	3 starch, 1 fat
10	8	—	45	960	1½ starch, 1 meat, ½ fat
12	4	—	—	810	3 starch, ½ meat
11	13	—	35	820	1½ starch, 1 meat, 1½ fat
9	8	—	30	960	3 starch, 1 fat

* Not available   ▉ More than 2 fat exchanges   ♥ Moderate to high sugar content

Products	SERVING SIZE	CALORIES	CARBO-HYDRATE (gm)
LUNCH BUCKET® LIGHT BALANCE® (The Dial Corporation)			
Microwaveable Meals			
Beef Americana	8.25 oz.	170	28
Beef & Pasta Bordeaux	8.25 oz.	180	31
Chicken Cacciatore	8.25 oz.	200	37
Chicken Fiesta	8.25 oz.	210	37
Pasta & Garden Vegetables	8.25 oz.	190	41
Mushroom Stroganoff	8.25 oz.	180	28
MORTONS® (ConAgra® Frozen Foods Co.)			
Dinners			
Beans & Franks	10 oz.	350	46
Fish	9.75 oz.	370	46
Ham	10 oz.	290	49
Meat Loaf	10 oz.	310	26
Mexican Style	10 oz.	300	44
Salisbury Steak	10 oz.	300	23
Sliced Beef	10 oz.	220	20
Spaghetti & Meatballs	10 oz.	200	39
Turkey	10 oz.	230	28
Veal Parmigian	10 oz.	260	35

PROTEIN (gm)	FAT (gm)	SAT. FAT (gm)	CHOLES- TEROL (mg)	SODIUM (mg)	EXCHANGES
9	3	1	15	700	1½ starch, 1 veg., ½ meat
12	1	<1	25	660	1½ starch, 1 veg., 1 lean meat
12	1	<1	25	730	2 starch, 1 veg., ½ lean meat
10	3	1	15	640	2 starch, 1 veg., ½ lean meat
6	1	<1	0	650	2 starch, 1 veg.
7	5	2	15	620	1½ starch, 1 veg., 1 fat
11	13	—	30	1490	3 starch, 1 high fat meat, ½ fat
18	13	—	65	910	2½ starch, 1 veg., 2 lean meat, 1 fat
15	4	—	45	1400	2½ starch, 1 veg., 1 lean meat
11	17	—	50	1520	1½ starch, 1 veg., 1 meat, 2 fat
9	10	—	20	1390	2½ starch, 1 veg., ½ meat, 1 fat
12	17	—	40	1420	1 starch, 1 veg., 1 meat, 2½ fat
24	5	—	65	950	1 starch, 1 veg., 3 lean meat
6	3	—	10	1090	2 starch, 1 veg., ½ lean meat
15	6	—	45	1300	1½ starch, 1 veg., 1½ lean meat
10	8	—	35	1510	2 starch, 1 veg., 1 meat

* Not available   ▯ More than 2 fat exchanges   ☕ Moderate to high sugar content

Products	SERVING SIZE	CALORIES	CARBO-HYDRATE (gm)
Western	10 oz.	290	29
Meat Pies			
Beef	7 oz.	430	27
Chicken	7 oz.	420	27
Turkey	7 oz.	420	27
OLD EL PASO® (PET, Inc.)			
Canned/Boxed Items (as prepared)			
Burrito Dinner (with filling)	1 burrito	299	36
Enchilada Dinner (with filling)	1 enchilada	145	11
Tamales	2	190	16
Dinner, Festive, Frozen			
Beef and Bean Burrito	11 oz.	470	72
Beef and Cheese Chimichanga	11 oz.	510	53
Beef Chimichanga	11 oz.	540	65
Beef Enchilada	11 oz.	390	56
Cheese Enchilada	11 oz.	590	51
Chicken Enchilada	11 oz.	460	54
Entrees, Frozen			
Bean and Cheese Chimichanga	1	350	36
Beef Chimichanga	1	380	35
Beef and Pork Chimichanga	1	340	35
Chicken Chimichanga	1	370	35

† For occasional use   ** Not recommended for use

PROTEIN (gm)	FAT (gm)	SAT. FAT (gm)	CHOLES- TEROL (mg)	SODIUM (mg)	EXCHANGES
14	14	—	35	1450	1½ starch, 1 veg., 1 meat, 1½ fat
11	31	—	30	740	1½ starch, 1 veg., 1 meat, 5 fat
14	28	—	35	740	1½ starch, 1 veg., 1 meat, 4½ fat
14	28	—	40	740	1½ starch, 1 veg., 1 meat, 4½ fat
11	13	4	23	430	2 starch, 1 meat, 1½ fat
7	8	3	21	325	1 starch, ½ meat, 1 fat
5	12	—	20	380	1 starch, 2 fat
23	9	—	—	1180	4½ starch, 2 lean meat
22	23	—	—	1400	3½ starch, 2 meat, 2 fat
23	21	—	—	1200	4 starch, 2 meat, 2 fat
24	8	—	—	1200	3½ starch, 2 lean meat
24	31	—	—	1200	3½ starch, 2 meat, 4 fat
21	18	—	—	770	3½ starch, 2 meat, 1 fat
12	17	—	—	700	2½ starch, 1 meat, 2 fat
10	23	—	—	470	2 starch, 1 meat, 3 fat
13	16	—	—	700	2 starch, 1 meat, 2 fat
10	21	—	—	460	2 starch, 1 meat, 3 fat

* Not available   ▤ More than 2 fat exchanges   ♥ Moderate to high sugar content

Products	SERVING SIZE	CALORIES	CARBO- HYDRATE (gm)
Beef Enchilada	1	210	16
Cheese Enchilada	1	250	24
Chicken Enchilada	1	220	20
⊟ Chicken Enchilada with Sour Cream Sauce	1	280	18
Individual Frozen Items Burritos, all varieties (average)	1	340	42
⊟ Chimichangas, all varieties (average)	1	365	34
ON-COR® (On-cor Frozen Foods, Inc.) Deluxe Entrees, frozen (32 oz. container) Beef Chop Suey without Rice	8 oz. (¼ pkg.)	90	9
Beef Stew	8 oz. (¼ pkg.)	147	21
Char-Broiled Beef Patties	8 oz. (¼ pkg.)	306	8
Chicken Fettucini	8 oz. (¼ pkg.)	190	22
⊟ Chicken Parmigiana	8 oz. (¼ pkg.)	352	27
Lasagna	8 oz. (¼ pkg.)	240	34
Macaroni & Cheese	8 oz. (¼ pkg.)	193	25
⊟ Meat Loaf	8 oz. (¼ pkg.)	488	22
Mostaccioli & Meatballs	8 oz. (¼ pkg.)	215	26
Salisbury Steak	8 oz. (¼ pkg.)	272	11
Sliced Beef	8 oz. (¼ pkg.)	91	7
Stuffed Cabbage	8 oz. (¼ pkg.)	200	22

† For occasional use   ** Not recommended for use

PROTEIN (gm)	FAT (gm)	SAT. FAT (gm)	CHOLES-TEROL (mg)	SODIUM (mg)	EXCHANGES
8	13	—	10	720	1 starch, 1 meat, 1 fat
10	12	—	—	830	1½ starch, 1 meat, 1 fat
8	12	—	—	740	1 starch, 1 meat, 1½ fat
10	19	—	—	520	1 starch, 1 meat, 3 fat
14	13	—	—	540-950	3 starch, 1 meat, 1 fat
12	20	—	—	470	2 starch, 1 meat, 3 fat
11	2	—	—	—	2 veg., 1 lean meat
10	3	—	—	—	1 starch, 1 veg., 1 lean meat
19	22	—	—	—	½ starch, 2½ meat, 2 fat
16	4	—	—	—	1½ starch, 1½ lean meat
14	21	—	—	—	2 starch, 1½ lean meat, 2½ fat
10	7	—	—	—	2 starch, 1 veg., 1 meat
9	6	—	—	—	1½ starch, 1 meat
21	35	—	—	—	1½ starch, 2 meat, 5 fat
11	8	—	—	—	2 starch, 1 meat
16	19	—	—	—	1 starch, 2 meat, 1½ fat
13	1	—	—	—	½ starch, 1½ lean meat
8	8	—	—	—	1 starch, 1 veg., 1 meat, ½ fat

* Not available   ⯑ More than 2 fat exchanges   🛒 Moderate to high sugar content

Products	SERVING SIZE	CALORIES	CARBO-HYDRATE (gm)
Stuffed Peppers	8 oz. (¼ pkg.)	190	20
Swedish Brand Sauce & Meat Balls	8 oz. (¼ pkg.)	340	19
Tomato Sauce & Italian Style Beef Patties	8 oz. (¼ pkg.)	374	18
Turkey & Dressing	8 oz. (¼ pkg.)	270	28
Turkey & Gravy	8 oz. (¼ pkg.)	136	9
Turkey Croquettes	8 oz. (¼ pkg.)	283	25
Veal Parmigiana	8 oz. (¼ pkg.)	363	27
Vegetable Beef Oriental	8 oz. (¼ pkg.)	190	25
Vegetable Lasagna	8 oz. (¼ pkg.)	270	37
Vegetable Manicotti Marinara	8 oz. (¼ pkg.)	220	29

PATIO® (ConAgra® Frozen Foods Co.)
Britos

Products	SERVING SIZE	CALORIES	CARBO-HYDRATE (gm)
Beef & Bean	½ pkg. (3.63 oz.)	250	33
Green Chile	½ pkg. (3.63 oz.)	250	33
Nacho Beef	½ pkg. (3.63 oz.)	270	30
Nacho Cheese	½ pkg. (3.63 oz.)	250	32
Red Chile	½ pkg. (3.63 oz.)	240	31
Spicy Chicken	½ pkg. (3.63 oz.)	250	33

Burritos

Products	SERVING SIZE	CALORIES	CARBO-HYDRATE (gm)
Beef & Bean	5 oz.	370	43
Beef & Bean Green Chile	5 oz.	330	43

† For occasional use   ** Not recommended for use

PROTEIN (gm)	FAT (gm)	SAT. FAT (gm)	CHOLES- TEROL (mg)	SODIUM (mg)	EXCHANGES
8	9	—	—	—	1 starch, 1 veg., 1 meat, ½ fat
20	20	—	—	—	1 starch, 2½ meat, 1½ fat
21	24	—	—	—	1 starch, 2½ meat, 2½ fat
13	11	—	—	—	2 starch, 1½ lean meat, ½ fat
12	6	—	—	—	½ starch, 1½ lean meat
14	14	—	—	—	1½ starch, 1½ lean meat, 2 fat
19	20	—	—	—	2 starch, 2 meat, 1½ fat
10	5	—	—	—	1 starch, 1 veg., 1 meat
11	9	—	—	—	2 starch, 1 veg., 1 meat
10	7	—	—	—	1½ starch, 1 veg., 1 meat
6	10	—	15	340	2 starch, ½ meat, 1 fat
6	10	—	15	420	2 starch, ½ meat, 1 fat
9	13	—	25	420	2 starch, 1 meat, 1 fat
7	10	—	20	330	2 starch, ½ meat, 1 fat
6	10	—	15	370	2 starch, ½ meat, 1 fat
6	10	—	25	330	2 starch, ½ meat, 1 fat
11	16	—	—	830	2½ starch, 1 meat, 2 fat
12	12	—	—	770	2½ starch, 1 meat, 1½ fat

* Not available   ▤ More than 2 fat exchanges   ☕ Moderate to high sugar content

Products	SERVING SIZE	CALORIES	CARBO-HYDRATE (gm)
Beef & Bean Red Chile	5 oz.	340	44
Red Hot	5 oz.	360	43
Mexican Dinners			
▤ Beef Enchilada	13.25 oz.	520	59
Cheese Enchilada	12.25 oz.	380	59
▤ Tamale	13 oz.	470	58
▤ Fiesta	12.25 oz.	470	55
▤ Mexican Style	13.25 oz.	540	64

QUAKER® OVEN STUFF® (Quaker Oats Company)

Products	SERVING SIZE	CALORIES	CARBO-HYDRATE (gm)
Beef Deli Meat	1 (4.74 oz.)	359	34
Chicken Turnover	1 (4.74 oz.)	336	32
Chicken Parmesan Turnover	1 (4.74 oz.)	323	25
Italian Sausage French Roll	1 (4.74 oz.)	345	35
Turkey Turnover	1 (4.74 oz.)	323	33
Turkey/Ham Deli Melt	1 (4.74 oz.)	332	27

RESER'S® (Reser's Fine Foods, Inc.)

Burritos

Products	SERVING SIZE	CALORIES	CARBO-HYDRATE (gm)
Bean & Cheese	5 oz.	339	48
Beef & Bean	5 oz.	366	46
Beef & Bean with Green Chili	5 oz.	353	46
Red Hot Beef	5 oz.	319	39

† For occasional use   ** Not recommended for use

PROTEIN (gm)	FAT (gm)	SAT. FAT (gm)	CHOLES- TEROL (mg)	SODIUM (mg)	EXCHANGES
11	13	—	—	810	2½ starch, 1 meat, 1½ fat
12	15	—	—	800	2½ starch, 1 meat, 2 fat
16	24	—	40	1810	3½ starch, 1 veg., 1 meat, 3 fat
14	10	—	20	2010	3½ starch, 1 veg., 1 meat
12	21	—	35	1850	3½ starch, 1 veg., ½ meat, 3 fat
16	20	—	30	2040	3 starch, 1 veg., 1 meat, 3 fat
15	25	—	45	1940	4 starch, 1 veg., 1 meat, 3 fat
23	15	—	25	538	2 starch, 2½ meat
18	15	—	27	413	2 starch, 2 meat, ½ fat
22	15	—	25	480	1½ starch, 2½ meat, ½ fat
18	15	—	55	565	2 starch, 2 meat, ½ fat
16	14	—	45	471	2 starch, 2 meat, ½ fat
23	15	—	19	695	2 starch, 2½ meat
12	11	—	—	—	3 starch, 1 meat, ½ fat
12	15	—	—	—	3 starch, 1 meat, 1 fat
12	13	—	—	—	3 starch, 1 meat, 1 fat
13	12	—	—	—	2½ starch, 1 meat, 1 fat

* Not available ⯐ More than 2 fat exchanges ⯐ Moderate to high sugar content

Products	SERVING SIZE	CALORIES	CARBO-HYDRATE (gm)
ROSITA - SI!® (Ruiz™ Food Products, Inc.)			
Burritos, all varieties (average)	4 oz.	290	37
Crispy Fried Burritos	4 oz.	330	36
Fiesta Lite Products Cheese Enchilada	8.25 oz.	310	35
Chicken Suiza	8.25 oz.	300	36
Shredded Beef Enchilada	8.25 oz.	290	43
RUIZ® (Ruiz™ Food Products, Inc.)			
Burritos, all varieties (average)	4 oz.	290	37
Crispy Fried Burritos	4 oz.	330	36
SARA LEE® (Kitchens of Sara Lee)			
Chicken and Broccoli Croissant	1	310	28
Ham and Swiss Cheese Croissant	1	310	29
STOUFFER'S® (Stouffer Foods Corp.)			
Beef Chop Suey with Rice	12 oz.	300	38
Beef Short Rib in Gravy	9 oz.	350	12
Beef Stroganoff with Parsley Noodles	9 ¾ oz.	390	28
Beef Teriyaki with Rice and Vegetables	9 ¾ oz.	290	33
Cashew Chicken in Sauce with Rice	9½ oz.	380	29
Cheese Enchiladas	10 ⅛ oz.	590	34
Chicken a la King with Rice	9½ oz.	290	34

PROTEIN (gm)	FAT (gm)	SAT. FAT (gm)	CHOLES-TEROL (mg)	SODIUM (mg)	EXCHANGES
9	11	—	—	420-500	2½ starch, ½ meat, 1 fat
9	16	—	—	480	2½ starch, ½ meat, 2 fat
15	13	—	—	680	2 starch, 1 veg., 1 meat, 1 fat
15	9	—	—	990	2 starch, 1 veg., 1 meat, 1 fat
10	9	—	—	700	2½ starch, 1 veg., ½ meat, 1 fat
9	11	—	—	420-500	2½ starch, ½ meat, 1 fat
9	16	-	—	480	2½ starch, ½ meat, 2 fat
13	17	—	15	430	2 starch, 1½ lean meat, 1½ fat
12	16	—	20	610	2 starch, 1 meat, 2 fat
16	9	—	—	1170	2 starch, 1 veg., 1½ meat
30	20	—	—	900	1 starch, 3½ meat
24	20	—	—	1090	2 starch, 2½ meat, 1 fat
22	8	—	—	1450	2 starch, 1 veg., 2 lean meat
31	16	—	—	1140	2 starch, 3½ lean meat, ½ fat
23	40	—	—	880	2 starch, 2½ high fat meat, 4 fat
19	9	—	—	890	2 starch, 1 veg., 2 lean meat

* Not available   ▤ More than 2 fat exchanges   🛒 Moderate to high sugar content

Products	SERVING SIZE	CALORIES	CARBO-HYDRATE (gm)
Chicken Chow Mein without Noodles	8 oz.	130	11
Chicken Divan	8½ oz.	320	11
⊟ Chicken Enchiladas	10 oz.	490	34
Chili Con Carne with Beans	8 ¾ oz.	260	24
⊟ Creamed Chicken	6½ oz.	300	8
Creamed Chipped Beef	½ of 11 oz. pkg.	230	9
⊟ Escalloped Chicken and Noodles	10 oz.	420	27
Fiesta Lasagna	10¼ oz.	430	35
Green Pepper Steak with Rice	10½ oz.	330	36
⊟ Ham and Asparagus Crepes	9½ oz.	510	31
Homestyle Chicken and Noodles	10 oz.	310	21
Lasagna	10½ oz.	360	33
⊟ Lobster Newburg	6½ oz.	380	9
Macaroni and Beef with Tomatoes	11½ oz.	340	30
Macaroni and Cheese	½ of 12 oz. pkg.	250	22
Meat Pies ⊟ Beef Pie	1-10 oz. pie	500	33
⊟ Chicken Pie	1-10 oz. pie	530	35
⊟ Turkey Pie	1-10 oz. pie	540	35
Pasta Shells, Cheese, with Tomato Sauce	9¼ oz.	330	32

† For occasional use   ** Not recommended for use

PROTEIN (gm)	FAT (gm)	SAT. FAT (gm)	CHOLES-TEROL (mg)	SODIUM (mg)	EXCHANGES
13	4	—	—	1080	2 veg., 1½ lean meat
24	20	—	—	780	½ starch, 1 veg., 3 lean meat, 2 fat
22	29	—	—	910	2 starch, 2½ meat, 3 fat
19	10	—	—	1270	1½ starch, 2 meat
19	21	—	—	670	½ starch, 2½ lean meat, 2½ fat
12	16	—	—	850	½ starch, 1½ meat, 1½ fat
21	25	—	—	1230	2 starch, 1 veg., 2 lean meat, 3 fat
24	22	—	—	960	2 starch, 1 veg., 2½ high fat meat
21	11	—	—	1440	2 starch, 1 veg., 2 meat
18	35	—	—	900	2 starch, 1 veg., 2 meat, 4 fat
23	15	—	—	1090	1½ starch, 2½ meat
28	13	—	—	1020	2 starch, 1 veg., 3 meat
14	32	—	—	870	½ starch, 2 lean meat, 5 fat
22	14	—	—	1620	2 starch, 2 meat, ½ fat
12	13	—	—	730	1½ starch, 1 meat, 1 fat
20	32	—	—	1300	2 starch, 1 veg., 2 meat, 3½ fat
22	33	—	—	1260	2 starch, 1 veg., 2 lean meat, 5 fat
20	36	—	—	1300	2 starch, 1 veg., 2 meat, 4 fat
17	15	—	—	850	2 starch, 1½ high fat meat, ½ fat

* Not available   ▉ More than 2 fat exchanges   🛒 Moderate to high sugar content

Products	SERVING SIZE	CALORIES	CARBO-HYDRATE (gm)
Salisbury Steak with Gravy	9⅞ oz.	250	9
Spaghetti with Meatballs	12⅝ oz.	380	42
Spaghetti with Meat Sauce	12⅞ oz.	370	49
Stuffed Green Peppers with Beef in Tomato Sauce	½ of 15½ oz. pkg.	200	19
Swedish Meatballs with Parsley Noodles	11 oz.	480	37
Tortellini			
Beef with Marinara Sauce	10 oz.	360	45
▐ Cheese in Alfredo Sauce	8⅞ oz.	600	32
Cheese with Tomato Sauce	9⅝ oz.	360	37
▐ Cheese with Vinaigrette Dressing	6⅞ oz.	400	24
▐ Grande	9⅝ oz.	530	34
Tuna Noodle Casserole	10 oz.	310	31
Turkey Casserole with Gravy and Dressing	9 ¾ oz.	360	29
Turkey Tetrazzini	10 oz.	380	28
Vegetable Lasagna	10½ oz.	420	29
▐ Welsh Rarebit	½ of 10 oz. pkg.	350	8

STOUFFER'S® DINNER SUPREME® (Stouffer Foods Corp.)

Baked Chicken Breast with Gravy	10 oz.	300	20
Barbecue-Style Chicken	10½ oz.	390	24
Cheese Stuffed Shells	11 oz.	310	29
Chicken Florentine	11 oz.	430	32

† For occasional use   ** Not recommended for use

PROTEIN (gm)	FAT (gm)	SAT. FAT (gm)	CHOLES-TEROL (mg)	SODIUM (mg)	EXCHANGES
21	14	—	—	1070	½ starch, 2½ meat, ½ fat
20	15	—	—	1510	3 starch, 2 meat
18	11	—	—	1510	3 starch, 1½ meat
11	9	—	—	940	1 starch, 1 veg., 1 meat, ½ fat
24	26	—	—	1510	2½ starch, 2½ meat, 2 fat
18	12	—	—	780	3 starch, 1½ meat
28	40	—	—	930	2 starch, 3 high fat meat, 3 fat
18	16	—	—	860	2 starch, 1 veg., 1½ meat, 1½ fat
15	27	—	—	540	1½ starch, 1½ high fat meat, 3 fat
24	33	—	—	910	2 starch, 2½ high fat meat, 2½ fat
17	13	—	—	1340	2 starch, 2 lean meat, 1 fat
23	17	—	—	1090	2 starch, 2½ meat, ½ fat
22	20	—	—	1170	2 starch, 1 veg., 2 lean meat, 2 fat
23	24	—	—	970	2 starch, 2½ meat, 1½ fat
13	30	—	—	680	½ starch, 1½ meat, 4½ fat
30	11	—	—	830	1 starch, 1 veg., 3½ lean meat
22	23	—	—	1250	1½ starch, 1 veg., 2 meat, 2 fat
16	14	—	—	1050	2 starch, 1½ meat, 1 fat
33	18	—	—	930	2 starch, 3½ meat

* Not available   ▯ More than 2 fat exchanges   🛒 Moderate to high sugar content

Products	SERVING SIZE	CALORIES	CARBO-HYDRATE (gm)
Chicken Parmigiana	11½ oz.	360	25
Chicken with Supreme Sauce	11⅜ oz.	360	29
Fried Chicken	10⅝ oz.	450	35
Glazed Ham Steak	10½ oz.	380	35
Homestyle Meatloaf	12 ⅛ oz.	410	29
Roast Turkey Breast	10 ¾ oz.	330	32
Salisbury Steak with Gravy and Mushrooms	11⅝ oz.	400	24
Veal Parmigiana	11¼ oz.	350	30

STOUFFER'S® LEAN CUISINE® (Stouffer Foods Corp.)

Beef and Bean Enchanadas	9¼ oz.	280	32
Beef and Pork Cannelloni with Mornay Sauce	9⅝ oz.	260	25
Beef Steak Ranchero	9¼ oz.	270	30
Breast of Chicken in Herb Cream Sauce	9½ oz.	260	17
Breast of Chicken Marsala with Vegetables	8 ⅛ oz.	190	11
Breast of Chicken Parmesan	10 oz.	260	19
Cheese Cannelloni with Tomato Sauce	9 ⅛ oz.	260	22
Chicken a l'Orange with Almond Rice	8 oz.	260	30
Chicken and Vegetables with Vermicelli	12 ¾ oz.	270	29
Chicken Cacciatore with Vermicelli	10⅞ oz.	250	26
Chicken Chow Mein with Rice	11¼ oz.	250	36

† For occasional use   ** Not recommended for use

PROTEIN (gm)	FAT (gm)	SAT. FAT (gm)	CHOLES-TEROL (mg)	SODIUM (mg)	EXCHANGES
31	15	—	—	1150	1½ starch, 1 veg., 3½ lean meat, ½ fat
33	12	—	—	990	1½ starch, 1 veg., 4 lean meat
25	23	—	—	990	2 starch, 1 veg., 3 meat, 1 fat
25	15	—	—	1960	2 starch, 1 veg., 3 lean meat, ½ fat
25	22	—	—	1170	1½ starch, 1 veg., 3 meat, 1 fat
27	10	—	—	1290	2 starch, 1 veg., 3 lean meat
25	23	—	—	1230	1 starch, 1 veg., 3 meat, 1½ fat
27	13	—	—	1090	2 starch, 1 veg., 3 lean meat
15	10	2	60	890	2 starch, 1 veg., 1 meat, ½ fat
17	10	4	45	950	1 starch, 1 veg., 2 lean meat, ½ fat
16	9	3	40	950	1½ starch, 1 veg., 1½ meat
26	10	3	80	910	1 starch, 1 veg., 3 lean meat
25	5	1	80	400	½ starch, 1 veg., 2½ lean meat
27	8	2	80	870	1 starch, 1 veg., 3 lean meat
21	10	5	35	910	1 starch, 1 veg., 2 meat
24	5	1	55	430	2 starch, 3 lean meat
20	8	2	45	980	1½ starch, 1 veg., 2 lean meat
21	7	1	45	860	1½ starch, 1 veg., 2 lean meat
14	5	1	35	980	2 starch, 1 veg., 1 lean meat

* Not available   ▊ More than 2 fat exchanges   🛒 Moderate to high sugar content

Products	SERVING SIZE	CALORIES	CARBO-HYDRATE (gm)
Chicken Enchanadas	9⅞ oz.	270	31
Chicken Oriental	9⅜ oz.	230	23
Fiesta Chicken	8½ oz.	250	29
Fillet of Fish Divan	12⅜ oz.	260	17
Fillet of Fish Florentine	9 oz.	230	13
Fillet of Fish Jardiniere with Souffléd Potatoes	11¼ oz.	290	18
Glazed Chicken with Vegetable Rice	8½ oz.	270	23
Lasagna with Meat and Sauce	10¼ oz.	270	24
Linguini with Clam Sauce	9⅝ oz.	270	35
Meatball Stew	10 oz.	250	20
Oriental Beef with Vegetables and Rice	8⅝ oz.	250	28
Rigatoni Bake with Meat Sauce and Cheese	9 ¾ oz.	260	25
Salisbury Steak with Italian Style Sauce and Vegetables	9½ oz.	280	12
Shrimp and Chicken Cantonese with Noodles	10 ⅛ oz.	270	25
Sliced Turkey Breast in Mushroom Sauce	8 oz.	240	20
Spaghetti with Beef and Mushroom Sauce	11½ oz.	280	38
Stuffed Cabbage with Meat in Tomato Sauce	10 ¾ oz.	220	19
Szechwan Beef with Noodles and Vegetables	9¼ oz.	260	22
Tuna Lasagna with Spinach Noodles and Vegetables	9 ¾ oz.	270	29
Turkey Dijon	9½ oz.	270	22

† For occasional use ** Not recommended for use

PROTEIN (gm)	FAT (gm)	SAT. FAT (gm)	CHOLES-TEROL (mg)	SODIUM (mg)	EXCHANGES
17	9	2	65	850	1½ starch, 1 veg., 1½ lean meat, 1 fat
22	6	1	100	790	1 starch, 1 veg., 2½ lean meat
21	6	1	45	880	1½ starch, 1 veg., 2 lean meat
31	7	2	85	750	½ starch, 1 veg., 4 lean meat
26	8	2	100	700	½ starch, 1 veg., 3 lean meat
31	10	4	110	840	1 starch, 4 lean meat
26	8	1	55	810	1 starch, 1 veg., 3 lean meat
25	8 *	3	60	970	1 starch, 1 veg., 3 lean meat
16	7	1	30	890	2 starch, 2 lean meat
21	10	3	85	940	1 starch, 1 veg., 2 meat
18	7	2	45	900	1½ starch, 1 veg., 2 lean meat
18	10	3	40	870	1 starch, 1 veg., 2 meat
25	15	5	100	840	½ starch, 1 veg., 3 lean meat, 1 fat
22	9	1	100	920	1 starch, 1 veg., 2½ lean meat
23	7	2	50	790	1 starch, 1 veg., 2½ lean meat
16	7	2	25	940	2 starch, 1 veg., 1 meat, ½ fat
14	10	2	55	930	1 starch, 1 veg., 1½ meat
20	10	3	100	680	1 starch, 1 veg., 2 meat
17	10	2	35	890	1½ starch, 1 veg., 2 lean meat, ½ fat
24	10	3	60	900	1 starch, 1 veg., 3 lean meat

* Not available   ▤ More than 2 fat exchanges   ☻ Moderate to high sugar content

Products	SERVING SIZE	CALORIES	CARBO-HYDRATE (gm)
Vegetable and Pasta Mornay with Ham	9⅜ oz.	280	29
Zucchini Lasagna	11 oz.	260	28
STOUFFER'S® RIGHT COURSE™ (Stouffer Foods Corp.)			
Beef Dijon with Pasta & Vegetables	9½ oz.	290	31
Beef Ragout with Rice Pilaf	10 oz.	300	38
Chicken Italiano with Fettucini & Vegetables	9⅝ oz.	280	29
Chicken Tenderloins in Barbecue Sauce	8 ¾ oz.	270	35
Chicken Tenderloins in Peanut Sauce	9¼ oz.	330	32
Fiesta Beef with Corn Pasta	8⅞ oz.	270	33
Homestyle Pot Roast	9¼ oz.	220	22
Sesame Chicken	10 oz.	320	34
Sliced Turkey in a Mild Curry Sauce with Rice Pilaf	8 ¾ oz.	320	40
Shrimp Primavera	9⅝ oz.	240	32
Vegetarian Chili	9 ¾ oz.	280	45
SUZI WAN™ (Uncle Ben's Foods)			
Dinner Recipes (as prepared)			
Honey Lemon Chicken	¼ recipe	370	45
Stir Fry Broccoli	¼ recipe	370	37
Sweet 'n Sour	¼ recipe	340	49
Teriyaki	¼ recipe	350	39

† For occasional use ** Not recommended for use

PROTEIN (gm)	FAT (gm)	SAT. FAT (gm)	CHOLES- TEROL (mg)	SODIUM (mg)	EXCHANGES
15	11	3	35	970	1½ starch, 1 veg., 1½ meat, ½ fat
21	7	2	25	975	1½ starch, 1 veg., 2 lean meat
20	9	2	40	580	2 starch, 2 lean meat, ½ fat
19	8	2	50	550	2½ starch, 2 lean meat
24	8	2	45	560	2 starch, 2½ lean meat
20	6	1	40	590	2 starch, 2 lean meat
27	10	2	50	570	2 starch, 3 lean meat
18	7	2	30	590	2 starch, 2 lean meat
17	7	2	35	550	1½ starch, 2 lean meat
25	9	2	50	590	2 starch, 3 lean meat
23	8	2	50	570	2½ starch, 2 lean meat
12	7	1	50	590	2 starch, 1 lean meat, ½ fat
9	7	1	0	590	3 starch, 1 fat
23	11	—	—	640	3 starch, 2½ lean meat
22	15	—	—	800	2 starch, 1 veg., 2 lean meats, 1½ fat
24	5	—	—	290	2 starch, 1 veg., 1 fruit, 2 lean meat†
22	12	—	—	970	2 starch, 1 veg., 2 lean meat, 1 fat

* Not available   ◫ More than 2 fat exchanges   🛒 Moderate to high sugar content

Products	SERVING SIZE	CALORIES	CARBO-HYDRATE (gm)
SWANSON® (Campbell Soup Co.)			
Canned Products			
Chicken a la King	5¼ oz.	180	9
Chicken and Dumplings	7½ oz.	220	19
Chicken Stew	7⅝ oz.	170	16
3-Compartment Frozen Dinners			
Beans and Franks	10½ oz.	440	55
Fried Chicken Platter	7 ¾ oz.	340	39
Macaroni and Beef	12 oz.	370	48
Macaroni and Cheese	12¼ oz.	380	49
Noodles and Chicken	10½ oz.	260	35
Spaghetti and Meatballs	12½ oz.	370	45
4-Compartment Frozen Dinners			
Beef	11¼ oz.	340	41
Beef in Barbecue Sauce	11 oz.	460	51
Beef Enchiladas	13 ¾ oz.	480	54
Chicken in Barbecue Sauce	11 ¾ oz.	460	57
Chicken Nuggets	8 ¾ oz.	460	40
Chopped Sirloin Beef	11 oz.	370	29
Fish 'n Chips	10 oz.	500	60

† For occasional use   ** Not recommended for use

PROTEIN (gm)	FAT (gm)	SAT. FAT (gm)	CHOLES-TEROL (mg)	SODIUM (mg)	EXCHANGES
10	12	—	—	690	½ starch, 1 lean meat, 2 fat
11	12	—	—	960	1 starch, 1 veg., 1 lean meat, 2 fat
9	7	—	—	960	1 starch, 1 lean meat, 1 fat
11	20	—	—	900	3½ starch, ½ high fat meat, 2½ fat
8	16	—	—	850	2½ starch, 1 lean meat, 2 fat
11	15	—	—	870	3 starch, 1 meat, 1½ fat
12	15	—	—	990	3 starch, 1 meat, 1½ fat
11	9	—	—	860	2 starch, 1 meat, ½ fat
12	16	—	—	1010	3 starch, 1 meat, 1½ fat
27	8	—	—	800	2 starch, 1 veg., 2½ lean meat
29	15	—	—	850	3 starch, 1 veg., 2½ meat
16	22	—	—	1300	3 starch, 1 veg., 1 meat, 3 fat
28	13	—	—	940	3½ starch, 1 veg., 2½ lean meat, ½ fat
19	25	—	—	710	2 starch, 1 veg., 2 lean meat, 3½ fat
21	19	—	—	850	1½ starch, 1 veg., 2 meat, 1½ fat
19	20	—	—	930	3½ starch, 1 veg., 1½ lean meat, 2½ fat

* Not available   ▯ More than 2 fat exchanges   ☷ Moderate to high sugar content

Products	SERVING SIZE	CALORIES	CARBO-HYDRATE (gm)
▤ Fish Nuggets	9½ oz.	410	43
Fried Chicken, BBQ Flavored	10+ oz.	520	53
▤ Fried Chicken, Dark Meat	9 ¾+ oz.	560	54
▤ Fried Chicken, White Meat	10¼+ oz.	560	61
Loin of Pork	10 ¾ oz.	310	28
▤ Meat Loaf	10 ¾ oz.	430	41
▤ Mexican Style Combination	14¼ oz.	520	60
Salibury Steak	10 ¾ oz.	410	43
⬥ Sweet 'n Sour Chicken	12 oz.	380	50
Swiss Steak	10 oz.	340	38
Turkey	11½ oz.	350	42
▤ Veal Parmigiana	12¼ oz.	450	40
Western Style	11½ oz.	450	43
Homestyle Recipe Entrees, frozen Chicken Cacciatore	11 oz.	260	33
▤ Chicken Nibbles	4¼+ oz.	340	21

† For occasional use   ** Not recommended for use

PROTEIN (gm)	FAT (gm)	SAT. FAT (gm)	CHOLES- TEROL (mg)	SODIUM (mg)	EXCHANGES
17	19	—	—	930	2½ starch, 1 veg., 1½ lean meat, 2½ fat
25	21	—	—	1000	3 starch, 1 veg., 2½ meat, 1½ fat
22	28	—	—	1110	3 starch, 1 veg., 2 meat, 3 fat
22	25	—	—	1380	3½ starch, 1 veg., 2 meat, 2½ fat
22	12	—	—	770	1½ starch, 1 veg., 2½ lean meat, ½ fat
17	22	—	—	1030	2½ starch, 1½ meat, 2½ fat
17	24	—	—	1580	3½ starch, 1 veg., 1 meat, 3½ fat
19	18	—	—	880	2½ starch, 1 veg., 2 meat, 1 fat
20	11	—	—	520	2 starch, 1 veg., 1 fruit, 2 lean meat, ½ fat†
23	11	—	—	740	2 starch, 1 veg., 2½ lean meat, ½ fat
20	11	—	—	1110	2½ starch, 1 veg., 2 lean meat, ½ fat
22	22	—	—	1100	2 starch, 1 veg., 2 meat, 2½ fat
22	21	—	—	1010	2½ starch, 1 veg., 2 meat, 2 fat
15	8	—	—	1030	2 starch, 1½ lean meat, ½ fat
10	24	—	—	480	1½ starch, 1 lean meat, 4 fat

* Not available   ▯ More than 2 fat exchanges   ☕ Moderate to high sugar content

Products	SERVING SIZE	CALORIES	CARBO-HYDRATE (gm)
⊟ Chicken Pie	8 oz.	380	40
Chili Con Carne	8¼ oz.	270	26
Fish 'N Fries	6½ oz.	350	35
⊟ Fried Chicken	7+ oz.	380	30
Lasagna with Meat Sauce	10½ oz.	400	39
Macaroni and Cheese	10 oz.	400	38
⊟ Salisbury Steak	10 oz.	480	22
Scalloped Potatoes and Ham	9 oz.	340	31
Seafood Creole with Rice	9 oz.	240	40
Sirloin Tips in Burgundy Sauce	7 oz.	270	27
Spaghetti with Italian Style Meatballs	13 oz.	460	56
Swedish Meatballs	8½ oz.	350	22
Turkey with Dressing & Potatoes	9 oz.	290	30
Veal Parmigiana	10 oz.	330	35
Hungry Man Dinners, frozen Boneless Chicken	17 ¾ oz.	700	65
⊟ Chopped Beef Steak	16 ¾ oz.	640	41
⊟ Fried Chicken, Dark Meat	14¼+ oz.	860	77
⊟ Fried Chicken, White Meat	14¼+ oz.	870	80

† For occasional use   ** Not recommended for use

PROTEIN (gm)	FAT (gm)	SAT. FAT (gm)	CHOLES-TEROL (mg)	SODIUM (mg)	EXCHANGES
13	19	—	—	860	2½ starch, 1 lean meat, 3 fat
20	10	—	—	740	1½ starch, 2 meat
15	17	—	—	690	2 starch, 1½ lean meat, 2 fat
18	21	—	—	1030	2 starch, 2 lean meat, 2½ fat
25	16	—	—	870	2½ starch, 2½ meat, ½ fat
15	21	—	—	980	2½ starch, 1½ high fat meat, 1 fat
22	34	—	—	1170	1½ starch, 2½ meat, 4 fat
19	16	—	—	990	2 starch, 2 meat, 1 fat
7	6	—	—	810	2½ starch, ½ lean meat, ½ fat
17	10	—	—	570	2 starch, 2 lean meat
16	19	—	—	1010	4 starch, 1 meat, 2 fat
17	22	—	—	780	1½ starch, 2 meat, 2 fat
17	13	—	—	1020	2 starch, 2 lean meat, 1 fat
19	13	—	—	960	2 starch, 2 lean meat, 1 fat
48	28	—	—	1530	4 starch, 1 veg., 5 lean meat, 2 fat
35	37	—	—	1600	2½ starch, 1 veg., 4 meat, 3 fat
36	45	—	—	1660	4½ starch, 1 veg., 4 meat, 4 fat
35	46	—	—	2150	5 starch, 1 veg., 3 meat, 5 fat

* Not available   🮱 More than 2 fat exchanges   ♟ Moderate to high sugar content

Products	SERVING SIZE	CALORIES	CARBO-HYDRATE (gm)
▤ Mexican	20¼ oz.	820	88
▤ Salisbury Steak	18¼ oz.	680	37
Sliced Beef	15¼ oz.	450	49
Turkey	17 oz.	550	61
Veal Parmigiana	18¼ oz.	560	64
Hungry Man Pot Pies, frozen			
▤ Beef	16 oz.	700	66
▤ Chicken	16 oz.	740	65
▤ Turkey	16 oz.	750	65
Pot Pies, frozen			
▤ Beef	7 oz.	380	37
▤ Chicken	7 oz.	370	35
Macaroni and Cheese	7 oz.	220	27
▤ Turkey	7 oz.	390	38
TUNA HELPER® (General Mills, Inc.)			
Main Dishes (as prepared)			
Buttery Rice	6 oz. (⅕ pkg.)	280	32
Cheesy Noodles	7.75 oz. (⅕ pkg.)	250	28
Creamy Mushroom	7 oz. (⅕ pkg.)	220	28
Creamy Noodles	8 oz. (⅕ pkg.)	300	30

† For occasional use   ** Not recommended for use

PROTEIN (gm)	FAT (gm)	SAT. FAT (gm)	CHOLES- TEROL (mg)	SODIUM (mg)	EXCHANGES
25	41	—	—	2080	5½ starch, 1 veg., 2 meat, 5 fat
41	41	—	—	1730	2 starch, 1 veg., 5 meat, 3 fat
37	12	—	—	1060	3 starch, 1 veg., 3½ lean meat
36	18	—	—	1810	3½ starch, 1 veg., 3 lean meat, 2 fat
30	23	—	—	2080	4 starch, 1 veg., 2½ meat, 1 fat
27	36	—	—	1530	4 starch, 1 veg., 2 meat, 5 fat
27	41	—	—	1630	4 starch, 1 veg., 2 lean meat, 6½ fat
27	42	—	—	1670	4 starch, 1 veg., 2 lean meat, 6½ fat
11	20	—	—	700	2 starch, 1 veg., ½ meat, 3 fat
10	22	—	—	810	2 starch, 1 veg., ½ lean meat, 4 fat
8	9	—	—	880	2 starch, ½ meat, 1½ fat
10	22	—	—	720	2 starch, 1 veg., ½ lean meat, 4 fat
13	11	—	—	1040	2 starch, 1½ lean meat, 1 fat
15	9	—	—	980	2 starch, 1½ meat
14	6	—	—	740	2 starch, 1½ lean meat
14	14	—	—	960	2 starch, 1½ lean meat, 1½ fat

* Not available ⯐ More than 2 fat exchanges 🛒 Moderate to high sugar content

Products	SERVING SIZE	CALORIES	CARBO-HYDRATE (gm)
Fettucini Alfredo	7 oz. (⅕ pkg.)	300	30
Tuna Au Gratin	6 oz. (⅕ pkg.)	280	30
▯ Tuna Pot Pie	5.1 oz. (⅙ pkg.)	420	31
▯ Tuna Salad	5.5 oz. (⅕ pkg.)	420	29
Tuna Tetrazzini	6 oz. (⅕ pkg.)	240	27

TYSON® GOURMET SELECTION® (Tyson Foods, Inc.)
Dinners

A L'Orange	9.5 oz.	300	36
Beef Champignon	10.5 oz.	370	31
Chicken & Beef Luau	10.5 oz.	330	42
Dijon	8.5 oz.	310	22
Francais	9.5 oz.	280	20
▯ Kiev	9.25 oz.	520	40
Lasagna	11.5 oz.	380	47
Marsala	10.5 oz.	300	26
Mesquite	9.5 oz.	320	35
Oriental	10.25 oz.	270	32
Parmigiana	11.25 oz.	380	37
Pasta Trio	11 oz.	450	53
Peking	10 oz.	390	34

† For occasional use   ** Not recommended for use

PROTEIN (gm)	FAT (gm)	SAT. FAT (gm)	CHOLES- TEROL (mg)	SODIUM (mg)	EXCHANGES
16	13	—	—	1000	2 starch, 1½ lean meat, 1½ fat
16	11	—	—	980	2 starch, 1½ meat, ½ fat
13	27	—	—	890	2 starch, 1½ lean meat, 4 fat
14	27	—	—	870	2 starch, 1½ lean meat, 4 fat
15	8	—	—	780	2 starch, 1½ meat, ½ fat
21	8	—	—	670	2 starch, 1 veg., 2 lean meat
27	15	—	—	830	1½ starch, 1 veg., 3 meat
18	10	—	—	1030	2½ starch, 1 veg., 1½ meat
17	17	—	—	840	1 starch, 1 veg., 2 meat, 1 fat
19	14	—	—	1130	1 starch, 1 veg., 2 meat, ½ fat
16	33	—	—	1200	2 starch, 1 veg., 1½ lean meat, 5½ fat
20	14	—	—	840	2½ starch, 1 veg., 1½ meat, 1½ fat
19	13	—	—	900	1½ starch, 1 veg., 2 lean meat, 1 fat
23	10	—	—	700	2 starch, 1 veg., 2½ lean meat
20	7	—	—	1140	2 starch, 1 veg., 2 lean meat
19	17	—	—	1100	2 starch, 1 veg., 2 lean meat, 2 fat
21	17	—	—	890	3 starch, 1 veg., 2 meat, 1 fat
18	20	—	—	860	2 starch, 1 veg., 2 lean meat, 2 fat

* Not available   **⯐** More than 2 fat exchanges   🛒 Moderate to high sugar content

Products	SERVING SIZE	CALORIES	CARBO-HYDRATE (gm)
Pepper Steak	11.25 oz.	330	38
Picatta	9 oz.	240	19
Salisbury Supreme	10 oz.	430	34
Short Ribs	11 oz.	470	38
Sweet & Sour	11 oz.	420	50
Turkey	11.5 oz.	380	51
TYSON® LOONEY TUNES™ (Tyson Foods, Inc.)			
Bugs Bunny™ Chicken Chunks	7.35 oz.	370	31
Daffy Duck™ Spaghetti & Meatballs	8.65 oz.	300	46
Road Runner™ Chicken Sandwich	6.95 oz.	320	46
Speedy Gonzales™ Beef Enchiladas	9.5 oz.	400	52
Sylvester™ Fish Sticks	6.25 oz.	300	29
Tweety™ Macaroni & Cheese	9.75 oz.	280	42
Wile E. Coyote™ Hamburger Pizza	6 oz.	300	37
Yosemite Sam™ BBQ Glazed Chicken	8 oz.	420	30
VAN CAMP'S® (Quaker Oats Co.)			
Noodlee Weenee®	1 cup	240	33
Spaghetee Weenee®	1 cup	240	35

† For occasional use   ** Not recommended for us

PROTEIN (gm)	FAT (gm)	SAT. FAT (gm)	CHOLES-TEROL (mg)	SODIUM (mg)	EXCHANGES
20	11	—	—	1130	2 starch, 1 veg., 2 meat
19	10	—	—	680	1 starch, 1 veg., 2 lean meat, ½ fat
16	26	—	—	810	2 starch, 1 veg., 1½ meat, 3 fat
25	24	—	—	950	2 starch, 1 veg., 3 meat, 1½ fat
22	15	—	—	850	2 starch, 1 veg., 1 fruit, 2 meat, ½ fat†
19	11	—	—	1350	3 starch, 1 veg., 1½ lean meat, ½ fat
17	20	—	—	770	1½ starch, 1 veg., 2 meat, 1½ fat
12	8	—	—	820	2½ starch, 1 veg., 1 meat
9	11	—	—	610	2½ starch, 1 veg., ½ meat, 1 fat
12	16	—	—	830	3 starch, 1 veg., 1 meat, 1½ fat
12	15	—	—	670	1½ starch, 1 veg., 1 meat, 2 fat
10	8	—	—	630	2½ starch, 1 veg. ½ meat, ½ fat
10	12	—	—	620	2½ starch, 1 meat, 1 fat
28	21	—	—	750	1½ starch, 1 veg., 3 meat, 1 fat
9	8	—	—	1250	2 starch, ½ high fat meat, ½ fat
9	7	—	—	1130	2 starch, ½ high fat meat, ½ fat

---

* Not available   ☰ More than 2 fat exchanges   🛒 Moderate to high sugar content

Products	SERVING SIZE	CALORIES	CARBO-HYDRATE (gm)
VELVEETA® (Kraft, Inc.)			
Shells and Cheese	¾ cup	260	32
WEIGHT WATCHER® (H.J. Heinz Co.)			
Entrees			
Angel Hair Pasta	10 oz.	210	23
Baked Cheese Ravioli	9 oz.	290	34
Beef Enchiladas Ranchero	9.12 oz.	230	17
Beef Fajitas	6.75 oz.	250	32
Beef Salisbury Steak Romana	8.75 oz.	190	13
Beef Sirloin Tips and Mushrooms in Wine Sauce	7.5 oz.	220	19
Beef Stroganoff	8.5 oz.	290	26
Breaded Chicken Cordon Bleu	8 oz.	220	14
Broccoli and Cheese Baked Potato	10.5 oz.	290	43
Cheese Enchiladas Ranchero	8.87 oz.	360	30
Cheese Manicotti	9.25 oz.	280	33
Cheese Tortellini	9.0 oz.	310	50
Chicken ala King	9 oz.	240	28
Chicken Burrito	7.62 oz.	310	34
Chicken Divan Baked Potato	11 oz.	280	42
Chicken Enchiladas Suiza	9 oz.	280	28
Chicken Fajitas	6.75 oz.	230	30
Chicken Fettucini	8.25 oz.	280	25

† For occasional use   ** Not recommended for use

PROTEIN (gm)	FAT (gm)	SAT. FAT (gm)	CHOLES-TEROL (mg)	SODIUM (mg)	EXCHANGES
12	10	5	25	720	2 starch, 1 meat, ½ fat
12	5	1	20	420	1½ starch, 1 meat
18	9	4	85	630	2 starch, 1 veg., 2 meat
20	10	3	40	720	1 starch, 1 veg., 2 meat
15	7	2	20	630	2 starch, 1 veg., 1 meat
20	7	2	40	470	½ starch, 1 veg., 2 lean meat
20	7	3	50	540	1 starch, 1 veg., 2 meat
22	9	4	25	600	1½ starch, 1 veg., 2 lean meat, ½ fat
19	9	5	50	630	½ starch, 1 veg., 2 meat
13	8	2	25	600	2½ starch, 1 veg., 1 meat
18	18	5	60	900	2 starch, 1½ meat, 2 fat
17	8	4	75	490	2 starch, 1 veg., 1½ meat
14	6	1	15	570	3 starch, 1 veg., ½ meat
17	6	3	20	490	1½ starch, 1 veg., 2 lean meat
15	13	4	60	790	2 starch, 1 veg., 1 fat
18	4	2	40	730	2 starch, 1 veg., 1½ lean meat
19	11	2	30	600	2 starch, 2 meat
17	5	2	30	590	2 starch, 1 veg., 1 lean meat
22	9	3	40	590	1½ starch, 3 lean meat

* Not available   ▤ More than 2 fat exchanges   ♛ Moderate to high sugar content

Products	SERVING SIZE	CALORIES	CARBO-HYDRATE (gm)
Chicken Kiev	7 oz.	230	23
Chicken Nuggets	5.9 oz.	270	24
Fettucini Alfredo	9.0 oz.	210	18
Fillet of Fish Au Gratin	9.25 oz.	200	11
Garden Lasagna	11 oz.	290	35
Ham Lorraine Baked Potato	11 oz.	250	31
Homestyle Chicken & Noodles	9 oz.	240	25
Homestyle Turkey Baked Potato	12 oz.	300	39
Imperial Chicken	9.25 oz.	240	32
Italian Cheese Lasagna	11 oz.	350	33
Lasagna with Meat Sauce	11 oz.	320	32
London Broil in Mushroom Sauce	7.37 oz.	140	9
Oven Fried Fish	7.08 oz.	240	23
Pasta Primavera	8.5 oz.	260	22
Pasta Rigati	10.63 oz.	300	35
Southern Fried Chicken	6.5 oz.	320	27
Spaghetti with Meat Sauce	10.5 oz.	280	32
Stuffed Turkey Breast	8½ oz.	260	24
🛒 Sweet 'n Sour Chicken Tenders	10.19 oz.	240	43
Veal Patty Parmigiana	8.44 oz.	190	12

PROTEIN (gm)	FAT (gm)	SAT. FAT (gm)	CHOLES-TEROL (mg)	SODIUM (mg)	EXCHANGES
13	9	3	30	610	1 starch, 1 veg., 1½ meat, ½ fat
15	12	4	50	540	1½ starch, 1½ meat, 1 fat
17	8	3	35	600	1 starch, 1 veg., 2 lean meat
25	6	1	60	700	½ starch, 1 veg., 2½ lean meat
19	7	2	20	670	2 starch, 1 veg., 2 meat
20	4	2	15	670	1½ starch, 1 veg., 2 lean meat
19	7	2	30	450	1 starch, 1 veg., 2 lean meat
21	6	3	60	670	2½ starch, 2 lean meat
21	3	1	35	640	1½ starch, 1 veg., 2 lean meat
29	12	4	30	690	2 starch, 1 veg., 3 lean meat
26	10	4	45	630	2 starch, 1 veg., 2 meat
18	3	1	40	510	2 veg., 2 lean meat
20	7	<1	15	380	1 starch, 1 veg., 2 lean meat
15	11	<1	5	800	1 starch, 1 veg., 1½ meat, ½ fat
20	9	2	25	490	2 starch, 1 veg., 2 lean meat
17	16	7	65	690	2 starch, 2 lean meat, 2 fat
20	7	3	35	610	2 starch, 1 veg., 1½ lean meat
20	10	4	80	910	1 starch, 1 veg., 2 lean meat, 1 fat
16	1	<1	40	600	2 starch, 1 veg., ½ fruit, 1 lean meat†
23	6	3	55	650	2 veg., 2½ lean meat

* Not available   🅱 More than 2 fat exchanges   🍬 Moderate to high sugar content

Products	SERVING SIZE	CALORIES	CARBO-HYDRATE (gm)
WOLF'S® (Quaker Oats Co.)			
Beef Stew	scant cup	180	18

CRACKERS

Products	SERVING SIZE	CALORIES	CARBO-HYDRATE (gm)
ESTEE® (Estee Corp.)			
6 Calorie Wheat Wafers	12 wafers	72	12
Unsalted Crackers	6	90	14
FEATHERWEIGHT® (Sandoz Nutrition)			
Crackers, Low Sodium	6	90	15
FRITO-LAY® (Frito-Lay, Inc.)			
Cheese Filled Crackers	1.5 oz.	210	24
Peanut Butter Filled Crackers	1.5 oz.	210	24
HAIN® (PET, Inc.)			
Sodium Values - Regular/No Salt Added			
Cheese	1 oz.	130	17
Onion	1 oz.	130	17
Rich	1 oz.	130	18
Rye	1 oz.	120	19
Sesame	1 oz.	140	16
Sour Cream & Chive	1 oz.	130	15
Sourdough	1 oz.	130	18
Vegetable	1 oz.	130	10
HEALTH VALLEY® (Health Valley Foods, Inc.)			
Graham:			
Amaranth, Honey, Rice Bran (average)	5	80	17
Rice Bran	6	110	16

PROTEIN (gm)	FAT (gm)	SAT. FAT (gm)	CHOLES-TEROL (mg)	SODIUM (mg)	EXCHANGES
10	8	—	—	1040	1 starch, 1 high fat meat
—	—	—	0	<60	1 starch
2	3	<1	0	0	1 starch, ½ fat
0	3	—	0	3	1 starch, ½ fat
4	10	—	5	470	1½ starch, 2 fat
6	10	—	0	450	1½ starch, 2 fat
3	6	—	—	180	1 starch, 1 fat
3	6	—	—	*160/ 5	1 starch, 1 fat
3	5	—	—	*160/ 15	1 starch, 1 fat
3	4	—	—	*200/ 10	1 starch, 1 fat
3	7	—	—	*210/ 10	1 starch, 1½ fat
3	6	—	—	*150/ 25	1 starch, 1 fat
3	5	—	—	*200/ 10	1 starch, 1 fat
3	5	—	—	*180/ 50	1 starch, 1 fat
2	2	—	0	32-89	1 starch
3	3	—	0	56	1 starch, ½ fat

* Not available   ▤ More than 2 fat exchanges   ☕ Moderate to high sugar content

Products	SERVING SIZE	CALORIES	CARBO-HYDRATE (gm)
Wheat Crackers All varieties except no salt added (average)	13	55	9
No Salt Added	13	55	9
KEEBLER® (Keebler Co.)			
Club	8	120	16
Melba Toast, long	5	75	18
Melba Toast, rounds, all varieties (average)	8	100	16
Oyster, large	30	92	15
Oyster, small	60	96	16
Toasted Snack, all varieties (average)	8	120	16
Town House®	8	140	16
Waldorf® Sodium Free	6	90	15
Whole Grain Wheat	5	90	15
Zesta® Saltines	8	100	16
Unsalted Tops	8	100	16
NABISCO® (Nabisco Brands, Inc.)			
American Classic®, all varieties, (average)	8 (1 oz.)	140	18
Bacon Flavored Thins®	14 (1 oz.)	140	18
Better Cheddars® Regular	20 (1 oz.)	140	16
Low Salt	20 (1 oz.)	140	16
Cheese Nips®	20 (¾ oz.)	105	14
Chicken in a Biskit®	14 (1 oz.)	160	16
Crown Pilot®	1 (½ oz.)	70	11
Dandy® Soup and Oyster Crackers	30 (¾ oz.)	90	15
Escort®	6 (1 oz.)	140	18
Harvest Crisps®, all varieties (average)	12 (1 oz.)	120	20
Meal Mates® Sesame Seed Wafers	6 (1 oz.)	140	18

PROTEIN (gm)	FAT (gm)	SAT. FAT (gm)	CHOLES- TEROL (mg)	SODIUM (mg)	EXCHANGES
1	2	—	0	80	½ starch, ½ fat
1	2	—	0	30	½ starch, ½ fat
2	8	—	0	300	1 starch, 1 fat
5	0	—	0	50	1 starch
4	0	—	0	120-140	1 starch
2	2	—	0	202	1 starch
2	2	—	0	210	1 starch
2	8	—	0	220-280	1 starch, 1 fat
2	8	—	0	240	1 starch, 1½ fat
2	3	—	0	0	1 starch, ½ fat
3	3	—	0	210	1 starch, ½ fat
2	3	—	0	300	1 starch, ½ fat
2	3	—	0	140	1 starch, ½ fat
2	6	—	<4	240-280	1 starch, 1 fat
2	8	2	<4	420	1 starch, 1½ fat
4	8	—	<4	260	1 starch, 1½ fat
4	8	—	<4	130	1 starch, 1½ fat
2	5	—	<3	200	1 starch, 1 fat
2	10	2	<4	260	1 starch, 2 fat
1	2	—	<2	70	1 starch
2	3	—	<3	330	1 starch, ½ fat
2	8	—	0	230	1 starch, 1½ fat
2	4	—	0	270	1 starch, 1 fat
2	6	—	0	320	1 starch, 1 fat

* Not available   ▌ More than 2 fat exchanges   🛒 Moderate to high sugar content

Products	SERVING SIZE	CALORIES	CARBO-HYDRATE (gm)
Oat Thins®	16 (1 oz.)	140	20
Oysterettes® Oyster Crackers	27 (1½ oz.)	90	15
Premium® Saltine			
Regular	6 squares	72	12
Low salt	6 squares	72	12
Unsalted Tops	6 squares	72	12
Whole Wheat	6 squares	72	12
Premium Bits®	24 (¾ oz.)	105	14
Ritz®			
Original	8 (1 oz.)	140	18
Low Salt	8 (1 oz.)	140	18
Ritz® Bits			
Regular	44 (1 oz.)	140	18
Cheese	44 (1 oz.)	140	18
Low Salt	44 (1 oz.)	140	18
Peanut Butter Sandwiches	12 (1 oz.)	160	16
Royal Lunch®	2 (1 oz.)	120	20
Sociables®	12 (1 oz.)	140	18
Swiss Cheese®	11 (¾ oz.)	105	17
Tid Bits®	32 (1 oz.)	140	16
Triscuit® Wafers			
Original	6 (1 oz.)	120	20
Low Salt	6 (1 oz.)	120	20
Wheat 'n Bran	6 (1 oz.)	120	20
Triscuit Bits®	16 (1 oz.)	120	20
Twigs® Snack Sticks	10 (1 oz.)	140	16
Uneeda® Biscuits, unsalted tops	6 (1 oz.)	120	20
Vegetable Thins®	14 (1 oz.)	140	16
Waverly®			
Original	8 (1 oz.)	140	20
Low Salt	8 (1 oz.)	140	20

† For occasional use   ** Not recommended for use

PROTEIN (gm)	FAT (gm)	SAT. FAT (gm)	CHOLES- TEROL (mg)	SODIUM (mg)	EXCHANGES
2	6	—	0	180	1 starch, 1 fat
2	2	—	0	210	1 starch
1	3	—	<2	216	1 starch
1	3	—	<2	138	1 starch
1	3	—	<2	162	1 starch
1	3	—	0	156	1 starch
2	4	—	0	240	1 starch, ½ fat
2	8	—	<4	240	1 starch, 1½ fat
2	8	—	<4	120	1 starch, 1½ fat
2	8	—	0	240	1 starch, 1½ fat
2	8	—	<2	300	1 starch, 1½ fat
2	8	—	0	120	1 starch, 1½ fat
4	8	—	0	160	1 starch, 1½ fat
2	4	—	<10	160	1 starch, 1 fat
2	6	—	<4	270	1 starch, 1 fat
2	5	—	<3	255	1 starch, 1 fat
2	8	2	<4	400	1 starch, 1½ fat
2	4	—	0	150	1 starch, 1 fat
2	4	—	0	70	1 starch, 1 fat
2	4	—	0	150	1 starch, 1 fat
2	4	—	0	150	1 starch, 1 fat
2	8	—	<4	280	1 starch, 1½ fat
2	4	—	0	200	1 starch, 1 fat
2	8	—	<4	280	1 starch, 1½ fat
2	6	—	0	320	1 starch, 1 fat
2	6	—	0	160	1 starch, 1 fat

* Not available   ▤ More than 2 fat exchanges   ☵ Moderate to high sugar content

Products	SERVING SIZE	CALORIES	CARBO-HYDRATE (gm)
Wheat Thins®			
Original	16 (1 oz.)	140	18
Low Salt	16 (1 oz.)	140	18
Nutty	14 (1 oz.)	160	16
Wheatsworth®	8 (1 oz.)	140	18
Zweiback Toast	3 (¾ oz.)	90	15
PEPPERIDGE FARM® (Campbell Soup Co.)			
Distinctive Crackers			
Butter Flavored	6	120	15
Cracked Wheat	5	135	18
English Water Biscuit	5	85	16
Goldfish Cheese Thins	4	70	8
Hearty Wheat	5	125	16
Sesame	6	120	15
Three Cracker Assortment	5	125	16
Toasted Wheat with Onion	6	120	15
Goldfish Crackers, all varieties (average)	45	140	18
Snack Sticks, all varieties (average)	8	130	18
RALSTON® (Ralston Purina Co.)			
Oat Bran Krisp®	4 triple crackers (1 oz.)	120	18
RyKrisp®, all varieties (average)	4 triple crackers (1 oz.)	90	20
SALERNO® (General Biscuit of America, Inc.)			
Graham Crackers, and Multi-Grain Graham (average)	5 crackers	88	15
Oyster	60 oysters (¾ oz.)	90	15
Saltines and Multi-Grain Saltines (average)	7 crackers	84	14
Saltines, unsalted tops	7 crackers	84	14

† For occasional use   ** Not recommended for use

PROTEIN (gm)	FAT (gm)	SAT. FAT (gm)	CHOLES-TEROL (mg)	SODIUM (mg)	EXCHANGES
2	6	—	0	240	1 starch, 1 fat
2	6	—	0	120	1 starch, 1 fat
2	8	—	0	340	1 starch, 1½ fat
2	6	—	0	270	1 starch, 1 fat
3	2	—	<3	—	1 starch
2	5	—	—	150	1 starch, 1 fat
3	5	—	—	250	1 starch, 1 fat
1	1	—	—	113	1 starch
1	3	—	—	110	½ starch, ½ fat
3	5	—	—	225	1 starch, 1 fat
3	5	—	—	165	1 starch, ½ fat
3	5	—	—	225	1 starch, 1 fat
5	5	—	—	165	1 starch, 1 fat
3	6	—	—	160-250	1 starch, 1 fat
3	6	—	—	320-390	1 starch, 1 fat
2	6	—	—	280	1 starch, 1 fat
2	2	—	—	150-210	1 starch
1	3	—	0	88	1 starch
3	3	—	0	165	1 starch
3	3	—	0	112-154	1 starch
3	3	—	0	91	1 starch

* Not available   ▌ More than 2 fat exchanges   ♥ Moderate to high sugar content

Products	SERVING SIZE	CALORIES	CARBO-HYDRATE (gm)
Tetris	40 pieces (1 oz.)	140	16
WEIGHT WATCHERS® (H.J. Heinz Co.)			
Crispbread, all varieties (average)	4 wafers	60	14

DESSERTS

Author's Note: Many of these products contain large amounts of refined sugars. We recommend that these products be used in moderation, if at all. If you decide to use them, work the specific product into your meal plan, using the nutrition information suppled here. And if you have diabetes, remember that when you decide to eat a high sugar food, do so with a meal, when it will be more slowly absorbed, or before exercise, so that it will be readily used for energy.

BARS, BROWNIES, COOKIES

BETTY CROCKER® (General Mills, Inc.)

Products	SERVING SIZE	CALORIES	CARBO-HYDRATE (gm)
⛟ Big Batch® Cookie Mix (as prepared) (average)	2 cookies	120	16
⛟ Brownie Mix, all varieties (as prepared) (average)	1 brownie	150	23
⛟ MicroRave® Brownie Mix, unfrosted, all varieties (as prepared) (average)	1 brownie	155	22
⛟ Date Bar Mix (as prepared)	1/24 package	60	9
DELICIOUS® (Delicious Cookie Co., Inc.)			
⛟ Almond Windmill	1	80	11
⛟ Animal Crackers	15	130	20
⛟ Bear Grahams, all varieties (average)	10	80	10
⛟ Chocolate Chip	1 oz.	127	20
⛟ Coconut Bars	1	70	10
⛟ Fig Bars	2	130	27
⛟ Fudge Grahams	1	141	20
⛟ Striped Shortbread	1 oz.	138	20

† For occasional use   ** Not recommended for use

PROTEIN (gm)	FAT (gm)	SAT. FAT (gm)	CHOLES- TEROL (mg)	SODIUM (mg)	EXCHANGES
2	8	—	0	210	1 starch, 1½ fat
<2	0	—	—	110	1 starch
1	6	—	—	100	1 starch, 1 fat†
1	6	1	15	75-120	1½ starch, 1 fat†
2	7	2	0	95-110	1½ starch, 1 fat†
1	2	1	0	35	½ starch, ½ fat†
1	3	<1	0	100	1 starch†
2	4	1	0	125	1 starch, 1 fat†
1	3	1	0	70-125	½ starch, 1 fat†
2	5	2	0	101	1 starch, 1 fat†
1	3	<1	0	190	1½ starch, ½ fat†
1	2	<1	0	70	1 starch, 1 fruit†
2	8	5	0	53	1 starch, 1½ fat†
2	6	4	0	68	1 starch, 1 fat†

* Not available   ▤ More than 2 fat exchanges   ☻ Moderate to high sugar content

Products	SERVING SIZE	CALORIES	CARBO-HYDRATE (gm)
🛒 Teenage Mutant Ninja Turtle Cookies, all varieties (average)	16-18 (1 oz.)	127	20
🛒 Vanilla Wafers	5	108	18
DUNCAN HINES® (Proctor & Gamble)			
🛒 Brownie Mixes, all varieties except Gourmet Turtle (as prepared) (average)	1 brownie	150	20
🛒 Gourmet Turtle Mix (as prepared)	1 brownie	200	27
🛒 Cookies, all varieties (average)	2 cookies	110	15
ENTENMANN'S® (Entenmann's, Inc.)			
🛒 Fat Free Cholesterol Free Oatmeal Raisin Cookies	2 (.8 oz.)	80	17
ESTEE® (Estee Corp.)			
Brownie Mix (as prepared)	2" x 4" piece	100	16
Chocolate Chip Cookie Mix (as prepared)	3 - 2" cookies	150	18
Cookies and Wafers, Dietetic Assorted Creme Filled Wafers	4	120	16
Chocolate or Vanilla Creme Filled Wafers	5	100	15
Cookies, all others, average	4	120	16
Sandwich Cookies, all varieties, average	3	150	15
Snack Wafers: Chocolate, Strawberry or Vanilla (average)	1	80	11
Snack Wafers, Chocolate Coated	1	130	14
FEATHERWEIGHT® SWEET PRETENDERS® (Sandoz Nutrition)			
Chocolate Chip Cookies	2	90	12
Chocolate Wafers	2	60	6
Creme Wafers, all varieties (average)	4	100	12

PROTEIN (gm)	FAT (gm)	SAT. FAT (gm)	CHOLES- TEROL (mg)	SODIUM (mg)	EXCHANGES
2	5	1	0	100- 128	1 starch, 1 fat†
1	3	1	0	80	1 starch, ½ fat†
1	8	—	—	90- 105	1 starch, 1½ fat†
2	9	—	—	125	1½ starch, 2 fat†
1	5	—	—	75- 90	1 starch, 1 fat†
1	0	—	—	120	1 starch†
2	4	<1	0	10	1 starch, ½ fat†
2-3	9	<1	0	120	1 starch, 1½ fat†
1	8	<1	0	20	1 starch, 1½ fat†
1-2	5	<1	0	25	1 starch, 1 fat†
1-2	4	0	<1	0	1 starch, 1 fat†
3	9	0-3	0	15- 105	1 starch, 1½ fat†
<1	4	<1	0	<5	½ starch, 1 fat†
2	7	3	0	10	1 starch, 1 fat†
2	4	0	0	12	1 starch, ½ fat†
0	4	—	—	24	½ fruit, 1 fat†
1-4	4	—	0	0	1 starch, ½ fat†

* Not available   ▤ More than 2 fat exchanges   ♥ Moderate to high sugar content

Products	SERVING SIZE	CALORIES	CARBO-HYDRATE (gm)
Lemon Cookies	2	90	12
Oatmeal Raisin Cookies	2	90	12
Peanut Butter Wafers	2	80	10
Vanilla Cookies	2	90	12
FRITO-LAY'S (Frito-Lay, Inc.)			
☕ Fudge Nut Brownie	2 oz.	240	37
☕ Peanut Butter Bar	1.75 oz.	270	30
FRUITSWEET PRODUCTS, INC. (Fruitsweet Products, Inc.)			
Cookies			
Coconut	1 oz.	140	16
Double Chocolate	1 oz.	130	16
Oatmeal	1 oz.	140	17
Peanut Butter	1 oz.	140	14
GRANDMA'S® (Frito-Lay, Inc.)			
Candied Animal Cookies	1 oz.	140	21
☕ Chocolate Chip Big Cookies	2 cookies (2.75 oz.)	370	50
☕ Glazed Gingerbread Cookies	1 oz.	120	21
☕ Peanut Butter Big Cookie	2 cookies (2.75 oz.)	410	43
☕ Raisin Big Cookie	2 cookies	320	54
☕ Sandwich Creme Cookies, all varieties (average)	1.8 oz.	260	36
HEALTH VALLEY® (Health Valley Foods, Inc.)			
Amaranth Cookies™	1	70	12
Fancy Fruit Chunks™, all varieties (average)	2	90	13
Fancy Peanut Chunks™	2	90	12
Fat Free Cookies, all varieties (average)	3	75	17
Fat Free Jumbos™	1	70	16
Fiber Jumbos™, all varieties (average)	1	100	14
Fruit and Fitness® Cookies	5	200	36

PROTEIN (gm)	FAT (gm)	SAT. FAT (gm)	CHOLES-TEROL (mg)	SODIUM (mg)	EXCHANGES
2	4	—	0	0	½ starch, 1 fat†
2	4	—	0	0	1 starch, ½ fat†
2	4	—	0	20	½ starch, 1 fat†
2	4	—	0	0	1 starch, ½ fat†
2	9	—	5	150	1 starch, 1½ fruit, 1½ fat†
2	16	—	0	65	1 starch, 1 fruit, 3 fat†
3	7	—	0	56	1 starch, 1½ fat†
3	6	—	0	69	1 starch, 1 fat†
4	6	—	0	55	1 starch, 1 fat†
4	8	—	0	46	1 starch, 1½ fat†
1	6	—	0	80	1 starch, 1 fat†
4	17	—	5	260	**
1	3	—	0	200	1 starch, ½ fat†
7	30	—	10	410	**
3	10	—	10	280	**
3	12	—	—	180-480	1 starch, 1½ fruit, 2 fat†
2	3	—	0	30	1 starch, ½ fat†
2	3	—	0	45-95	1 starch, ½ fat†
2	3	—	0	55	1 starch, ½ fat†
2	0	—	0	40	1 starch†
2	0	—	0	35	1 starch†
2	3	—	0	45	1 starch, ½ fat†
4	6	—	0	115	1 starch, 1 fruit, 1 fat†

* Not available   ☰ More than 2 fat exchanges   ☞ Moderate to high sugar content

Products	SERVING SIZE	CALORIES	CARBO-HYDRATE (gm)
Fruit Jumbos™, all varieties (average)	1	70	10
Honey Jumbos™, all varieties (average)	2	140	20
Oat Bran Animal Cookies	7	110	17
Oat Bran Fruit Jumbos™	1	70	12
Oat Bran Fruit & Nut Cookie	2	110	17
The Great Tofu Cookie™	2	90	14
The Great Wheat Free Cookie™	2	80	14
KEEBLER® (Keebler Co.)			
☕ Buttercup Cookies	4	93	15
☕ Commodore Cookies	2	120	20
☕ Fiber Enriched Cookies, all varieties (average)	2	140	18
☕ French Vanilla Cremes	2	160	24
☕ Homeplate Cookies	2	120	20
☕ Keebies Cakies	2	160	24
☕ Old Fashion Cookies, all varieties (average)	2	160	22
☕ Pitter Patter® Sandwich Cookies	1	90	12
☕ Vanilla Wafers	6	120	15
NABISCO® (Nabisco Brands, Inc.)			
☕ Almost Home® Cookies, all varieties (average)	2 (1 oz.)	140	20
☕ Animal Crackers	8 (¾ oz.)	90	17
☕ Baker's Own®, all varieties (average)	1 (½ oz.)	70	12
☕ Brown Edge Wafers	5 (1 oz.)	140	20
☕ Chocolate Grahams	2 (1 oz.)	120	14
☕ Famous Chocolate Wafers	4	112	18
☕ Giggles® Sandwich Cookies	2	120	16
☕ Lorna Doone® Shortbread	6 (1 oz.)	140	18

PROTEIN (gm)	FAT (gm)	SAT. FAT (gm)	CHOLES-TEROL (mg)	SODIUM (mg)	EXCHANGES
2	3	—	0	30-35	½ starch, ½ fat†
4	5	—	0	50-70	1 starch, 1 fat†
2	4	—	0	50	1 starch, ½ fat†
2	2	—	0	35	1 starch†
3	4	—	0	70	1 starch, ½ fat†
2	3	—	0	30	1 starch, ½ fat†
2	3	—	0	35	1 starch, ½ fat†
1	4	—	0	147	1 starch, ½ fat†
2	4	—	0	130	1 starch, ½ fat†
<2	6	—	0	100-120	1 starch, 1 fat†
<2	8	—	0	160	1½ starch, 1 fat†
2	4	—	0	260	1 starch, 1 fat†
2	6	—	0	160	1½ starch, 1 fat†
2	8	—	0	130-200	1½ starch, 1 fat†
2	4	—	0	115	1 starch, ½ fat†
<2	6	1	0	90	1 starch, 1 fat†
2	6	<1	<4	80-160	1 starch, 1 fat†
2	3	<1	<3	105	1 starch, ½ fat†
<1	2	<1	0	80	1 fruit†
2	6	<2	<4	90	1 starch, 1 fat†
2	5	4	<4	60	1 starch, 1 fat†
2	3	0	<3	175	1 starch, ½ fat†
2	6	<1	<4	40	1 starch, 1 fat†
2	8	<1	<10	130	1 starch, 1½ fat†

* Not available   目 More than 2 fat exchanges   🛒 Moderate to high sugar content

Products	SERVING SIZE	CALORIES	CARBO-HYDRATE (gm)
National® Arrowroot Biscuit	5	100	15
Newtons®			
Apple, Raspberry or Strawberry	1 (¾ oz.)	80	15
Fig	2 (1 oz.)	120	22
Nilla® Wafers	5 (¾ oz.)	90	17
Old Fashioned Ginger Snaps	3 (¾ oz.)	90	18
Oreo®	2 (1 oz.)	100	16
Oreo®, Mini	5 cookies (½ oz.)	70	10
Social Tea® Biscuit	5	100	16
Teddy Grahams®, all varieties (average)	17 (¾ oz.)	90	17

NATURES WAREHOUSE™ (Natures Warehouse, Inc.)
Fruit Juice Sweetened Cookies

Almond Butter	2 (1 oz.)	122	19
Carob Fudge	2 (1 oz.)	116	21
Chocolate Chocolate Chip	2 (1 oz.)	130	16
Cinnamon Nut	2 (1 oz.)	113	19
Coconut	2 (1 oz.)	130	14
Fig Bars, all varieties (average)	2 (1 oz.)	98	19
Oat Bran Chocolate Chip	2 (1 oz.)	139	17
Oatmeal Raisin	2 (1 oz.)	135	17
Peanut Butter	2 (1 oz.)	128	18
Peanut Butter Chocolate Chip	2 (1 oz.)	139	14
Wheat Free Oat Bran	2 (1 oz.)	129	16

PEPPERIDGE FARM® (Campbell Soup, Co.)

American Collection Cookies, all varieties (average)	1	120	15
Fruit Cookies, all varieties (average)	3	150	23

PROTEIN (gm)	FAT (gm)	SAT. FAT (gm)	CHOLES-TEROL (mg)	SODIUM (mg)	EXCHANGES
0	5	<1	<10	75	1 fruit, 1 fat†
1	2	<1	<2	45-60	1 starch†
2	2	<1	<4	120	1 starch, ½ fruit†
2	3	<1	7	68	1 starch, ½ fat†
<3	3	<3	<6	135	1 starch, ½ fat†
2	4	<2	<4	150	1 starch, ½ fat†
1	3	<1	0	85	½ starch, ½ fat†
<3	3	<5	<10	100	1 starch, ½ fat†
2	3	<1	0	135	1 starch, ½ fat†
2	4	—	—	41	1 starch, 1 fat†
1	3	—	—	78	½ starch, 1 fruit, ½ fat†
3	6	—	—	69	1 starch, 1 fat†
1	4	—	—	71	1 starch, 1 fat†
1	8	—	—	20	1 starch, 1½ fat†
1	2	—	—	—	1 starch, ½ fat†
4	6	—	—	55	1 starch, 1 fat†
2	6	—	—	44	1 starch, 1 fat†
4	6	—	—	29	1 starch, 1 fat†
4	8	—	—	46	1 starch, 1½ fat†
2	6	—	—	54	1 starch, 1 fat†
1	7	—	—	70-110	1 starch, 1 fat†
1	6	—	—	70-80	½ starch, 1 fruit, 1 fat†

* Not available   ▐ More than 2 fat exchanges   🛒 Moderate to high sugar content

Products	SERVING SIZE	CALORIES	CARBO-HYDRATE (gm)
☕ Kitchen Hearth Cookies, all varieties (average)	3	160	21
☕ Old Fashioned Cookies, all varieties except Gingerman, Molasses Crisps (average)	3	150	19
☕ Gingerman and Molasses Crisps (average)	4	130	18
☕ Special Collection Cookies, all varieties (average)	2	140	15
R. W. FROOKIES® (R. W. Frookies™, Inc.)			
Cookies, fruit juice sweetened, all varieties (average)	2 cookies	90	12
ROBIN HOOD® (General Mills, Inc.)			
☕ Fudge Brownie Mix (as prepared)	¹⁄₁₆ mix	100	16
SALERNO® (General Biscuit of America, Inc.)			
☕ Almond Crescent	5 (1 oz.)	130	20
☕ Animal Cookies	16 (1 oz.)	120	18
☕ Bonnie Shortbread	4 (1 oz.)	130	19
☕ Butter Cookies	4	112	16
☕ Dinosaur Cookies - Large	1	70	13
☕ Dinosaur Cookies, mini, all varieties (average)	14	110	18
☕ Gingerbread	5	117	16
☕ Ginger Snaps	4	105	17
☕ Jingles	5	117	18
☕ Royal Grahams, small	2	93	12
☕ Royal Stripes	1	70	10
☕ Super Mario	8	104	17
WEIGHT WATCHERS® (H. J. Heinz Co.)			
☕ Chocolate Brownie, frozen	1.25 oz. (⅓ pkg.)	100	16

† For occasional use   ** Not recommended for use

PROTEIN (gm)	FAT (gm)	SAT. FAT (gm)	CHOLES-TEROL (mg)	SODIUM (mg)	EXCHANGES
1	8	—	—	60-80	1 starch, 1½ fat†
1	8	—	—	70-170	1 starch, 1½ fat†
1	5	—	—	105	1 starch, 1 fat†
2	8	—	—	50-80	1 starch, 1½ fat†
<2	4	2	0	50-80	1 starch, ½ fat†
1	4	—	—	85	1 starch, ½ fat†
2	5	—	0	105	1 starch, 1 fat†
2	4	—	—	—	1 starch, 1 fat†
2	5	—	—	—	1 starch, 1 fat†
2	5	—	10	104	1 starch, 1 fat†
1	2	—	0	50	1 starch†
2	3	—	—	15-30	1 starch, ½ fat†
2	5	—	3	104	1 starch, 1 fat†
2	3	—	—	—	1 starch, ½ fat†
2	4	—	0	83	1 starch, 1 fat†
1	5	—	0	63	½ starch, 1 fat†
1	3	—	0	45	½ starch, ½ fat†
2	3	—	0	92	1 starch, ½ fat†
3	3	1	5	150	1 starch, ½ fat†

* Not available   █ More than 2 fat exchanges   ♥ Moderate to high sugar content

CAKE, CAKE MIXES

Author's Note: Some of these products contain large amounts of sugars and fats. If you decide to use them occasionally, make them part of your meal plan and use them with a meal or before exercise.

Products	SERVING SIZE	CALORIES	CARBO-HYDRATE (gm)
BETTY CROCKER® (General Mills, Inc.)			
Angel Food Cake Mix, all varieties (as prepared) (average)	1/12 cake	150	34
Boston Cream Pie Mix (as prepared)	1/8 cake	270	50
Gingerbread Mix (as prepared)	1/9 cake	220	35
Golden Pound Cake Mix (as prepared)	1/12 cake	200	28
Lemon Chiffon Cake Mix (as prepared)	1/12 cake	200	36
MicroRave® Cake Mix			
All varieties except those below (as prepared) (average)	1/6 cake	310	37
Apple Streusel	1/6 cake	240	33
Cinnamon Pecan Streusel	1/6 cake	280	39
Pineapple Upside Down Cake Mix (as prepared)	1/9 cake	250	39
Pudding Cake Mix, all varieties (as prepared) (average)	1/6 cake	230	45
Supermoist® Cake Mix			
all varieties except those listed below (as prepared) (average)	1/12 cake	260	36
Cherry Chip	1/12 cake	190	37
Chocolate Chip	1/12 cake	280	36

† For occasional use   ** Not recommended for use

PROTEIN (gm)	FAT (gm)	SAT. FAT (gm)	CHOLES-TEROL (mg)	SODIUM (mg)	EXCHANGES
3	0	—	0	170-300	2 starch†
4	6	—	—	390	2 starch, 1 fruit, 1 fat††
3	7	2	30	330	2 starch, 1 fat†
2	9	3	35	170	2 starch, 1 fat†
4	5	—	—	200	2 starch, ½ fat **or** 1 starch, 1 fruit, 1 fat†
2	17	5	35-45	210-300	**
2	11	3	45	190	1 starch, 1 fruit, 2 fat†
3	13	3	45	210	1 starch, 1½ fruit, 2½ fat†
2	10	4	40	210	1 starch, 1½ fruit, 1½ fat†
2	5	—	—	250-270	1 starch, 2 fruit, 1 fat†
3	12	3	55	270-470	2 starch, 2 fat **or** 1 starch, 1½ fruit, 2 fat†
3	3	1	0	270	2½ starch **or** 1 starch, 1½ fruit, ½ fat†
3	14	3	55	320	2 starch, 2½ fat, **or** 1 starch, 1½ fruit, 2½ fat†

* Not available　　🮲 More than 2 fat exchanges　　🍮 Moderate to high sugar content

Products	SERVING SIZE	CALORIES	CARBO-HYDRATE (gm)
Sour Cream White	½ cake	180	36
Supermoist® Light Cake Mix Standard Recipe (as prepared) (average)	½ cake	190	36
No Cholesterol Recipe (as prepared) (average)	½ cake	180	36
DUNCAN HINES® (Proctor & Gamble)			
Angel Food (as prepared)	½ cake	140	30
Layer Cake Mixes, all varieties (as prepared using original directions) (average)	½ cake	270	35
ENTENMANN'S® (Entenmann's, Inc.)			
Fat Free Cholesterol Free Cakes Chocolate Loaf	1 oz. slice	70	16
Golden Loaf	1 oz. slice	80	16
ESTEE® (Estee Corp.)			
Cake Mixes, dietetic with sorbitol, all varieties (as prepared) (average)	⅟₁₀ cake	100	18
PEPPERIDGE FARMS® (Campbell Soup Co.)			
Cakes, supreme, all varieties (average)	3 oz.	290	40
Cream Cakes, supreme, all varieties (average)	2 oz.	190	29
Layer Cakes, all varieties (average)	1⅝ oz.	180	23
Old Fashioned Cakes, all varieties (average)	1 oz.	130	16
PILLSBURY® (The Pillsbury Co.)			
Bundt® Brand Cake Mix, all varieties (as prepared) (average)	⅟₁₆ cake	260	38
Gingerbread Mix (as prepared)	1½" x 3" piece	95	18

† For occasional use   ** Not recommended for use

PROTEIN (gm)	FAT (gm)	SAT. FAT (gm)	CHOLES-TEROL (mg)	SODIUM (mg)	EXCHANGES
3	3	1	0	300	2 starch, ½ fat, **or** 1 starch, 1½ fruit, ½ fat†
3	4	1	55	320-360	2 starch, ½ fat†
3	3	1	0	330-380	2 starch, ½ fat†
3	0	—	—	130	2 starch†
3	13	3-4	65	240-470	2 starch, 2½ fat†
1	0	—	0	130	1 starch†
2	0	—	0	90	1 starch†
1	2	<1	0	65-100	1 starch, ½ fat†
3	14	—	—	140-220	**
2	7	—	—	120-130	1 starch, 1 fruit, 1 fat†
1	9	—	—	110-170	1 starch, ½ fruit, 1½ fat†
1	7	—	—	90-150	1 starch, 1 fat†
3	9	—	—	300-310	2 starch, ½ fruit, 2 fat†
1	2	—	—	155	1 starch†

* Not available   🡇 More than 2 fat exchanges   🛒 Moderate to high sugar content

Products	SERVING SIZE	CALORIES	CARBO-HYDRATE (gm)
☕ Lovin' Lites™ Cake Mix, all varieties (as prepared with water & egg whites) (average)	½₂ cake	165	34
Microwave Cake Mix (as prepared)			
☕ Chocolate, Lemon and Yellow (average)	⅛ cake	220	23
☕ Streusel Swirl Cinnamon	⅛ cake	240	33
☕ Double Chocolate, Double Lemon, Tunnel of Fudge® Bundt (average)	⅛ cake	300	39
☕ Microwave Cake Mix and Frosting, all varieties (as prepared) (average)	¹⁄₁₆ cake	150	18
☕ Pillsbury Plus® Cake Mix, all varieties (as prepared) (average)	¹⁄₂₄ cake	125	17
☕ Streusel Swirl® Cake Mix, all varieties (as prepared) (average)	¹⁄₁₆ cake	270	38
SARA LEE® (Kitchens of Sara Lee)			
Free & Light			
☕ Chocolate	1 slice (⅛ cake)	110	26
☕ Pound	1 slice (1 oz.)	70	17
Lights			
☕ Apple Crisp Cake	1 cake	150	31
☕ Black Forest	1 cake	150	24
☕ Carrot	1 cake	170	30
☕ Double Chocolate	1 cake	150	23
☕ Lemon Cream	1 cake	180	29
☕ Pound Cake, original	¹⁄₁₀ cake (1 oz.)	130	14
Single Layer Cakes, iced			
☕ Banana	⅛ cake	170	28
☕ Carrot	⅛ cake	250	30

PROTEIN (gm)	FAT (gm)	SAT. FAT (gm)	CHOLES- TEROL (mg)	SODIUM (mg)	EXCHANGES
3	2	<1	0	310- 380	2 starch†
2	13	—	—	170- 260	1 starch, ½ fruit, 2½ fat†
2	11	—	—	180	1 starch, 1 fruit, 2 fat†
3	17	—	—	210- 340	**
1	9	—	—	110- 150	1 starch, 1½ fat†
2	6	—	—	145- 150	1 starch, 1 fat†
3	11	—	—	200- 340	2 starch, ½ fruit, 2 fat†
2	0	—	0	140	1 starch, ½ fruit†
1	0	—	0	90	1 starch†
1	2	—	5	105	1 starch, 1 fruit†
3	5	0	5	55	1½ starch, ½ fat†
4	4	—	5	75	2 starch, ½ fat†
4	5	—	10	85	1½ starch, ½ fat†
3	6	—	10	60	2 starch, ½ fat†
2	7	—	—	85	1 starch, 1 fat†
1	6	<1	—	160	1 starch, 1 fruit, 1 fat†
3	13	—	25	240	1 starch, 1 fruit, 2½ fat†

* Not available   ▤ More than 2 fat exchanges   ♥ Moderate to high sugar content

Products	SERVING SIZE	CALORIES	CARBO-HYDRATE (gm)
Snack Cakes			
☕ All Butter Pound	1	200	23
☕ Chocolate Fudge	1	190	24
☕ Classic Cheesecake	1	200	16
☕ Deluxe Carrot	1	180	26
☕ Three Layer Cakes, all varieties (average)	⅛ cake (2.25 oz.)	220	27
☕ Two Layer Cakes, all varieties (average)	⅛ cake	190	28
WEIGHT WATCHERS® (Foodways National, Inc.)			
☕ Black Forest Cake, frozen	3 oz. (½ pkg.)	180	32
☕ Carrot Cake, frozen	3 oz. (½ pkg.)	170	27
☕ Chocolate Cake, frozen	2½ oz. (½ pkg.)	190	31
☕ German Chocolate cake, frozen	2½ oz. (½ pkg.)	200	31

DESSERTS

Author's Note: Some of these products contain large amounts of sugars and fats. If you decide to use them occasionally, make them part of your meal plan and use them with a meal or before exercise.

D-ZERTA® (General Foods Corp.)

Low Calorie Gelatin, all flavors (as prepared) (average)	½ cup	8	0

ESTEE® (Estee Corp.)

Gelatin Desserts, dietetic, all flavors (average)	½ cup	8	<1

FEATHERWEIGHT® (Sandoz Nutrition)

Gelatin, dietetic, all flavors (average)	½ cup	10	1

JELL-O® (General Foods Corp.)

☕ Cheesecake (as prepared)	⅛ of 8" cake	280	36
☕ Gelatin, all flavors (average)	½ cup	80	19

† For occasional use   ** Not recommended for use

PROTEIN (gm)	FAT (gm)	SAT. FAT (gm)	CHOLES- TEROL (mg)	SODIUM (mg)	EXCHANGES
2	11	—	—	190	1½ starch, 2 fat†
2	10	—	—	125	1½ starch, 1½ fat†
4	14	—	—	150	1 starch, 2½ fat†
3	7	—	—	200	1½ starch, 1 fat†
3	12	—	20-30	110-150	1 starch, 1 fruit, 2 fat†
2	8	—	—	90-105	1 starch, 1 fruit, 1½ fat†
4	5	1	5	280	1 starch, 1 fruit, 1 fat†
4	5	<1	5	310	1 starch, 1 fruit, 1 fat†
5	5	<1	5	250	1 starch, 1 fruit, 1 fat†
4	7	<1	5	350	1 starch, 1 fruit, 1½ fat†
2	0	—	0	0	Free
1	0	0	0	10	Free
2	0	—	0	0	Free
5	13	—	0	350	2 starch, ½ fruit, 2 fat†
2	0	-	0	35-75	1 starch†

---

* Not available   ▌ More than 2 fat exchanges   🛒 Moderate to high sugar content

Products	SERVING SIZE	CALORIES	CARBO-HYDRATE (gm)
Sugar Free Gelatin, all flavors (average)	½ cup	8	0
Jell-O 1-2-3®, all flavors (average)	⅔ cup	130	27
KNOX® (Thomas J. Lipton, Co.)			
Orange Flavored Drinking Gelatin with Nutrasweet®	1 envelope	40	4
SARA LEE® (Kitchens of Sara Lee)			
Cheesecake, original			
Plain	⅙ cake	230	27
Cherry or Strawberry	⅙ cake	230	34
Cheesecake, Classic, snack cake	1 snack cake	200	16
Classics			
Chocolate Mousse	1 slice (⅛ pkg.)	260	23
French Cheesecake	1 slice (⅛ pkg.)	250	23
Strawberry French Cheesecake	1 slice (⅛ pkg.)	240	28
Free & Light Strawberry Yogurt Dessert	1 slice (1⁄10 pkg.)	120	26
Lights			
Chocolate Mousse	1 cake	170	20
French Cheesecake	1 cake	150	24
Strawberry French Cheesecake	1 cake	150	29
STOUFFER'S® (Stouffer Foods Corp.)			
Escalloped Apples	⅓ of 12 oz. pkg.	130	27
WEIGHT WATCHERS® (Foodways National, Inc.)			
Cheesecake, brownie, frozen	3.5 oz. (½ pkg.)	200	30
Cheesecake, plain	3.9 oz. (½ pkg.)	220	30

† For occasional use ** Not recommended for use

PROTEIN (gm)	FAT (gm)	SAT. FAT (gm)	CHOLES-TEROL (mg)	SODIUM (mg)	EXCHANGES
1	0	—	0	50-80	Free
2	2	—	0	55	1 starch, 1 fruit†
6	0	—	0	17	1 lean meat
5	11	—	—	153	2 starch, 2 fat†
4	8	—	—	171-184	1½ starch, ½ fruit, 1½ fat†
4	14	—	—	150	1 starch, 2½ fat†
3	17	—	20	100	1½ starch, 3 fat†
4	16	—	20	120	1½ starch, 3 fat†
3	13	—	20	125	1½ starch, ½ fruit, 2 fat†
2	1	—	0	90	1½ starch†
4	8	—	10	60	1½ starch, 1½ fat†
5	4	—	15	90	1½ starch, ½ fat†
3	2	—	5	65	1½ starch, ½ fruit†
0	2	—	—	15	2 fruit†
9	6	3	15	310	2 starch, 1 fat†
10	7	1	25	280	1 starch, 1 skim milk, 1 fat†

* Not available   ▊ More than 2 fat exchanges   ♥ Moderate to high sugar content

Products	SERVING SIZE	CALORIES	CARBO-HYDRATE (gm)
☕ Cheesecake, strawberry, frozen	3.9 oz. (½ pkg.)	180	28

ICE CREAM, FROZEN DESSERTS

Author's Note: Some of these products contain large amounts of sugars and fats. If you decide to use them occasionally, make them part of your meal plan and use them with a meal or before exercise.

BLUE BUNNY® (Wells' Dairy, Inc.)

Products	SERVING SIZE	CALORIES	CARBO-HYDRATE (gm)
☕ Dairy Dessert, nonfat, all varieties (average)	½ cup	93	19
☕ Dairy Dessert, lite, all varieties (average)	½ cup	120	19
Frozen Yogurt, nonfat, all varieties (average)	½ cup	80	20
Ice Cream, all plain varieties (average)	½ cup	130	16
Ice Milk, all varieties (average)	½ cup	120	20
Sherbet, all varieties	½ cup	120	28
Ice Cream Novelties			
☕ Frozen Yogurt and Fruit Snack, all varieties (average)	1 ¾ fl. oz.	50	10
Nutrasweet Citrus Bars	1 ¾ fl. oz.	16	4
Nutrasweet Fudge Bars	1 ¾ fl. oz.	35	5
Nutrasweet Sugar Free Pops, all varieties (average)	1 ¾ fl. oz.	8	2
☕ Strawberry Yogurt Oat Bran Sandwich	3.5 fl. oz.	140	24

COMET® (Nabisco Brands, Inc.)

Products	SERVING SIZE	CALORIES	CARBO-HYDRATE (gm)
Cones	1	40	9
Cups	1	20	4

CRYSTAL LIGHT® (General Foods Corp.)

Products	SERVING SIZE	CALORIES	CARBO-HYDRATE (gm)
Crystal Light Bars®, all flavors (average)	1	14	2

PROTEIN (gm)	FAT (gm)	SAT. FAT (gm)	CHOLES-TEROL (mg)	SODIUM (mg)	EXCHANGES
7	5	1	20	230	1 starch, 1 fruit, 1 fat†
3	0	—	0	35	1 starch†
3	4	—	—	40-60	1 starch, 1 fat†
3	0	—	0	60-67	1 starch†
2	7	—	—	70	1 starch, 1 fat†
3	4	—	—	65	1 starch, 1 fat†
0	1	—	—	35	2 fruit†
1	1	—	—	20	1 fruit†
0	0	—	—	10	Free
3	0	—	—	45	½ starch
0	0	—	—	10	Free
3	5	—	10	90	1 starch, ½ fruit, ½ fat†
1	0	—	—	35	½ starch
0	0	—	—	5	Free
0	0	—	0	10	Free

* Not available   ▊ More than 2 fat exchanges   ☕ Moderate to high sugar content

Products	SERVING SIZE	CALORIES	CARBO-HYDRATE (gm)
Cool N'Creamy Bars®, all flavors (average)	1	50	7
ESKIMO PIE® (Eskimo Pie Corp.)			
Light Bar	1 bar (2.5 oz.)	140	12
Regular Bar	1 bar (3 oz.)	180	16
Sugar Free Bar, chocolate or crisped rice coated (average)	1 bar (2.5 oz.)	145	12
Sugar Free Sandwiches	1 (3.2 oz.)	170	26
Sugar Freedom™ Sundae Cones	1 (4.2 oz.)	230	23
JELLO® (General Foods Corp.)			
Gelatin Pops®, all flavors (average)	1 bar	35	8
Pudding Pops®, all flavors, not chocolate-coated (average)	1 bar	80	13
Snowbursts, all flavors (average)	1 bar	45	12
KEEBLER® (Keebler Company)			
Ice Cream Cones			
Sugar Cone	1	45	11
Vanilla Cup	1	15	4
Waffle Bowl	1	60	12
Waffle Cone	1	97	20
KEMPS® (Marigold Foods, Inc.)			
Frozen Yogurt, all varieties (average)	4 oz.	100	20
Frozen Yogurt, nonfat, all varieties (average)	4 oz.	90	20
Ice Cream (average)	½ cup	130	17
Ice Milk, light (average)	½ cup	100	17
Lite Fudge Jr's.	1 bar	45	8
Lite Pops	1 pop	12	3
Sherbet (average)	½ cup	120	27

PROTEIN (gm)	FAT (gm)	SAT. FAT (gm)	CHOLES-TEROL (mg)	SODIUM (mg)	EXCHANGES
2	2	—	0	25-60	1½ fruit, ½ fat†
2	9	—	—	25	1 starch, 1½ fat†
2	12	—	—	35	1 starch, 2 fat†
3	11	—	—	36-40	1 starch,2 fat†
4	6	—	—	142	1½ starch, 1 fat†
5	12	—	15	80	1½ starch, 2 fat†
1	0	—	0	25	½ fruit†
2	2	—	0	55-90	1 starch†
0	0	—	0	10	1 fruit†
1	<1	<1	0	35	½ starch
<1	<1	<1	0	20	Free
1	<1	<1	0	<1	1 starch
1	<1	<1	0	<1	1 starch
3	1	—	7	50	1 starch†
3	0	—	0	60	1 starch†
2	6	—	—	—	1 starch, 1 fat†
2	2	—	10	60	1 starch†
2	<1	—	—	50	½ starch†
0	0	—	—	0	Free
1	1	—	—	—	2 starch†

* Not available   ⯄ More than 2 fat exchanges   ⯅ Moderate to high sugar content

Products	SERVING SIZE	CALORIES	CARBO-HYDRATE (gm)
KOOL-AID® (General Foods Corp.)			
☕ Cream Pops®, all flavors (average)	1 bar	50	9
☕ Kool Pops®, all flavors (average)	1 bar	40	10
LAND O'LAKES® (Land O'Lakes, Inc.)			
☕ Frozen Yogurt, strawberry	½ cup	110	20
☕ Ice Cream, all varieties (average)	½ cup	140	16
☕ Ice Milk, all varieties (average)	½ cup	110	17
☕ Sherbet, all varieties (average)	½ cup	130	27
MOCHA MIX™ (Presto Food Products, Inc.)			
☕ Non-Dairy Frozen Dessert, all varieties (average)	½ cup	140	17
SIMPLE PLEASURES® (The Simplesse Co.)			
Frozen Dairy Dessert Light, all varieties (average)	4 oz.	80-90	15-20
Praline Pecan	4 oz.	140	25
3 MUSKETEERS® (Dove International)			
3 Musketeers® Snack Bar, sugar free	1 bar (.63 oz.)	50	5
WEIGHT WATCHERS® (H.J. Heinz Co.)			
Frozen Novelties			
☕ Chocolate Dip Bar	1 bar (1.7 oz.)	110	10
Chocolate Mousse Bar	1 bar (1.75 oz.)	35	9
Double Fudge Bar	1 bar (1.75 oz.)	60	12
☕ English Toffee Crunch Bar	1 bar (1.7 oz.)	120	11
Fruit Juice Bar	1 bar (1.7 oz.)	35	9
Peanut Butter Fudge Bar	1 bar (1.75 oz.)	60	12

† For occasional use   ** Not recommended for use

PROTEIN (gm)	FAT (gm)	SAT. FAT (gm)	CHOLES- TEROL (mg)	SODIUM (mg)	EXCHANGES
1	2	—	5	20	½ fruit, ½ fat†
0	0	—	0	10	1 fruit†
3	3	2	10	60	1 starch, ½ fat†
2	7	4	30	60	1 starch, 1½ fat†
3	3	2	10	55	1 starch, ½ fat†
1	2	1	5	25	2 fruit†
<1	7	2	0	80	1 starch, 1 fruit†
5	<1	—	15	90-110	1 starch†
6	2	—	5	60	1½ starch, ½ fat†
1	4	—	—	15	1 fat†
2	7	3	5	35	½ starch, 1½ fat†
2	<1	—	5	30	½ starch†
3	1	—	5	50	1 starch†
2	8	4	5	45	1 starch, 1 fat†
0	0	0	0	10	½ fruit
2	<1	—	—	120	1 starch†

* Not available   ▤ More than 2 fat exchanges   ♥ Moderate to high sugar content

Products	SERVING SIZE	CALORIES	CARBO-HYDRATE (gm)
Treat Bars			
Chocolate	1 bar (2.75 oz.)	100	18
Chocolate Mint	1 bar (1.75 oz.)	60	12
Sugar Free Orange Vanilla	1 bar (1.75 oz.)	30	8
☕ Vanilla Sandwich Bar	1 bar	150	28
☕ Grand Collection® Premium Ice Milk, all varieties (average)	½ cup	110	18
WELCH'S® (Welch Foods)			
Fruit Juice Bars, all varieties (average)	1.75 oz.	45	11
	3 oz.	80	19
No Sugar Added Juice Bars, all varieties (average)	3 oz.	25	6

PIES, PUDDINGS, PIE CRUST

Author's Note: Some of these products contain large amounts of sugars and fats. If you decide to use them occasionally, make them part of your meal plan and use them with a meal or before exercise.

BANQUET® (ConAgra® Frozen Foods Co.)			
☕ Cream Pies, all varieties (average)	⅛ of 14 oz. pie	135	16
☕ Fruit Pies, all varieties (average)	⅙ of 20 oz. pie	195	29
☕ Pumpkin Pie	⅙ of 20 oz. pie	150	22
BETTY CROCKER® (General Mills, Inc.)			
Pie Crust Mix	1/16 package	120	10
Pie Crust Sticks	⅛ stick	120	10
D-ZERTA® (General Foods Corp.)			
Reduced Calorie Pudding, all varieties (as prepared) (average)	½ cup	70	12

† For occasional use ** Not recommended for use

PROTEIN (gm)	FAT (gm)	SAT. FAT (gm)	CHOLES-TEROL (mg)	SODIUM (mg)	EXCHANGES
4	1	—	—	75	1 starch†
2	1	—	—	50	1 starch†
2	<1	—	5	40	½ starch†
3	3	2	5	170	1 starch, 1 fruit, ½ fat†
3	3	1-2	5-10	75-80	1 starch, ½ fat†
0	0	0	0	0	1 fruit
0	0	0	0	0	1 fruit
0	0	0	0	0	½ fruit
2	8	—	—	80-110	1 starch, 1½ fat†
2	8	—	—	195-278	1 starch, 1 fruit, 1½ fat†
2	6	—	—	263	1 starch, ½ fruit, 1 fat†
1	8	2	0	140	½ starch, 1½ fat
1	8	2	0	140	½ starch, 1½ fat
4	0	—	0	65-70	1 skim milk **or** 1 starch†

* Not available   ⒏ More than 2 fat exchanges   ☻ Moderate to high sugar content

Products	SERVING SIZE	CALORIES	CARBO-HYDRATE (gm)
ESTEE® (Estee Corp.)			
Mousse, dietetic, all varieties (as prepared) (average)	½ cup	70	9
Puddings, dietetic, all varieties (as prepared) (average)	½ cup	70	13
FEATHERWEIGHT® SWEET PRETENDERS® (Sandoz Nutrition)			
Chocolate Mousse Mix (as prepared)	½ cup	100	14
Instant Pudding Mix, all varieties (as prepared) (average)	½ cup	100	19
Ready to Serve Puddings, all varieties (average)	½ cup	100	21
Vanilla Custard Mix (as prepared) (average)	½ cup	80	14
FLAKO® (Quaker Oats Co.)			
⊟ Pie Crust Mix	⅙ of 9" crust	250	24
JELL-O® (General Foods Corp.)			
Americana			
⛟ Golden Egg Custard Mix (as prepared with skim milk)	½ cup	130	23
⛟ Rice Pudding (as prepared with skim milk)	½ cup	140	30
⛟ Tapioca Pudding, all varieties (as prepared with skim milk) (average)	½ cup	130	27
Mousse			
⛟ Chocolate Mousse Pie, filling only (as prepared with skim milk)	⅛ pie	230	25
⛟ Rich and Luscious® Mousse, all varieties (as prepared with skim milk) (average)	½ cup	120	21

PROTEIN (gm)	FAT (gm)	SAT. FAT (gm)	CHOLES- TEROL (mg)	SODIUM (mg)	EXCHANGES
3	3	2	0	50	½ starch, ½ fat†
4	1	<1	2	75	1 starch **or** 1 skim milk†
3	5	—	5	65	1 starch, ½ fat†
4	0	—	5	190	1 starch†
0	1	—	0	110- 160	1½ fruit†
5	0	—	5	105	1 starch **or** 1 skim milk†
4	15	5	9	390	1½ starch, 3 fat
5	2	—	80	200	1 starch, ½ skim milk†
5	1	—	15	160	1 starch, ½ skim milk **or** 1 starch, 1 fruit†
4	1	—	15	170	1 starch, ½ skim milk **or** 1 starch, 1 fruit†
4	9	—	0	430	1 starch, ½ skim milk, 2 fat†
5	3	—	10	75	1 starch, ½ skim milk **or** 1 starch, ½ fruit†

* Not available   ▊ More than 2 fat exchanges   ♛ Moderate to high sugar content

Products	SERVING SIZE	CALORIES	CARBO-HYDRATE (gm)
Pudding Snacks			
All varieties (average)	4 oz. cup	170	28
	5.5 oz. cup	240	38
Light Pudding Snacks, all varieties (average)	4 oz. cup	100	21
Pudding and Pie Filling			
Cooked or Instant, filling only, all varieties (as prepared with skim milk) (average)	½ cup	140	28
Microwave Pudding, all varieties (as prepared with skim milk) (average)	½ cup	120	27
Sugar Free Cooked or Instant, filling only, all varieties (as prepared with skim milk) (average)	½ cup	70	13
KEEBLER® (Keebler Company)			
Dessert Shells			
Ready Crust, 9 inch, all varieties (average)	⅛	100	14
Ready Crust, 3 inch, all varieties (average)	1	110	15
MRS SMITH'S® (Mrs. Smith's® Frozen Foods, A Kellogg Company)			
Lemon Meringue Pie	⅙ of 8" pie (3 oz.)	210	38
Pie in Minutes™ Pies			
Fruit, all varieties (average)	⅛ pie	215	30
Pecan	⅛ pie	330	51
Pumpkin	⅛ pie	190	30
Pie Shells			
9" (shallow)	⅛ pie shell	80	8
9-⅝"	⅛ pie shell	120	12

† For occasional use ** Not recommended for use

PROTEIN (gm)	FAT (gm)	SAT. FAT (gm)	CHOLES- TEROL (mg)	SODIUM (mg)	EXCHANGES
3	6	—	0	130-140	1 starch, 1 fruit, 1 fat†
4	8	—	0	170-190	1½ starch, 1 fruit, 1½ fat†
3	2	—	5	125	1½ starch†
4	1	—	15	160-480	1 starch, ½ skim milk **or** 1 starch, 1 fruit†
4	2	—	15	120-160	1 starch, ½ skim milk **or** 1 starch, ½ fruit†
4	1	—	10	160-390	1 skim milk **or** 1 starch†
1	5	1	0	120-130	1 starch, 1 fat
1	5	1	0	135-145	1 starch, 1 fat
2	5	1	30	130	1 starch, 1½ fruit, 1 fat†
2	9	2	0	190-250	1 starch, 1 fruit, 1½ fat†
3	13	2	35	200	**
3	6	2	35	230	1 starch, 1 fruit, 1 fat†
1	5	2	0	105	½ starch, 1 fat
2	7	2	0	160	1 starch, 1 fat

* Not available   █ More than 2 fat exchanges   ♥ Moderate to high sugar content

Products	SERVING SIZE	CALORIES	CARBO-HYDRATE (gm)
PEPPERIDGE FARM® (Campbell Soup Co.)			
Apple Dumplings	3 oz.	260	33
Fruit Squares, all varieties (average)	1	225	28
Puff Pastry Shells	1	210	17
Puff Pastry Sheets	¼ sheet	260	22
Turnovers, all varieties (average)	1	310	33
PET-RITZ® (PET, Inc.)			
Frozen Pies			
Cream, all varieties (average)	⅙ pie	180	25
Custard, all varieties (average)	⅙ pie	200	28
Fruit, all varieties (average)	⅙ pie	330	50
Pie Shells			
Graham Cracker	⅙ shell	110	8
Regular	⅙ shell	110	11
Tart Shells (3 inch)	1 shell	150	12
PILLSBURY® (The Pillsbury Co.)			
All-Ready Pie Crust	⅛ of 2 crust pie	240	24
Pastry Pockets	1 pocket	230	25
Pie Crust Mix or Sticks (as prepared)	⅙ of 2 crust pie	270	25
SARA LEE® (Kitchens of Sara Lee)			
Free & Light			
Streusel Pies, all varieties (average)	1 slice (⅛ pie)	160	35
Homestyle (9 inch)			
Fruit Pies, all varieties (average)	1 slice (¹⁄₁₀ pie)	290	40
Pecan	1 slice (¹⁄₁₀ pie)	400	56
Pumpkin	1 slice (¹⁄₁₀ pie)	240	34

† For occasional use   ** Not recommended for use

PROTEIN (gm)	FAT (gm)	SAT. FAT (gm)	CHOLES-TEROL (mg)	SODIUM (mg)	EXCHANGES
2	13	—	—	230	1 starch, 1 fruit, 2½ fat†
2	12	—	—	170-190	1 starch, 1 fruit, 2 fat†
2	15	—	—	180	1 starch, 3 fat
4	17	—	—	290	1½ starch, 3 fat
3	18	—	—	240-300	**
2	8	—	—	145-185	1 starch, 1 fruit, 1 fat†
5	8	—	—	—	2 starch, 1 fat†
3	12	—	—	320-385	**
1	6	—	7	80	½ starch, 1 fat
1	7	—	7	110	1 starch, 1 fat
3	10	—	7	150	1 starch, 2 fat
2	15	—	15	210	1 1/2 starch, 3 fat
4	13	5	5	550	1½ starch, 2½ fat
4	17	—	—	420	1½ starch, 3½ fat
2	2	—	0	70	1 starch, 1½ fruit†
2	13	—	0	150-340	**
4	18	—	55	290	**
4	10	—	40	250	2 starch, 2 fat†

Products	SERVING SIZE	CALORIES	CARBO-HYDRATE (gm)
Homestyle High Pie (10 inch) ⏚ Apple	1 slice (⅒ pie)	400	46
WEIGHT WATCHERS® (H. J. Heinz Co.)			
Mousse, frozen ⏚ Chocolate	2.5 oz. (½ pkg.)	170	24
⏚ Praline Pecan	2.71 oz. (½ pkg.)	190	27
⏚ Raspberry	2.5 oz. (½ pkg.)	150	21
Mousse Mix, all varieties (as prepared with skim milk) (average)	½ cup	60	9
Pie, frozen ⏚ Apple	3.5 oz. (½ pkg.)	200	39
⏚ Boston Cream Pie	3 oz. (½ pkg.)	190	35
⏚ Chocolate Mocha	2.75 oz. (½ pkg.)	160	23
Pudding Mix, instant, all varieties (as prepared with skim milk) (average)	½ cup	90	17
YOPLAIT® (General Mills, Inc.)			
⏚ Yoplait Pudding, all varieties (average)	4 oz.	160	26

WHIPPED TOPPINGS
BIRD'S EYE® (General Foods Corp.)

Products	SERVING SIZE	CALORIES	CARBO-HYDRATE (gm)
Cool Whip® Extra Creamy Dairy Recipe Whipped Topping	1 Tbsp.	14	1
	¼ cup	56	4
Cool Whip® Lite Whipped Topping	2 Tbsp.	16	2
	¼ cup	32	4
Cool Whip® Non-Dairy Whipped Topping	1 Tbsp.	12	1
	¼ cup	48	4
DREAM WHIP® (General Foods Corp.)			
Whipped Topping Mix (as prepared)	1 Tbsp.	10	1

† For occasional use   ** Not recommended for use

PROTEIN (gm)	FAT (gm)	SAT. FAT (gm)	CHOLES-TEROL (mg)	SODIUM (mg)	EXCHANGES
3	23	—	0	450	**
6	6	<1	5	190	1½ starch, 1 fat†
5	7	1	5	180	2 starch, 1 fat†
5	6	<1	5	150	1½ starch, 1 fat†
4	3	—	—	45-75	½ milk, ½ fat **or** ½ starch, ½ fat
2	5	1	5	280	1 starch, 1½ fruit, ½ fat†
4	4	1	5	280	1 starch, 1 fruit, 1 fat†
5	5	3	5	150	1½ starch, 1 fat†
5	0	—	—	510	1 skim milk **or** 1 starch†
6	4	—	—	80-105	1 starch, ½ milk, 1 fat†
0	1	—	0	0	Free
0	4	—	0	0	1 fat
0	1	—	0	0	Free
0	2	—	0	0	½ fat
0	1	—	0	0	Free
0	4	—	0	0	1 fat
0	0	—	0	0	Free

* Not available   ▤ More than 2 fat exchanges   ♛ Moderate to high sugar content

Products	SERVING SIZE	CALORIES	CARBO-HYDRATE (gm)
D-ZERTA® (General Foods Corp.)			
Reduced Calorie Whipped Topping Mix (as prepared)	1 Tbsp.	8	0
	¼ cup	32	0
ESTEE® (Estee Corp.)			
Whipped Topping Mix (as prepared)	¼ cup	16	1
FEATHERWEIGHT® SWEET PRETENDERS® (Sandoz Nutrition)			
Whipped Topping Mix (as prepared)	1 Tbsp.	4	0
KRAFT® (Kraft, Inc.)			
Real Cream Topping	¼ cup	25	2
Whipped Topping	¼ cup	35	2
LA CREME® (Kraft, Inc.)			
Whipped Topping	1 Tbsp.	12	1
	¼ cup	48	4
PET® (PET, Inc.)			
La Creme	1 Tbsp.	16	1
	¼ cup	64	4
Pet Whip	1 Tbsp.	14	1
	¼ cup	56	4

FATS: BUTTER, MARGARINE, OIL, SOUR CREAM

BAC*OS® (General Mills, Inc.)			
Bac*os®	1 tsp.	13	1
BLUE BONNET® (Nabisco Brands, Inc.)			
Butter Blend, soft or stick	1½ tsp.	45	0
Margarine	1½ tsp.	50	0
Soft Margarine	1½ tsp.	50	0
Spread (48% fat)	2 tsp.	40	0
Spread Stick (75% fat)	1½ tsp.	45	0
Whipped Margarine (stick)	2 tsp.	47	0

† For occasional use   ** Not recommended for use

PROTEIN (gm)	FAT (gm)	SAT. FAT (gm)	CHOLES-TEROL (mg)	SODIUM (mg)	EXCHANGES
0	1	—	0	5	Free
0	4	—	0	20	1 fat
1	1	<1	0	0	Free
0	0	—	0	5	Free
0	2	2	10	10	½ fat
0	3	3	0	10	1 fat
0	1	—	-	5	Free
0	4	—	—	20	1 fat
0	1	—	<1	5	Free
0	4	—	<4	20	1 fat
0	1	—	—	0	Free
0	4	—	—	0	1 fat
1	<1	—	0	45	Free
0	6	1	0	48	1 fat
0	6	1	0	48	1 fat
0	6	1	0	48	1 fat
0	5	<1	0	74	1 fat
0	6	1	0	48	1 fat
0	5	<1	0	47	1 fat

* Not available   ▯ More than 2 fat exchanges   ♥ Moderate to high sugar content

Products	SERVING SIZE	CALORIES	CARBO- HYDRATE (gm)
BLUE BUNNY® (Wells' Dairy Inc.)			
Lite Sour Cream Dairy Blend	1 oz.	30	2
CARNATION® (Calreco®, Inc.)			
Coffee-Mate, liquid	1 Tbsp.	16	2
Lite Non-dairy Creamer	1 tsp.	8	2
CHIFFON® (Kraft, Inc.)			
Soft Margarine, cup or stick (average)	1½ tsp.	45	0
Soft Unsalted Margarine	1½ tsp.	45	0
Whipped Margarine	2 tsp.	46	0
COUNTRY MORNING® BLEND (Land O'Lakes, Inc.)			
Margarine, all varieties (average)	1½ tsp.	50	0
Light, all varieties (average)	2 tsp.	40	0
FLEISHMANN'S® (Nabsico Brands, Inc.)			
Extra Light Corn Oil Spread	1 Tbsp.	50	0
Light Corn Oil Spread	2 tsp.	54	0
Margarine			
Diet	1 Tbsp.	50	0
Soft	1½ tsp.	50	0
Squeeze	1½ tsp.	45	0
Stick	1½ tsp.	50	0
Sweet Unsalted, soft or stick (average)	1½ tsp.	50	0
Whipped, lightly salted	2 tsp.	47	0
HAIN® (PET, Inc.)			
Margarine			
Safflower, regular and soft	1½ tsp.	50	0
Safflower, unsalted	1½ tsp.	50	0
KEMPS® (Marigold Foods, Inc.)			
Sour Cream, lite	2 Tbsp. (1 oz.)	30	2

† For occasional use   ** Not recommended for use

PROTEIN (gm)	FAT (gm)	SAT. FAT (gm)	CHOLES-TEROL (mg)	SODIUM (mg)	EXCHANGES
2	2	—	—	20	½ fat
0	1	0	0	5	Free
0	0	<1	0	0	Free
0	5	1	0	50-55	1 fat
0	5	1	0	0	1 fat
0	5	<1	0	53	1 fat
0	5	2	8	43-58	1 fat
0	6	2	5	60	1 fat
0	6	1	0	55	1 fat
0	5	1	0	47	1 fat
0	6	1	0	50	1 fat
0	6	1	0	48	1 fat
0	5	<1	0	48	1 fat
0	6	1	0	48	1 fat
0	6	1	0	0	1 fat
0	5	1	0	40	1 fat
0	6	1	0	85	1 fat
0	6	1	0	1	1 fat
1	2	—	—	35	½ fat

Products	SERVING SIZE	CALORIES	CARBO-HYDRATE (gm)
KRAFT® (Kraft, Inc.)			
"Touch of Butter" Spread, bowl (40% fat)	1 Tbsp.	50	0
"Touch of Butter" Spread, stick (50% fat)	2 tsp.	45	0
LAND O'LAKES® (Land O'Lakes, Inc.)			
Butter			
Sweet Cream	1 tsp.	35	0
Whipped	1½ tsp.	38	0
Margarine, all varieties (average)	1 tsp.	35	0
Spread with Sweet Cream, all varieties (average)	1½ tsp.	45	0
Sour Cream	1 Tbsp.	30	1
Sour Cream Dairy Blend, light, all varieties (average)	1 Tbsp.	20	2
Sour Half and Half	2 Tbsp.	50	4
MAZOLA® (Best Foods, CPC International)			
Diet Mazola, reduced calorie margarine	1 Tbsp.	50	0
Margarine	1½ tsp.	50	0
No-Stick Vegetable Spray Coating	2.5 second spray	6	0
MIRACLE® (Kraft, Inc.)			
Margarine, whipped, stick or soft (average)	2 tsp.	45	0
NUCOA® (Best Foods, CPC International)			
Margarine	1½ tsp.	50	0
Soft Margarine	1½ tsp.	45	0
OLD HOME® (Old Home® Foods, Inc.)			
Sour Cream	2 Tbsp.	60	2
Sour Lean	1 Tbsp.	20	1
PARKAY® (Kraft, Inc.)			
Light Corn Oil Spread	2 tsp.	47	0
Light Spread (50% vegetable oil)	2 tsp.	40	0

† For occasional use   ** Not recommended for use

PROTEIN (gm)	FAT (gm)	SAT. FAT (gm)	CHOLES- TEROL (mg)	SODIUM (mg)	EXCHANGES
0	6	1	0	110	1 fat
0	5	1	0	70	1 fat
0	4	2	10	38	1 fat
0	4	3	8	38	1 fat
0	4	—	—	35	1 fat
0	5	2	0	0-53	1 fat
<1	3	2	5	10	1 fat
1	1	<1	5	15-75	Free
2	4	2	10	20	1 fat
0	6	1	0	130	1 fat
0	6	1	0	50	1 fat
0	1	0	0	0	Free
0	5	<1	0	44-47	1 fat
0	6	1	0	80	1 fat
0	5	1	0	75	1 fat
2	4	—	—	16	1 fat
1	1	—	—	8	Free
0	5	1	0	74	1 fat
0	5	1	0	74	1 fat

* Not available   ▤ More than 2 fat exchanges   ♥ Moderate to high sugar content

Products	SERVING SIZE	CALORIES	CARBO-HYDRATE (gm)
Margarine, stick or soft (average)	1 tsp.	34	0
Soft Diet, reduced calorie margarine	1 Tbsp.	50	0
Squeeze® Margarine	1 tsp.	34	0
Whipped Margarine, cup or stick (average)	2 tsp.	40	0
PET/DAIRY MATE® (PET, Inc.)			
Imitation Sour Cream	2 Tbsp.	50	1
PROGRESSO® (PET, Inc.)			
Olive Oil, all varieties (average)	1 tsp.	40	0
WEIGHT WATCHERS® (H. J. Heinz Co.)			
Cooking Spray, all varieties (average)	1 second	2	0
Margarine			
Corn Oil	1 Tbsp.	50	0
Light Spread	1 Tbsp.	50	0
Reduced Calorie	2 tsp.	45	0
Sweet Unsalted	1 Tbsp.	50	0
Sour Cream, light	2 Tbsp. (1 oz.)	35	2

FRUIT DRINKS, JUICES

Author's Note: Some of these products contain large amounts of refined sugars. If you decide to use them occasionally, make them part of your meal plan and use them with a meal or before exercise.

BACARDI® (Coca-Cola Foods)
Tropical Fruit Mixers, frozen concentrated (as prepared)

Daiquiri, all flavors, without rum (average)	8 oz.	135	32
Margarita, without rum	8 oz.	100	25
Pina Colada, without rum	8 oz.	160	28

† For occasional use   ** Not recommended for use

PROTEIN (gm)	FAT (gm)	SAT. FAT (gm)	CHOLES-TEROL (mg)	SODIUM (mg)	EXCHANGES
0	4	1	0	35	1 fat
0	6	1	0	110	1 fat
0	4	1	0	34	1 fat
0	5	1	0	44-47	1 fat
1	4	—	1	50	1 fat
0	5	1	0	0	1 fat
0	<1	—	—	0	Free
0	6	1	0	130	1 fat
0	6	1	0	130	1 fat
0	5	1	0	87	1 fat
0	6	1	0	0	1 fat
2	2	—	—	40	½ fat
0	0	—	—	20	**
0	0	—	—	20	**
0	2	—	—	30	**

* Not available   ⏱ More than 2 fat exchanges   🛒 Moderate to high sugar content

Products	SERVING SIZE	CALORIES	CARBO-HYDRATE (gm)
BRIGHT AND EARLY® (Coca-Cola Foods)			
Imitation Orange Beverage	4 oz.	60	15
CAMPBELL'S® (Campbell Soup Co.)			
Tomato Juice	6 oz.	35	8
V-8	6 oz.	35	8
V-8, No Salt Added	6 oz.	40	9
Spicy Hot V-8	6 oz.	35	8
COUNTRY TIME® (General Foods Corp.)			
Drink Mix, sugar sweetened, all flavors (average)	6 oz.	60	15
Sugar Free Drink Mix, all flavors (average)	8 oz.	4	0
CRYSTAL LIGHT® (General Foods Corp.)			
Sugar Free Drink Mix, all flavors (average)	8 oz.	4	1
FEATHERWEIGHT® (Sandoz Nutrition)			
Tomato Juice, Low Sodium	6 oz.	35	8
FIVE ALIVE® (Coca-Cola Foods)			
All flavors (average)	4 oz.	60	15
HEALTH VALLEY® (Health Valley Foods)			
Coolers, all varieties (average)	12 oz.	140	32
HI-C® (Coca-Cola Foods)			
Fruit Drinks, all flavors (average)	4 oz.	65	16
Fruit Drink Box, all flavors (average)	8.45 oz.	130	32
KOOL-AID® (General Foods Corp.)			
Kool Bursts™ Soft Drink, all varieties (average)	6.75 oz.	130	34
Koolers® Juice Drink, all flavors (average)	8.45 oz.	140	35

† For occasional use   ** Not recommended for use

PROTEIN (gm)	FAT (gm)	SAT. FAT (gm)	CHOLES-TEROL (mg)	SODIUM (mg)	EXCHANGES
0	0	—	—	12	1 fruit†
1	0	—	—	570	1½ veg. **or** 1½ fruit
1	0	—	—	600	1½ veg. **or** 1½ fruit
1	0	—	—	45	1½ veg. **or** 1½ fruit
1	0	—	—	600	1½ veg. **or** 1½ fruit
0	0	—	0	11-15	1 fruit†
0	0	—	0	0	Free
0	0	—	0	0	Free
1	0	—	—	10	1 veg. **or** ½ fruit
0	0	—	—	14	1 fruit†
1	1	—	—	12-30	**
0	0	—	—	17	1 fruit†
0	0	—	—	25	2 fruit†
0	0	0	0	10	2 fruit†
0	0	—	0	10	**

* Not available   ▤ More than 2 fat exchanges   ☙ Moderate to high sugar content

Products	SERVING SIZE	CALORIES	CARBO-HYDRATE (gm)
Soft Drink Mix, unsweetened, all flavors (as packaged) (average)	1 package, powder only	2	0
☕ Soft Drink Mix, unsweetened, all flavors (as prepared with sugar) (average)	8 oz.	100	25
☕ Soft Drink Mix, sugar sweetened, all flavors (average)	8 oz.	80	20
Sugar Free Soft Drink Mix, all flavors (average)	8 oz.	4	0
LAND O'LAKES® (Land O'Lakes, Inc.)			
☕ Flavored Fruit Drinks, all flavors (average)	4 oz.	60	15
MINUTE MAID® (Coca-Cola Foods)			
☕ Flavored Ades (average)	4 oz.	55	14
☕ Flavored Punches (average)	4 oz.	62	15
Juices To Go, cans, all flavors (average)	11.5 z.	175	43
On the Go® Bottled Juices and Punch (average)	10 oz.	150	38
OCEAN SPRAY® (Ocean Spray Cranberries, Inc.)			
Cranberry Juice Cocktail	4 oz. (½ cup)	70	17
Cranapple® Juice Drink	4 oz. (½ cup)	85	21
Cran•Blueberry Drink	4 oz. (½ cup)	80	20
Cran•Grape® Drink	4 oz. (½ cup)	70	17
Cranicot® Juice Drink	4 oz. (½ cup)	70	17
Cran•Raspberry® Drink	4 oz. (½ cup)	70	17
Cran•Tastic® Blended Juice Drink	4 oz. (½ cup)	70	17
Low Calorie Cranberry Juice Cocktail	8 oz. (1 cup)	60	15

PROTEIN (gm)	FAT (gm)	SAT. FAT (gm)	CHOLES-TEROL (mg)	SODIUM (mg)	EXCHANGES
0	0	—	0	0-35	Free
0	0	—	0	0-25	**
0	0	—	0	0-25	**
0	0	—	0	0-35	Free
<1	0	—	0	0-5	1 fruit†
0	0	—	—	14	1 fruit†
0	0	—	—	10	1 fruit†
1	0	—	—	33-74	3 fruit
1	0	—	—	29-38	2½ fruit
0	0	0	0	7	1 fruit
0	0	0	0	<10	1½ fruit†
0	0	0	0	7	1 fruit
0	0	0	0	<10	1 fruit†
0	0	0	0	<10	1 fruit†
0	0	0	0	<10	1 fruit†
0	0	0	0	10	1 fruit†
0	0	0	0	15	1 fruit

* Not available   ▯ More than 2 fat exchanges   ♥ Moderate to high sugar content

Products	SERVING SIZE	CALORIES	CARBO-HYDRATE (gm)
Low Calorie Cranapple® Juice Drink	8 oz. (1 cup)	60	15
Low Calorie Cran^Raspberry Juice Drink	8 oz. (1 cup)	60	15
Mauna La'I™ Hawaiian Fruit Drink, all varieties (average)	4 oz. (½ cup)	67	17
SQUEEZIT® (General Mills, Inc.)			
🛒 Fruit Drink, all flavors (average)	6.75 oz.	110	27
SUNDANCE® (Stroh Foods, Inc.)			
Natural Juice Sparkler, fruit juice and sparkling water, all flavors (average)	10 oz.	120-134	26-31
TANG® (General Foods Corp.)			
🛒 Breakfast Beverage Crystals (as prepared)	6 oz.	90	22
🛒 Fruit Box Juice Drink, all flavors (average)	8.45 oz.	130	34
Sugar Free Breakfast Beverage Crystals (as prepared)	6 oz.	6	1
WELCH'S® (Welch Foods)			
Grape Juice, all varieties (average)	4 oz. (½ cup)	80	20
Juice Cocktail, 10 oz. bottles — all varieties (average)	10 oz.	170	43
Orchard® Juice Cocktail, all varieties (average)	4 oz.	73	18
Orchard® Cocktails In-A-Box, all varieties (average)	8.45 oz.	150	38
Sparkling Juices, all varieties (average)	4 oz.	75	19
Tomato Juice	6 oz. (¾ cup)	35	7
Tropical Drinks Juice Cocktail, all varieties (average)	4 oz.	67	17
Welchade Grape Drink	6 oz. (¾ cup)	90	23

† For occasional use   ** Not recommended for use

PROTEIN (gm)	FAT (gm)	SAT. FAT (gm)	CHOLES-TEROL (mg)	SODIUM (mg)	EXCHANGES
0	0	0	0	15	1 fruit
0	0	0	0	15	1 fruit
0	0	0	0	7	1 fruit
<1	<1	—	—	5-30	2 fruit†
<1	0	0	0	22-47	2 fruit
0	0	0	0	0	1½ fruit†
0	0	—	—	10	**
0	0	0	—	0	Free
0	0	—	0	3-10	1 fruit
0	0	0	0	0-95	3 fruit
0	0	0	0	13	1 fruit
0	0	0	0	20	2½ fruit
0	0	0	0	3-20	1 fruit
1	0	—	0	550	1 veg. **or** ½ fruit
0	0	0	0	13	1 fruit
0	0	—	0	25	1½ fruit†

* Not available   ▤ More than 2 fat exchanges   ♥ Moderate to high sugar content

Products	SERVING SIZE	CALORIES	CARBO-HYDRATE (gm)
WYLER'S® (Thomas J. Lipton, Inc.)			
Beverage Flavor Crystals (as prepared) (average)	8 oz.	85	21
Fruit Punch, canned	6 oz. (½ can)	84	21
Fruit Slush, all flavors (average)	4 oz.	157	39
Fruit Tea Punch, canned	6 oz. (½ can)	118	30
Lemonade, canned	6 oz. (½ can)	64	17

JAMS, JELLIES, PRESERVES

DIA-MEL® (Estee Corp.)			
Preserves and Jellies, Dietetic, all varieties (average)	1 tsp.	2	0
FEATHERWEIGHT® (Sandoz Nutrition)			
Low Calorie Fruit Spreads, sweetened with fructose, all varieties (average)	1 Tbsp.	12	3
KRAFT® (Kraft, Inc.)			
Jams, Jellies, Preserves, all varieties (average)	1 tsp.	17	4
Reduced Calorie Grape Jelly	1 tsp.	8	2
Reduced Calorie Strawberry Preserves	1 tsp.	8	2
NUTRADIET® (S and W Fine Foods)			
Reduced Calorie Jams, Jellies and Preserves, dietetic, all varieties (average)	1 tsp.	4	1
POLANER® (M. Polaner, Inc.)			
All Fruit™, spreadable fruit, all varieties (average)	1 tsp.	14	4
SMUCKER'S® (J. M. Smucker Co.)			
Low Sugar Spread (½ the sugar of regular), all varieties (average)	1 tsp.	8	2

† For occasional use   ** Not recommended for use

PROTEIN (gm)	FAT (gm)	SAT. FAT (gm)	CHOLES-TEROL (mg)	SODIUM (mg)	EXCHANGES
0	0	0	0	18	1½ fruit†
0	0	0	0	8	1½ fruit†
0	0	0	0	10	**
0	0	0	0	10	**
0	0	0	0	33	1 fruit†
0	0	0	0	<1	Free
0	0	—	0	0-5	Free
0	0	0	0	0	Free
0	0	0	0	10	Free
0	0	0	0	10	Free
0	0	—	—	0-10	Free
0	0	—	—	0	Free
0	0	—	—	0	Free

* Not available   ▤ More than 2 fat exchanges   ♥ Moderate to high sugar content

Products	SERVING SIZE	CALORIES	CARBO-HYDRATE (gm)
Simply Fruit®, spreadable fruit, all varieties (average)	1 tsp.	16	4
WEIGHT WATCHERS® (H. J. Heinz Co.) Fruit Spreads, all varieties (average)	2 tsp.	16	4
WELCH® (Welch Foods) Jam, Jellies and Preserves, all varieties (average)	1 tsp.	18	5
	2 tsp.	35	9
Totally Fruit™, spreadable fruit, all varieties (average)	1 tsp.	14	4

MEAT, FISH, POULTRY

CHICKEN

BANQUET® (ConAgra® Frozen Foods Co.)

Chicken Products			
Fried Chicken	⅕ pkg. (6.4 oz.)	330	29
Fried Chicken, Breast Portions	½ pkg. (5.75 oz.)	220	13
Fried Chicken, Thighs and Drumsticks	½ pkg. (6.25 oz.)	250	14
Hot 'n Spicy Fried Chicken	⅕ pkg. (6.4 oz.)	330	29
Hot 'n Spicy Snack'n Chicken	¼ pkg. (3.75 oz.)	140	8

BANQUET® HOT BITES® (ConAgra® Frozen Foods Co.)

Boneless Chicken (¼ package)			
Breast Patties	2.63 oz.	210	13
Breast Tenders	2.25 oz.	150	12
Chicken Drum-Snackers	2.63 oz.	220	13
Chicken Nuggets	2.63 oz.	210	11
Chicken Nuggets with Cheddar	2.63 oz.	250	11

† For occasional use   ** Not recommended for use

PROTEIN (gm)	FAT (gm)	SAT. FAT (gm)	CHOLES-TEROL (mg)	SODIUM (mg)	EXCHANGES
0	0	—	—	0	Free
0	0	0	0	0	Free
0	0	0	0	3	Free
0	0	0	0	5	½ fruit†
0	0	—	—	5	Free
18	19	—	—	1210	2 starch, 2 meat, 1 fat
16	11	—	—	710	1 starch, 2 meat
14	14	—	—	790	1 starch, 2 meat, ½ fat
18	19	—	—	1210	2 starch, 2 meat, 1 fat
6	9	—	—	480	½ starch, 1 meat, ½ fat
11	13	—	—	460	1 starch, 1 meat, 1 fat
11	6	—	—	280	1 starch, 1 meat
10	15	—	—	530	1 starch, 1 meat, 1½ fat
11	14	—	—	550	1 starch, 1 meat, 1 fat
11	18	—	—	560	1 starch, 1 meat, 2 fat

* Not available   ▊ More than 2 fat exchanges   🛒 Moderate to high sugar content

Products	SERVING SIZE	CALORIES	CARBO-HYDRATE (gm)
Chicken Sticks	2.63 oz.	220	11
Hot 'n Spicy Chicken Nuggets	2.63 oz.	250	10
Southern Fried Breast Patties	2.63 oz.	210	13
Southern Fried Breast Tenders	2.25 oz.	160	13
Southern Fried Chicken Nuggets	2.63 oz.	220	13
Microwave Chicken Breast Pattie and Bun	4 oz.	310	32
Breast Tenders	4 oz.	260	24
Chicken Nuggets with Sweet and Sour Sauce	4.5 oz.	360	22
Hot 'n Spicy Chicken Nuggets with BBQ Sauce	4.5 oz.	360	23
Southern Fried Breast Pattie and Biscuit	4 oz.	320	37
Southern Fried Chicken Breast Nuggets with BBQ Sauce	4.5 oz.	370	20

COUNTRY PRIDE® (ConAgra® Frozen Foods Co.)

Products	SERVING SIZE	CALORIES	CARBO-HYDRATE (gm)
Chicken Chunks	¼ of 12 oz. pkg.	240	15
⊟ Chicken Nuggets	¼ of 12 oz. pkg.	250	14
Chicken Patties	¼ of 12 oz. pkg.	250	14
⊟ Chicken Sticks	¼ of 12 oz. pkg.	240	16
⊟ Southern Fried Chicken Chunks	¼ of 12 oz. pkg.	280	14
⊟ Southern Fried Chicken Patties	¼ of 12 oz. pkg.	240	13

HORMEL® CHICKEN BY GEORGE® (Geo. A. Hormel and Co.)

Products	SERVING SIZE	CALORIES	CARBO-HYDRATE (gm)
All varieties (average)	5 oz.	175	5

PROTEIN (gm)	FAT (gm)	SAT. FAT (gm)	CHOLES-TEROL (mg)	SODIUM (mg)	EXCHANGES
10	15	—	—	350	1 starch, 1 meat, 1 fat
10	19	—	—	380	1 starch, 1 meat, 2 fat
11	12	—	—	620	1 starch, 1 meat, 1 fat
10	7	—	—	340	1 starch, 1 meat
10	14	—	—	530	1 starch, 1 meat, 1 fat
15	14	—	—	670	2 starch, 1½ meat, 1 fat
19	10	—	—	560	1½ starch, 2 meat
20	21	—	—	770	1½ starch, 2 meat, 2 fat
20	21	—	—	820	1½ starch, 2 meat, 2 fat
12	14	—	—	980	2½ starch, 1 meat, 1 fat
19	23	—	—	930	1 starch, 2½ meat, 2 fat
10	15	—	—	560	1 starch, 1 lean meat, 2 fat
11	16	—	—	460	1 starch, 1 lean meat, 2½ fat
12	16	—	—	570	1 starch, 1½ lean meat, 2 fat
10	15	—	—	400	1 starch, 1 lean meat, 2½ fat
10	20	—	—	690	1 starch, 1 lean meat, 3½ fat
11	16	—	—	630	1 starch, 1 lean meat, 2½ fat
27	6	—	55-90	340-680	3 lean meat

* Not available   ▌ More than 2 fat exchanges   🛒 Moderate to high sugar content

Products	SERVING SIZE	CALORIES	CARBO-HYDRATE (gm)
SWANSON® (Campbell Soup Co.)			
Chicken, canned			
Chunk Style Mixin' Chicken	2½ oz.	130	0
Chunk Chicken Spread	1 oz.	60	2
Premium Chunk White Chicken	2½ oz.	100	0
Premium Chunk White and Dark Chicken	2½ oz.	100	0
Chicken Duet Entrees, frozen			
Creamy Broccoli	6 oz.	320	18
Creamy Green Bean	6 oz.	330	19
Saucy Tomato	6 oz.	340	21
Savory Wild Rice	6 oz.	330	19
Chicken Duet Gourmet Nuggets, frozen			
Ham and Cheese	2.70 oz.	190	11
Mexican Style	2.70 oz.	200	12
Pizza Style	2.70 oz.	190	13
Spinach and Herb	2.70 oz.	200	13
Chicken, Plump & Juicy, frozen			
Chicken Dipsters	3 oz. edible portion	220	12
Chicken Drumlets	3 oz. edible portion	220	11
Chicken Nibbles	3½ oz. edible portion	300	18
Fried Chicken, Breast Portions	4½ oz. edible portion	360	20

† For occasional use   ** Not recommended for use

PROTEIN (gm)	FAT (gm)	SAT. FAT (gm)	CHOLES-TEROL (mg)	SODIUM (mg)	EXCHANGES
14	8	—	—	230	2 meat
4	4	—	—	140	½ high fat meat
15	4	—	—	240	2 lean meat
16	4	—	—	240	2 lean meat
20	19	—	—	590	1 starch, 1 veg., 2 lean meat, 2 fat
21	19	—	—	570	1 starch, 1 veg., 2 lean meat, 2½ fat
23	18	—	—	600	1 starch, 1 veg., 2½ lean meat, 2 fat
19	20	—	—	580	1 starch, 1 veg., 2 lean meat, 2½ fat
10	12	—	—	370	1 starch, 1 meat, 1 fat
10	12	—	—	370	1 starch, 1 meat, 1 fat
10	11	—	—	400	1 starch, 1 meat, 1 fat
10	12	—	—	380	1 starch, 1 meat, 1 fat
12	14	—	—	390	1 starch, 1½ meat, 1 fat
13	14	—	—	370	1 starch, 1½ meat, 1 fat
12	20	—	—	660	1 starch, 1½ meat, 2 fat
21	22	—	—	770	1 starch, 2½ meat, 2 fat

* Not available   ▊ More than 2 fat exchanges   🛒 Moderate to high sugar content

Products	SERVING SIZE	CALORIES	CARBO-HYDRATE (gm)
1 lb. Take-Out Pre-Fried Chicken	3¼ oz. edible portion	270	13
Take-Out Fried Chicken	3¼ oz. edible portion	270	14
Thighs and Drumsticks	3¼ oz. edible portion	280	11
TYSON® (Tyson Foods, Inc.) Breaded Boneless Chicken, frozen			
Breast Chunks	3 oz.	240	10
Chick'n Cheddar	2.6 oz.	220	11
Diced Meat	3 oz.	150	0
Microwave Chunks	3.5 oz.	220	11
Microwave Tenders	3.5 oz.	230	19
Southern Fried Breast Patties	2.6 oz.	220	9
Southern Fried Breast Tenders	3 oz.	220	15
Microwave Sandwiches, frozen			
BBQ Sandwich	4 oz.	230	27
Breast Sandwich	3.5 oz.	275	27
Mini Sandwich	3.5 oz.	230	39
Tyson Wings, all varieties (average)	6-7 wings (3.5 oz.)	220	0

FISH
CAPTAIN JAC® (SeaFest/JAC Creative Foods)

Imitation Crab	3 oz.	70	9
Imitation Lobster	2 oz.	60	7

† For occasional use   ** Not recommended for use

PROTEIN (gm)	FAT (gm)	SAT. FAT (gm)	CHOLES-TEROL (mg)	SODIUM (mg)	EXCHANGES
15	17	—	—	590	1 starch, 2 meat, 1 fat
15	17	—	—	630	1 starch, 2 meat, 1 fat
16	19	—	—	550	1 starch, 2 meat, 1 fat
13	17	—	30	430	1 starch, 1½ lean meat, 1½ fat
11	15	—	40	310	1 starch, 1 meat, 1½ fat
26	5	—	70	50	3 lean meat
10	15	—	—	—	1 starch, 1 lean meat, 2 fat
16	11	—	—	600	1 starch, 2 lean meat, 1 fat
11	15	—	35	460	½ starch, 1½ lean meat, 2 fat
14	11	—	25	630	1 starch, 2 lean meat, ½ fat
16	6	—	—	510	2 starch, 1½ lean meat
14	12	—	—	520	2 starch, 1½ lean meat, 1 fat
12	5	—	—	540	2½ starch, ½ lean meat
23	14	—	—	400	3 meat
9	<1	—	15	700	½ starch, 1 lean meat
7	<1	—	6	420	½ starch, ½ lean meat

* Not available   ⬛ More than 2 fat exchanges   🛒 Moderate to high sugar content

Products	SERVING SIZE	CALORIES	CARBO-HYDRATE (gm)
FEATHERWEIGHT® (Sandoz Nutrition)			
Salmon-Pink, Low Sodium, canned	2 oz.	70	0
Tuna, Low Sodium, canned	2 oz.	60	0
GORTON'S® (The Gorton Group, Division of General Mills, Inc.)			
Fish Fillets			
Crispy Batter	2 fillets	300	18
Crispy Batter (larger cut)s	1 fillet	320	20
Crunchy	2 fillets	320	24
Light Recipe™, lightly breaded	1 fillet	180	16
Light Recipe™, Tempura	1 fillet	200	8
Microwave	2 fillets	340	17
Microwave (larger cut)	1 fillet	320	20
Potato Crisp™	2 fillets	310	19
Ranch (larger cut)	1 fillet	330	24
Value Pack	1 fillet	180	15
Microwave Entrees			
Baked Scrod	1 package	320	17
Fillets Almondine	1 package	340	2
Fillets in Herb Butter	1 package	190	3
Haddock in Lemon Butter	1 package	360	19
Shrimp Scampi	1 package	470	33
Sole in Lemon Butter	1 package	380	17
Sole in Wine Sauce	1 package	180	3

PROTEIN (gm)	FAT (gm)	SAT. FAT (gm)	CHOLES-TEROL (mg)	SODIUM (mg)	EXCHANGES
11	3	—	20	45	1½ lean meat
13	1	—	30	30	1½ lean meat
12	20	8	35	580	1 starch, 1½ lean meat, 3 fat
12	21	—	—	680	1 starch, 1½ lean meat, 3 fat
12	20	7	35	400	1½ starch, 1 lean meat, 3 fat
11	8	3	30	380	1 starch, 1 lean meat, 1 fat
10	14	4	30	400	½ starch, 1 lean meat, 2 fat
10	26	12	30	400	1 starch, 1 lean meat, 4½ fat
11	22	10	35	500	1 starch, 1 lean meat, 4 fat
14	20	6	30	380	1 starch, 2 lean meat, 2½ fat
12	21	—	—	520	1½ starch, 1 lean meat, 3½ fat
7	10	—	—	450	1 starch, 1 lean meat, 1 fat
22	18	4	80	420	1 starch, 3 lean meat, 1½ fat
27	25	10	100	450	3½ lean meat, 3 fat
26	8	5	90	450	3½ lean meat
23	21	10	100	730	1 starch, 3 lean meat, 2½ fat
12	32	14	130	720	2 starch, 1 lean meat, 5½ fat
25	24	11	120	560	1 starch, 3 lean meat, 3 fat
25	8	3	90	770	3 lean meat

* Not available   ▐ More than 2 fat exchanges   🛒 Moderate to high sugar content

Products	SERVING SIZE	CALORIES	CARBO-HYDRATE (gm)
Stuffed Flounder	1 package	350	21
Specialty Butterfly Shrimp	4 oz.	160	16
▤ Microwave Crunchy Clam Strips	3.5 oz.	330	24
▤ Microwave Crunchy Whole Shrimp	5 oz.	380	35
▤ Shrimp Crisps	4 oz.	280	26
MRS. PAUL'S® (Campbell Soup Co.) Catfish Light Fillets	4¼ oz.	250	24
Fillet Strips	4 oz.	240	21
Clams, fried	2½ oz.	240	22
▤ Combination Seafood Platter	9 oz.	600	55
Crab Deviled Crabs	1 cake	170	19
Deviled Crabs Miniatures	3½ oz.	250	29
Fish Cakes Fish Cakes	2 cakes	250	27
Fish Cake Thins	2 cakes	290	29
Fish Fillets ▤ Batter Dipped	2 fillets	430	27
Buttered	2 fillets	160	1

† For occasional use   ** Not recommended for use

PROTEIN (gm)	FAT (gm)	SAT. FAT (gm)	CHOLES-TEROL (mg)	SODIUM (mg)	EXCHANGES
25	18	7	120	850	1½ starch, 3 lean meat, 1½ fat
19	<1	—	—	540	1 starch, 2 lean meat
10	22	6	30	430	1½ starch, 1 lean meat, 3½ fat
14	20	3	65	870	2 starch, 1½ lean meat, 3 fat
9	15	—	—	740	1½ starch, 1 lean meat, 2½ fat
17	10	—	—	389	1½ starch, 2 lean meat, ½ fat
10	13	—	—	290	1½ starch, 1 lean meat, 1½ fat
8	13	—	—	380	1½ starch, 1 lean meat, 1½ fat
19	33	8	85	408	3½ starch, 2 lean meat, 4½ fat
8	7	—	—	300	1 starch, 1 lean meat, 1 fat
8	12	—	—	480	2 starch, ½ lean meat, 1½ fat
11	11	—	—	840	2 starch, 1 lean meat, 1½ fat
15	13	—	—	1210	2 starch, 1½ lean meat, 1½ fat
17	28	4	50	800	2 starch, 2 lean meat, 3½ fat
21	8	5	105	230	3 lean meat

* Not available   ▤ More than 2 fat exchanges   🛒 Moderate to high sugar content

Products	SERVING SIZE	CALORIES	CARBO-HYDRATE (gm)
Crispy Crunchy	2 fillets	220	23
Crunchy Batter	2 fillets	280	26
Supreme Light Batter	1 fillet	210	21
Fish Sticks			
Crispy Crunchy	4 sticks	190	18
Crunchy (Minced)	4 oz.	200	18
Crunchy Batter	4 sticks	180	16
Flounder			
Crispy Crunchy	2 fillets	300	17
Crunchy Batter	2 fillets	260	20
Light Fillets	4¼ oz.	260	28
Haddock			
Crispy Crunchy	2 fillets	280	23
Crunchy Batter	2 fillets	280	25
Light Fillets	4¼ oz.	220	24
Light Seafood Entrees			
Fish Dijon	8 ¾ oz.	200	17
Fish Florentine	8 oz.	215	10
Fish Mornay	9 oz.	230	12
Seafood Lasagna	9½ oz.	290	39
Seafood Rotini	9 oz.	240	34
Shrimp Cajun Style	9 oz.	230	37

† For occasional use   ** Not recommended for use

PROTEIN (gm)	FAT (gm)	SAT. FAT (gm)	CHOLES- TEROL (mg)	SODIUM (mg)	EXCHANGES
13	9	2	22	380	1½ starch, 1 lean meat, 1 fat
12	14	3	22	810	2 starch, 1 lean meat, 1½ fat
9	12	—	—	540	1½ starch, 1 lean meat, 1 fat
9	8	1	25	560	1 starch, 1 lean meat, 1 fat
10	10	—	—	340	1 starch, 1 lean meat, 1 fat
8	10	2	25	560	1 starch, 1 lean meat, 1 fat
14	19	3	45	520	1 starch, 2 lean meat, 2½ fat
13	14	—	—	610	1 starch, 1½ lean meat, 2 fat
14	11	—	—	536	2 starch, 1½ lean meat, ½ fat
16	14	2	40	460	1½ starch, 2 lean meat, 1 fat
11	15	—	—	580	2 starch, 1 lean meat, 1½ fat
19	5	—	—	456	1½ starch, 2 lean meat
21	5	2	60	650	1 starch, 2½ lean meat
25	8	4	93	820	½ starch, 3 lean meat
24	10	4	80	670	1 starch, 3 lean meat
14	8	3	57	750	2½ starch, 1 lean meat, 1 fat
12	6	2	25	570	2 starch, 1½ lean meat
9	5	1	60	740	2 starch, 1 veg., ½ lean meat, ½ fat

* Not available   ⊟ More than 2 fat exchanges   ♛ Moderate to high sugar content

Products	SERVING SIZE	CALORIES	CARBO-HYDRATE (gm)
Shrimp and Clams with Linguini	10 oz.	240	36
Shrimp Primavera	9½ oz.	180	28
Ocean Perch Crispy Crunchy	2 fillets	310	19
Light Fillets	4½ oz.	270	19
Pollock Light Fillets	4¼ oz.	240	18
Scallops, fried	3 oz.	200	22
Shrimp, fried	3 oz.	200	16
Sole Light Fillets	4¼ oz.	260	28
NUTRADIET® (S and W Fine Foods)			
Salmon, Low Sodium	½ cup	188	0
SEAFEST™ (SeaFest/JAC Creative Foods)			
Crab Tasties™, Surimi Seafood Blend, all varieties (average)	2 oz.	50	6
Lobster Tasties™, Sirimi Seafood Blend, all varieties (average)	2 oz.	60	7
UNDERWOOD® (PET, Inc.)			
Sardines in Soya Oil, all varieties (average)	3 oz.	230	1
Sardines in Sauce	3.75 oz.	220	2
VAN DE KAMP'S® (PET, Inc.)			
Battered Items Fish Fillets	1	170	14
Fish Sticks	4	170	14

PROTEIN (gm)	FAT (gm)	SAT. FAT (gm)	CHOLES-TEROL (mg)	SODIUM (mg)	EXCHANGES
12	5	2	40	750	2 starch, 1 lean meat, ½ fat
11	3	1	125	840	1½ starch, 1 lean meat
14	20	4	40	460	1 starch, 1½ lean meat, 3 fat
18	13	—	—	391	1 starch, 2 lean meat, 1½ fat
17	11	—	—	530	1 starch, 2 lean meat, 1 fat
9	8	—	—	410	1½ starch, 1 lean meat, ½ fat
9	11	—	—	430	1 starch, 1 lean meat, 1 fat
14	11	—	—	536	2 starch, 1½ lean meat, 1 fat
22	11	—	—	45	3 lean meat
6	0	—	2-10	400	1 lean meat
7	<1	—	6	420	1 lean meat
16	18	—	35	400	2 high fat meat, ½ fat
16	16	—	6	400-650	2 high fat meat
9	9	—	25	340	1 starch, 1 lean meat, 1 fat
9	9	—	25	340	1 starch, 1 lean meat, 1 fat

* Not available ▮ More than 2 fat exchanges ⛽ Moderate to high sugar content

Products	SERVING SIZE	CALORIES	CARBO-HYDRATE (gm)
Haddock Fillets	2	250	20
Halibut Fillets	2	180	14
Perch Fillets	2	260	20
Breaded Items Fish Fillets	2	260	23
Fish Sticks	4	190	18
Haddock Fillets	2	260	23
Crispy Microwave Fish Fillets	1	130	9
Fish Sticks	3	150	11
Light Fillets Cod	1	250	19
Flounder	1	240	19
Haddock	1	250	19
Ocean Perch	1	260	19
Sole	1	240	19

PROCESSED MEATS (COLD CUTS, WIENERS, ETC.)
HEALTH VALLEY® (Health Valley Foods, Inc.)

Wieners Chicken	1	96	1
Turkey	1	96	1

JONES DAIRY FARM® (Jones Dairy Farm)

Sausage Products, cooked Brown & Serve/Bacon (as purchased) (10/8 oz.)	2 links	180	0
Brown & Serve/Beef (as purchased) (10/8 oz.)	2 links	180	0

† For occasional use   ** Not recommended for use

PROTEIN (gm)	FAT (gm)	SAT. FAT (gm)	CHOLES- TEROL (mg)	SODIUM (mg)	EXCHANGES
12	13	—	50	520	1 starch, 1½ lean meat, 1½ fat
9	9	—	35	340	1 starch, 1 lean meat, 1 fat
13	14	—	50	520	1 starch, 1½ lean meat, 2 fat
10	15	—	30	430	1½ starch, 1 lean meat, 2 fat
7	10	—	25	280	1 strch, 1 lean meat, 1 fat
10	15	—	30	430	1½ starch, 1 lean meat, 2 fat
7	7	—	15	250	½ starch, 1 lean meat, 1 fat
8	8	—	20	270	1 starch, 1 lean meat, 1 fat
16	12	2	40	430	1 starch, 2 lean meat, 1 fat
15	12	2	45	460	1 starch, 2 lean meat, 1 fat
17	12	2	35	380	1 starch, 2 lean meat, 1 fat
17	13	2	40	400	1 starch, 2 lean meat, 1½ fat
15	12	2	45	460	1 starch, 2 lean meat, 1 fat
5	8	—	49	90	1 high fat meat
5	8	—	35	112	1 high fat meat
6	16	—	38	280	1 high fat meat, 1½ fat
6	17	—	36	380	1 high fat meat, 2 fat

* Not available   ▤ More than 2 fat exchanges   🛒 Moderate to high sugar content

Products	SERVING SIZE	CALORIES	CARBO-HYDRATE (gm)
Brown & Serve/Light (as purchased) (10/8 oz.)	2 links	120	2
Brown & Serve/Regular (as purchased) (10/8 oz.)	2 links	200	0
Golden Brown Beef Link (as purchased) (10/8 oz.)	2 links	160	0
Golden Brown Light Link (as purchased) (10/8 oz.)	2 links	120	2
Golden Brown Mild Link (as purchased) (10/8 oz.)	2 links	200	0
Golden Brown Mild Patties (as purchased) (6/8 oz.)	1 patty	150	0
Golden Brown Spicy Link (as purchased) (10/8 oz.)	2 links	200	0
Sausage Products, uncooked Beef (as purchased) (12 slices/12 oz.)	1 slice	130	0
Dinner Link (as purchased) (8/1 lb.)	1 link	280	0
Hot Country (as purchased) (12 slices/12 oz.)	1 slice	110	0
Italian Sausage (as purchased) (8/1 lb.)	1 link	160	0
Light Link (as purchased) (16/1 lb.)	2 links	140	2
Original (as purchased) (12 slices/12 oz.)	1 slice	100	0
Sausage Patties (as purchased) (8/12 oz.)	1 patty	150	0
Smoked/Luncheon Meats Bacon (as purchased) (20 slices/1 lb.)	1 slice	130	0
Canadian Bacon (as purchased (12 slices/6 oz.)	2 slices	60	0
Ham Slices (as purchased) (10 slices/1 lb.)	2 slices	60	0
Liver Sausage, chub (as purchased) (8 slices/8 oz.)	1 slice	80	0
Liver Sausage, sliced (as purchased) (10 slices/8 oz.)	1 slice	80	0

† For occasional use ** Not recommended for use

PROTEIN (gm)	FAT (gm)	SAT. FAT (gm)	CHOLES-TEROL (mg)	SODIUM (mg)	EXCHANGES
6	9	—	32	280	1 high fat meat
5	20	—	38	300	1 high fat meat, 2 fat
7	14	—	36	160	1 high fat meat, 1 fat
6	9	—	32	260	1 high fat meat
5	19	—	36	300	1 high fat meat, 2 fat
5	14	—	29	220	1 high fat meat, 1 fat
5	18	—	36	300	1 high fat meat, 2 fat
3	13	—	25	160	½ high fat meat, 2 fat
6	28	—	48	310	1 high fat meat, 4 fat
4	10	—	24	170	½ high fat meat, 1 fat
8	14	—	44	420	1 high fat meat, 1 fat
8	10	—	42	420	1 high fat meat, ½ fat
4	10	—	24	180	½ high fat meat, 1 fat
6	14	—	36	270	1 high fat meat, 1 fat
2	13	—	25	150	2½ fat
6	2	—	14	320	1 lean meat
9	2	—	42	400	1 lean meat
5	7	—	43	250	1 high fat meat
3	7	—	43	180 ½ fat	½ high fat meat,

* Not available   ▤ More than 2 fat exchanges   ♥ Moderate to high sugar content

Products	SERVING SIZE	CALORIES	CARBO-HYDRATE (gm)
Scrapple (as purchased) (10 slices/ 1 lb.)	1 slice	90	5
LAND-O-FROST® (Land-O-Frost, Inc.)			
Thin Sliced Meats: Beef, Chicken, Corned Beef, Ham, Pastrami, Turkey (average)	1 oz. (5 slices)	50	1
Turkey Lunch Meats: Roasted Breast, Ham, Pastrami, Salami, White Meat (average)	1 oz. (1 slice)	40	1
Turkey Bologna	1 oz. (1 slice)	40	1
OSCAR MAYER® (Oscar Mayer and Co.)			
Bacon (22-25 slices/1 lb.)	3 slices cooked	105	0
Bacon, Lower Salt	3 slices, cooked	95	0
Bacon Bits (real bacon)	2 tsp.	14	0
Beef Franks (10/1 lb.)	1	145	1
Canadian Style Bacon (93% fat free)	2 slices (2 oz.)	50	1
Lean 'n Tasty™ Breakfast Strips, beef or pork (as prepared) (average)	2 strips	100	<1
Cold Cuts, sliced Bar-B-Q Loaf (90% fat free)	2 slices (2 oz.)	92	2
Bologna, Beef Bologna (average)	2 slices	180	1
Beef Lebanon Bologna	2 slices (1⅔ oz.)	94	1
Bologna with Cheese (10 slices/8 oz.)	2 slices (1⅔ oz.)	150	1
Braunschweiger Liver Sausage	2 slices (2 oz.)	190	1
Chopped Ham	2 slices (2 oz.)	105	2
Cotto Salami, all varieties (10 slices/ 8 oz.) (average)	2 slices	105	1

† For occasional use   ** Not recommended for use

PROTEIN (gm)	FAT (gm)	SAT. FAT (gm)	CHOLES-TEROL (mg)	SODIUM (mg)	EXCHANGES
4	6	—	24	230	½ starch, ½ high fat meat
6	2	—	—	370-430	1 lean meat
5	2	—	—	300-470	1 lean meat
4	6	—	—	340	½ high fat meat, ½ fat
5	9	4	15	355	1 high fat meat
6	7	3	15	355	1 high fat meat
2	1	<1	4	125	Free
5	13	—	—	460	½ high fat meat, 2 fat
9	2	1	20	570	1 lean meat
6	9	3	27	400	1 high fat meat
9	5	2	28	665	1 meat
6	17	7	36	610-675	1 high fat meat, 2 fat
9	6	3	32	610	1 meat
5	14	5	30	465	1 high fat meat, 1 fat
8	17	6	100	655	1 high fat meat, 2 fat
9	7	2	34	650	1 high fat meat
6	9	4	38	580-605	1 high fat meat

* Not available   ▌ More than 2 fat exchanges   ♨ Moderate to high sugar content

Products	SERVING SIZE	CALORIES	CARBO-HYDRATE (gm)
Genoa Salami (25 slices/ 8 oz.)	3 slices (1 oz.)	100	0
Head Cheese	2 slices (2 oz.)	110	0
Liver Cheese (6 slices/8 oz.)	1 slice	114	0
Loaf Luncheon Meats Ham and Cheese Loaf	2 slices (2 oz.)	130	2
Honey Loaf	2 slices	70	2
Jalapeno Loaf	2 slices (2 oz.)	145	5
Old Fashioned Loaf	2 slices (2 oz.)	135	5
Olive Loaf	2 slices (2 oz.)	120	6
Peppered Loaf (93% fat free)	2 slices (2 oz.)	80	2
Pickle and Pimiento Loaf	2 slices (2 oz.)	135	7
Picnic Loaf	2 slices (2 oz.)	120	2
Luncheon Meat	2 slices	190	1
New England Brand Sausage (10 slices/8 oz.)	2 slices	60	1
Salami for Beer, all varieties (average) (10 slices/8 oz.)	2 slices	110	1
Salami, hard (25 slices/ 8 oz.)	3 slices (1 oz.)	100	0
Summer Sausage, all varieties (average) (10 slices/8 oz.)	2 slices	140	0
"Our Leanest Cuts" Cold Cuts (95% or more fat free) Baked Cooked Ham (8 slices/6 oz.)	2 slices	42	1
Boiled Ham (8 slices/ 6 oz.)	2 slices	46	0

† For occasional use   ** Not recommended for use

PROTEIN (gm)	FAT (gm)	SAT. FAT (gm)	CHOLES-TEROL (mg)	SODIUM (mg)	EXCHANGES
6	8	4	27	485	1 high fat meat
9	8	3	52	695	1 high fat meat
6	10	4	80	418	1 meat, 1 fat
9	10	5	38	720	1 high fat meat, ½ fat
10	2	1	32	760	1½ lean meat
6	11	5	20	930	1 high fat meat, 1 fat
8	8	3	32	675	1 high fat meat
6	8	3	28	785	1 high fat meat
10	3	2	28	730	1½ lean meat
6	8	3	28	805	1 high fat meat
9	9	3	32	665	1 high fat meat
7	17	7	40	640	1 high fat meat, 2 fat
8	3	1	28	585	1 lean meat
6	9	4	32	570	1 high fat meat
6	8	4	24	505	1 high fat meat
7	12	5	37	650	1 high fat meat, 1 fat
8	1	<1	22	475	1 lean meat
8	1	1	24	550	1 lean meat

* Not available   ▉ More than 2 fat exchanges   🛒 Moderate to high sugar content

Products	SERVING SIZE	CALORIES	CARBO-HYDRATE (gm)
Corned Beef (10 slices/6 oz.)	2 slices	32	0
Cracked Black Pepper Ham (8 slices/6 oz.)	2 slices	44	0
Ham, Lower Salt (8 slices/6 oz.)	2 slices	48	1
Honey Ham (8 slices/6 oz.)	2 slices	46	1
Oven Roasted Chicken Breast (6 slices/6 oz.)	2 slices (2 oz.)	60	1
Oven Roasted Turkey (8 slices/6 oz.)	2 slices	46	1
Pastrami (10 slices/6 oz.)	3 slices	48	0
Smoked Beef (12 slices/6 oz.)	4 slices (2 oz.)	52	0
Smoked Chicken Breast (8 slices/6 oz.)	2 slices	52	1
Smoked Cooked Ham (8 slices/6 oz.)	2 slices	44	0
Smoked Turkey Breast (8 slices/6 oz.)	3 slices	57	1
Lunchables®			
Lunch Combinations Bologna and American	4.5 oz.	460	23
Ham and Swiss	4.5 oz.	340	21
Salami and Mozzarella	4.5 oz.	420	20
Turkey and Cheddar	4.5 oz.	340	22
Lunch Combinations, deluxe Chicken and Roast Beef	5.5 oz.	410	25
Chicken and Turkey	5.5 oz.	420	24
Ham and Roast Beef	5.5 oz.	410	24
Turkey and Ham	5.5 oz.	390	24

PROTEIN (gm)	FAT (gm)	SAT. FAT (gm)	CHOLES-TEROL (mg)	SODIUM (mg)	EXCHANGES
7	1	<1	14	405	1 lean meat
8	1	1	22	570	1 lean meat
7	1	1	20	330	1 lean meat
8	1	1	24	535	1 lean meat
10	1	<1	32	830	1 lean meat
8	1	<1	18	580	1 lean meat
10	1	1	21	650	1 lean meat
10	1	<1	28	710	1 lean meat
11	1	<1	30	800	1 lean meat
8	1	1	24	530	1 lean meat
13	1	<1	27	900	1 lean meat
17	33	—	80	1500	1½ starch, 2 high fat meat, 3 fat
22	19	—	70	1630	1½ starch,, 2½ meat, 1 fat
20	29	—	65	1350	1½ starch, 2 meat, 3½ fat
22	18	—	70	1540	1½ starch, 2½ meat, 1 fat
25	24	—	80	1740	1½ starch, 3 meat, 1½ fat
26	24	—	80	1610	1½ starch, 3 meat, 1½ fat
24	24	—	80	1920	1½ starch, 3 meat, 1½ fat
26	21	—	70	1980	1½ starch, 3 meat, 1 fat

* Not available　　　🔋 More than 2 fat exchanges　　　🛒 Moderate to high sugar content

Products	SERVING SIZE	CALORIES	CARBO-HYDRATE (gm)
Meat Spreads in Saran Tube			
Ham and Cheese	2 oz.	135	1
Ham Salad	2 oz.	120	7
Sandwich	2 oz.	130	8
Sausage Links			
Beef Smokies	1 link (1½ oz.)	125	1
Cheese Smokies	1 link (1½ oz.)	130	1
Little Friers® Pork Sausage	2 links	160	1
Little Smokies	3 links (1 oz.)	85	0
Smokie Links	1 link (1½ oz.)	130	1
Wieners and Franks			
Bacon and Cheddar Cheese Hot Dogs (10/1 lb.)	1	140	1
Beef Franks (5/½ lb.)	1	145	1
Beef Franks with Cheddar (10/1 lb.)	1	135	1
Bun-Length™ Beef Franks (8/1 lb.)	1	185	2
Bun-Length™ Wieners (8/1 lb.)	1	185	2
Cheese Hot Dogs (10/2 lb.)	1	145	1
Little Wieners (48/1 lb.)	3 (1 oz.)	85	1
Wieners (10/1 lb.)	1	145	1

SANDWICH SHOP® (Land O'Frost, Inc.)

Thin Sliced Meat Products, all varieties (average)	1 oz. (≈3 slices)	35	1

UNDERWOOD® (PET, Inc.)

Herring Steaks, all varieties (average)	2.8 oz.	150	0

PROTEIN (gm)	FAT (gm)	SAT. FAT (gm)	CHOLES-TEROL (mg)	SODIUM (mg)	EXCHANGES
9	10	5	30	646	1 meat, 1 fat
5	8	3	20	540	½ starch, ½ meat, 1 fat
4	10	4	20	540	½ starch, ½ meat, 1 fat
5	11	5	27	430	1 high fat meat, ½ fat
6	11	4	29	450	1 high fat meat, ½ fat
8	14	5	32	390	1 high fat meat, 1½ fat
4	8	3	18	275	½ high fat meat, 1 fat
5	11	4	28	425	1 high fat meat, ½ fat
6	12	5	30	500	1 high fat meat, 1 fat
5	13	6	30	460	1 high fat meat, 1 fat
6	12	5	27	505	1 high fat meat, 1 fat
6	17	7	34	570	1 high fat meat, 2 fat
6	17	6	33	575	1 high fat meat, 2 fat
5	13	5	30	485	1 high fat meat, 1 fat
3	8	3	15	275	½ high fat meat, 1 fat
5	13	5	28	465	1 high fat meat, 1 fat
6	1	—	—	290-360	1 lean meat
19	8	—	30	470-510	2½ lean meat

* Not available   𝔹 More than 2 fat exchanges   🛒 Moderate to high sugar content

Products	SERVING SIZE	CALORIES	CARBO-HYDRATE (gm)
Meat Spreads,			
Chicken, chunky	2 ⅛ oz.	150	3
Chicken, smoky	2 ⅛ oz.	119	3
Corn Beef	2 ⅛ oz.	120	—
Deviled Ham	2 ⅛ oz.	220	—
Deviled Ham, smoked	2 ⅛ oz.	190	<1
Liver Pate	2 ⅛ oz.	190	4
Liverwurst	2 ⅛ oz.	180	4
Roast Beef	2 ⅛ oz.	140	—
Roast Beef, mesquite smoked	2 ⅛ oz.	126	4
Meat Spreads, light			
Chunky Chicken	2 ⅛ oz.	80	2
Deviled Ham	2 ⅛ oz.	120	2
Roast Beef	2 ⅛ oz.	90	1
Salad Singles			
Chicken	3.5 oz.	170	7
Crab	3.5 oz.	150	13
Ham	3.5 oz.	180	9
Seafood	3.5 oz.	160	13
Tuna	3.5 oz.	150	10

WEAVER® (Tyson Foods, Inc.)

Cold Meats			
Chicken Bologna	2 slices	88	1
Chicken Roll	2 slices	52	1
Hickory Smoked Breast	2 slices	52	1
Oven Roasted Breast	2 slices	50	1
Turkey Breast	2 slices	40	1
Turkey Ham	2 slices	46	0

TURKEY

HORMEL® TURKEY BY GEORGE® (Geo A. Hormel and Co.)

All varieties (average)	5 oz.	165	4

PROTEIN (gm)	FAT (gm)	SAT. FAT (gm)	CHOLES- TEROL (mg)	SODIUM (mg)	EXCHANGES
10	11	—	35	575	1½ meat, ½ fat
9	8	—	—	330	1 meat, ½ fat
6	10	—	45	605	1 meat, 1 fat
9	20	—	40	640	1 meat, 3 fat
9	17	—	—	290	1 meat, 2½ fat
8	16	—	90	470	1 meat, 2 fat
8	15	—	90	470	1 meat, 2 fat
11	10	—	50	515	1½ meat, ½ fat
9	8	—	—	241	1 meat, ½ fat
11	3	—	—	300	1½ lean meat
11	8	—	—	250	1½ meat
11	5	—	—	260	1½ lean meat
12	11	1	55	590	½ starch, 1½ lean meat, 1 fat
7	7	1	15	860	1 starch, 1 meat
7	13	3	25	890	½ starch, 1 meat, 1½ fat
7	9	1	20	680	1 starch, 1 meat, ½ fat
9	9	1	15	610	½ starch, 1 meat, ½ fat
4	7	—	—	370	½ meat, 1 fat
6	3	—	—	306	1 lean meat
8	2	—	—	390	1 lean meat
8	2	—	—	370	1 lean meat
8	1	—	—	272	1 lean meat
6	2	—	—	364	1 lean meat
29	5	—	55-65	510-680	3 lean meat

* Not available   ▤ More than 2 fat exchanges   ♥ Moderate to high sugar content

Products	SERVING SIZE	CALORIES	CARBO-HYDRATE (gm)
SWANSON® (Campbell Soup Co.)			
Canned			
Premium Chunk White Turkey	2½ oz.	90	0
Premium Chunk White and Dark Turkey	2½ oz.	90	1

MILK, MILK BEVERAGES

Author's Note: Some of these products contain large amounts of sugars and fats. If you decide to use them occasionally, make them part of your meal plan and use them with a meal or before exercise.

Products	SERVING SIZE	CALORIES	CARBO-HYDRATE (gm)
BLUE BUNNY® (Wells' Dairy Inc.)			
Lite Chocolate Nonfat Milk with NutraSweet	1 cup	90	13
FEATHERWEIGHT® SWEET PRETENDERS® (Sandoz Nutrition)			
Hot Cocoa Mix, low calorie, all varieties (as prepared) (average)	6 oz.	50	8
HEALTH VALLEY® (Health Valley Foods)			
Soo Moo®, soy beverage	8 oz.	120	12
HERSHEY'S® (Hershey Foods Corp.)			
☕ Chocolate Milk Mix	1 level Tbsp.	90	22
KRAFT® (Kraft, Inc.)			
☕ Instant Malted Milk, all flavors (as prepared) (average)	3 tsp. powder and 8 oz. skim milk	180	28
LAND O'LAKES® (Land O'Lakes, Inc.)			
☕ Chocolate Lowfat Milk, ½%	8 oz.	150	26
Chocolate Lowfat Milk with NutraSweet	8 oz.	110	14
MOCHA MIX® (Presto Food Products, Inc.)			
Non Dairy Creamer	1 Tbsp.	20	1
	¼ cup	80	4

† For occasional use   ** Not recommended for use

PROTEIN (gm)	FAT (gm)	SAT. FAT (gm)	CHOLES-TEROL (mg)	SODIUM (mg)	EXCHANGES
16	2	—	—	260	2 lean meat
15	3	—	—	280	2 lean meat
10	1	—	—	210	1 skim milk
2	1	—	0	110	½ skim milk **or** ½ starch
6	6	—	—	55	1 skim milk, 1 fat
1	4	—	0	40	1 starch, ½ fat†
10	1	—	—	160-210	1 fruit, 1 skim milk†
8	1	1	5	170	1 fruit, 1 skim milk†
8	3	2	5	200	1 skim milk, ½ fat
<1	2	0	0	5	Free
<1	8	0	0	20	1½ fat

* Not available   ▤ More than 2 fat exchanges   🛒 Moderate to high sugar content

Products	SERVING SIZE	CALORIES	CARBO-HYDRATE (gm)
NESTLÉ® (Nestlé Foods Corp.)			
☕ Hot Cocoa Mix	1.25 oz.	150	26
☕ Quik, chocolate or strawberry flavor (average)	2 tsp.	90	20
Quik, sugar free	1 heaping tsp. (5.8 grams)	18	3
☕ Quik Syrup	1 oz.	80	18
OVALTINE® (Sandoz Nutrition)			
Cocoa Mix			
50 Calorie Mix (as prepared with water)	6 oz. prepared	50	7
☕ Hot 'N Rich Mix (as prepared with water)	1 oz. dry (6 oz. prepared)	120	22
Lactose Free Mix (as prepared with water)	1 oz. dry (6 oz. prepared)	130	21
Sugar Free Mix (as prepared with water)	6 oz.	40	6
☕ Ovaltine, chocolate or malt flavor, reconstituted with 8 oz. skim milk (average)	¾ oz. mix and 8 oz. skim milk	160	30
SOYAMEL® (Worthington Foods, Inc.)			
Non-Dairy Powdered Soy Milk	1 oz. dry (8 oz. prepared)	130	10
SWISS MISS® (Beatrice/Hunt-Wesson)			
☕ Hot Cocoa Mix (add water)	2 heaping scoops (1 oz.)	110	24
Sugar Free Hot Cocoa Mix	2 rounded scoops (.53 oz.)	50	10
WEIGHT WATCHERS® (H. J. Heinz Co.)			
Shake Mixes, all varieties (as prepared) (average)	1 envelope	70	11

PROTEIN (gm)	FAT (gm)	SAT. FAT (gm)	CHOLES-TEROL (mg)	SODIUM (mg)	EXCHANGES
3	4	—	—	110	1 starch, ½ fruit, 1 fat **or** 1 fruit, 1/2 skim milk, 1 fat†
1	0	—	—	0-35	1½ fruit†
1	<1	—	—	40	Free
<1	0	—	—	35	1 fruit†
1	2	—	—	150	½ skim milk **or** ½ starch
2	3	—	—	170	½ starch, 1 fruit, ½ fat **or** 1 fruit, ½ skim milk, ½ fat†
4	2	—	—	115	1 starch, ½ fruit, ½ fat **or** 1 fruit, ½ skim milk, ½ fat†
1	2	—	—	160	½ milk **or** ½ starch
9	1	—	—	185-260	1 starch, 1 milk, **or** 1 fruit, 1 milk†
7	7	1	0	210	1 skim milk, 1 fat
2	1	—	5	125	1 starch, ½ fruit **or** 1 fruit, ½ skim milk†
3	<1	—	2	125	Free
6	1	—	—	160-210	1 skim milk **or** 1 starch

* Not available   ▤ More than 2 fat exchanges   ⬛ Moderate to high sugar content

Products	SERVING SIZE	CALORIES	CARBO-HYDRATE (gm)

NUTS, NUT BUTTERS, SEEDS

EAGLE® (Eagle Snacks, Inc.)

Cashews, lightly salted	1 oz.	170	7
Cashew & Peanut Mix	1 oz.	170	8
Mixed Nuts	1 oz.	180	6
▤ Mixed Nuts, deluxe	1 oz.	180	6
Peanuts Honey Roasted	1 oz.	170	7
Lightly Salted	1 oz.	170	5

FISHER® (Fisher Nut Co.)

Almonds, raw	1 oz.	170	6
▤ Cashews, dry, honey or oil roasted, salted (average)	1 oz.	160	8
Mixed Nuts, dry or oil roasted, salted (average)	1 oz.	170	6
Peanuts, dry, honey or oil roasted (average)	1 oz.	155	5
Pistachios, shelled, roasted, salted	1 oz.	170	7
Nut Toppings, oil roasted, salted	1 oz.	160	7
Sunflower Seeds, shelled, dry or oil roasted, salted (average)	1 oz.	170	5
▤ Walnuts, English, raw (average)	1 oz.	180	5

FRITO-LAY'S® (Frito-Lay, Inc.)

▤ Cashews	1 oz.	170	9
Peanuts Dry Roasted	1 ⅛ oz.	190	7
Salted in Shell	1 oz.	160	6
Salted Peanuts	1 oz.	170	6
▤ Sunflower Kernels	1 oz.	180	5
Sunflower Seeds	1 oz.	170	4

† For occasional use   ** Not recommended for use

PROTEIN (gm)	FAT (gm)	SAT. FAT (gm)	CHOLES-TEROL (mg)	SODIUM (mg)	EXCHANGES
6	14	—	0	90	1 meat, 2 fat
5	13	—	0	130	½ starch, 1 meat, 1½ fat
5	16	—	0	130	1 meat, 2 fat
4	17	—	0	130	½ starch, ½ meat, 2½ fat
7	13	—	0	130	½ fruit, 1 meat, 1½ fat
7	15	—	0	90	1 meat, 2 fat
6	15	3	0	0	1 meat, 2 fat
5	13	3	0	90-110	½ starch, ½ meat, 2½ fat
6	16	2	0	50-125	1 meat, 2 fat
7	14	2	0	65-210	1 meat, 2 fat
5	14	2	0	85	1 meat, 2 fat
6	14	2	0	115	1 meat, 2 fat
6	16	2	0	170-200	1 meat, 2 fat
4	18	2	0	0	1 meat, 2½ fat
4	14	—	—	115	½ meat, 2½ fat
7	16	—	—	300	1 meat, 2 fat
7	14	—	—	265	1 meat, 2 fat
6	15	—	—	170	1 meat, 2 fat
5	17	—	—	170	1 meat, 2½ fat
8	16	—	—	50	1 meat, 2 fat

* Not available   ▊ More than 2 fat exchanges   ♣ Moderate to high sugar content

Products	SERVING SIZE	CALORIES	CARBO-HYDRATE (gm)
HAIN® (PET, Inc.)			
Nut Butters			
Almond, raw	2 Tbsp.	190	3
Cashew, raw	2 Tbsp.	190	8
Toasted Almond	2 Tbsp.	210	3
Toasted Cashew	2 Tbsp.	190	8
PARKERS FARM (Parkers Farm, Inc.)			
Peanut Butter, no sugar added	2 Tbsp.	210	5
PLANTERS® (Nabisco Brands, Inc.)			
Mixed Nuts			
Lightly Salted	1 oz.	180	6
Select Mix	1 oz.	170	7
Peanuts			
Cocktail	1 oz.	170	5
Dry Roasted	1 oz.	160	6
Dry Roasted, lite	1 oz.	135	8
Honey Roasted	1 oz.	160	7
Sweet•N•Crunchy™	1 oz.	140	15
Unsalted	1 oz.	170	5

PASTA/PASTA SIDE DISHES

BETTY CROCKER® SUDDENLY SALADS® (General Mills, Inc.)

Pasta Salads (as prepared)			
Caesar	½ cup	170	20
Classic Pasta	½ cup	160	23
Creamy Macaroni	½ cup	200	21
Italian Pasta	½ cup	150	20
Pasta Primavera	½ cup	190	20
Ranch and Bacon	½ cup	210	22
Tortellini Italiano	½ cup	160	21
BIRDS EYE FOR ONE® (General Foods Corp.)			
Cheese Tortellini in Tomato Sauce	5.5 oz.	210	31

† For occasional use   ** Not recommended for use

PROTEIN (gm)	FAT (gm)	SAT. FAT (gm)	CHOLES-TEROL (mg)	SODIUM (mg)	EXCHANGES
8	18	2	0	5	1 meat, 2½ fat
6	15	3	0	5	1 meat, 2 fat
8	19	2	0	5	1 meat, 3 fat
6	16	3	0	5	1 meat, 2 fat
8	17	—	0	112	1 high fat meat, 2 fat
5	16	2	0	80	1 meat, 2 fat
5	14	2	0	100	1 meat, 2 fat
7	14	2	0	110	1 meat, 2 fat
7	14	2	0	250	1 meat, 2 fat
9	9	2	0	270	1 meat, 1 fat
7	13	2	0	90	1 meat, 1½ fat
4	7	1	0	20	1 fruit, ½ meat, 1 fat†
7	15	2	0	0	1 meat, 2 fat
4	8	—	—	450	1½ starch, 1½ fat
4	6	—	—	530	1½ starch, 1 fat
4	10	—	—	280	1½ starch, 2 fat
5	6	—	—	380	1½ starch, 1 fat
4	10	—	—	340	1½ starch, 2 fat
6	11	—	—	320	1½ starch, 2 fat
4	7	—	—	450	1½ starch, 1 fat
11	5	—	30	500	2 starch, 1 lean meat

* Not available   ▯ More than 2 fat exchanges   ♣ Moderate to high sugar content

Products	SERVING SIZE	CALORIES	CARBO-HYDRATE (gm)
COUNTRY RECIPE™ (Uncle Ben's Foods)			
Pasta Salads (as prepared)			
Bacon Vinaigrette Pasta Salad	⅛ recipe	140	24
Creamy Dijon Salad	⅛ recipe	190	24
Creamy Italian Pasta Salad	⅛ recipe	160	22
Ranch Pasta Salad	⅛ recipe	140	19
CREAMETTE® (The Creamette Co.)			
Egg Noodles	2 oz. uncooked (1 cup cooked)	220	40
Macaroni, Spaghetti, Miscellaneous Pasta	2 oz. uncooked (1 cup cooked)	210	41
GOLDEN GRAIN® (Quaker Oats Company)			
Noodle Roni® (as prepared)			
Chicken & Mushroom	½ cup	160	25
Creamy Garlic	½ cup	300	29
Fettuccini	½ cup	300	29
Herb & Butter	½ cup	160	19
Parmesano	½ cup	240	23
Romanoff	½ cup	240	28
Stroganoff	½ cup	350	37
GREEN GIANT® (The Pillsbury Company)			
One Serving Side Dish			
Cheese Tortellini Marinara	5.5 oz.	260	37
Macaroni and Cheese	5.75 oz.	230	28
Pasta Marinara	6 oz.	180	29
Pasta Parmesan with Sweet Peas	5.5 oz.	170	24
Pasta Accents®			
Creamy Cheddar	½ cup	100	12

PROTEIN (gm)	FAT (gm)	SAT. FAT (gm)	CHOLES-TEROL (mg)	SODIUM (mg)	EXCHANGES
4	4	—	—	210	1½ starch, ½ fat
4	10	—	—	310	1½ starch, 1½ fat
4	7	—	—	340	1½ starch, 1 fat
4	5	—	—	300	1 starch, 1 fat
8	3	1	70	3	2½ starch
8	2	0-1	0-65	0-65	2½ starch
6	4	1	19	550	1½ starch, 1 fat
7	17	2	29	630	2 starch, 3 fat
7	18	2	27	560	2 starch, 3 fat
5	7	1	19	290	1 starch, 1½ fat
7	13	1	19	470	1½ starch, 2½ fat
8	11	2	23	730	2 starch, 2 fat
11	17	2	42	1190	2½ starch, 3½ fat
8	9	—	—	930	2 starch, 1 veg., 1½ fat
9	9	4	25	590	2 starch, 1½ fat
5	5	<1	0	730	2 starch, ½ fat
9	5	2	10	510	1½ starch, ½ meat, ½ fat
4	5	2	5	310	½ starch, 1 veg., 1 fat

* Not available   ▌ More than 2 fat exchanges   🛒 Moderate to high sugar content

Products	SERVING SIZE	CALORIES	CARBO-HYDRATE (gm)
Garden Herb	½ cup	80	11
Garlic Seasoning	½ cup	110	13
Pasta Primavera	½ cup	110	13
LIPTON® (Thomas J. Lipton, Inc.)			
Noodles and Sauce, all varieties (as prepared) (average)	½ cup	135	23
Pasta and Sauce, all varieties (as prepared) (average)	½ cup	143	26
Pasta Salad, all varieties (as prepared) (average)	½ cup	120	23
MINUTE® (General Foods Corp.)			
Microwave Dishes (as prepared with butter)			
Chicken Flavored Noodles	½ cup	160	23
Noodles Alfredo	½ cup	170	23
Parmesan Noodles	½ cup	170	23
Pasta and Cheddar Cheese	½ cup	160	20
RESER'S® (Reser's Fine Foods, Inc.)			
Macaroni/Pasta Salads			
Italian Pasta	3.5 oz.	120	11
⊟ Macaroni	3.5 oz.	225	19
Macaroni with Shrimp	3.5 oz.	196	18
Mexicale	3.5 oz.	196	23
⊟ Pesto Pasta	3.5 oz.	267	16
STOUFFERS® (Stouffer Foods Corp.)			
⊟ Fettucini Alfredo	½ of 10 oz. package	270	17
Noodles Romanoff	⅓ of 12 oz. package	170	15

PROTEIN (gm)	FAT (gm)	SAT. FAT (gm)	CHOLES- TEROL (mg)	SODIUM (mg)	EXCHANGES
3	3	<1	5	220	½ starch, 1 veg., ½ fat
3	5	2	5	280	½ starch, 1 veg., 1 fat
5	5	2	5	180	½ starch, 1 veg., 1 fat
5	3	—	—	346- 643	1½ starch, ½ fat
5	2	—	—	356- 545	2 starch
5	1	—	—	118- 342	1½ starch
6	5	—	35	570	1½ starch, 1 fat
6	7	—	45	670	1½ starch, 1½ fat
6	6	—	45	470	1½ starch, 1 fat
6	7	—	15	520	1 starch, 1½ fat
1	7	—	<1	511	1 starch, 1 fat
3	15	—	10	450	1 starch, 3 fat
4	12	—	8	370	1 starch, ½ lean meat, 2 fat
4	10	—	6	610	1½ starch, 2 fat
4	21	—	17	630	1 starch, 4 fat
8	19	—	—	560	1 starch, 1 meat, 2½ fat
7	9	—	—	840	1 starch, 1 meat, ½ fat

* Not available   ⯅ More than 2 fat exchanges   ⛟ Moderate to high sugar content

Products	SERVING SIZE	CALORIES	CARBO-HYDRATE (gm)
▤ Pasta Carbonara	9 ¾ oz.	620	34
Pasta Casino	9¼ oz.	300	44
▤ Pasta Mexicali	10 oz.	490	36
▤ Pasta Oriental	9⅞ oz.	300	35
▤ Pasta Primavera	10⅝ oz.	270	13

PIZZA, PIZZA MIXES

BANQUET® ZAP™ (ConAgra® Frozen Foods Co.)

Cheese French Bread Pizza	4.5 oz.	310	41
Deluxe French Bread Pizza	4.8 oz.	330	39
Pepperoni French Bread Pizza	4.5 oz.	350	36

CELESTE® (Quaker Oats Co.)

Cheese Pizza	¼ of 17 ¾ oz. pizza	330	28
▤ Deluxe Pizza	¼ of 22¼ oz. pizza	390	32
Pepperoni Pizza	¼ of 19 oz. pizza	370	30
Sausage Pizza	¼ of 20 oz. pizza	390	31
Suprema	¼ of 23 oz. pizza	410	31
▤ Pizza-For-One Cheese	1 pizza (6½ oz.)	500	48
▤ Deluxe	1 pizza (8¼ oz.)	600	54

† For occasional use   ** Not recommended for use

PROTEIN (gm)	FAT (gm)	SAT. FAT (gm)	CHOLES- TEROL (mg)	SODIUM (mg)	EXCHANGES
19	45	—	—	780	2 starch, 2 high fat meat, 5½ fat
9	10	—	—	800	3 starch, 1½ fat
16	31	—	—	1020	2½ starch, 1½ high fat meat, 3½ fat
8	14	—	—	760	2 starch, 3 fat
7	21	—	—	580	1 starch, 1 high fat meat, 2½ fat
14	10	—	35	800	2½ starch, 1 meat, 1 fat
13	13	—	25	890	2½ starch, 1 meat, 1½ fat
15	16	—	40	1040	2½ starch, 1 meat, 2 fat
14	17	7	20	770	2 starch, 1½ meat, 1½ fat
15	22	7	20	910	2 starch, 1½ meat, 2½ fat
15	21	7	15	1000	2 starch, 1½ high fat meat, 1½ fat
16	22	7	15	910	2 starch, 1½ high fat meat, 2 fat
16	24	7	15	1090	2 starch, 1½ high fat meat, 2 fat
21	24	11	40	1070	3 starch, 2 meat, 2½ fat
22	32	10	20	1370	3½ starch, 2 meat, 4 fat

* Not available   ▤ More than 2 fat exchanges   ▼ Moderate to high sugar content

Products	SERVING SIZE	CALORIES	CARBO-HYDRATE (gm)
▤ Pepperoni	1 pizza (6 ¾ oz.)	540	50
▤ Sausage	1 pizza (7½ oz.)	580	50
▤ Sausage and Mushroom	1 pizza (8½ oz.)	600	54
▤ Suprema	1 pizza (9 oz.)	690	58
FOX DELUXE® (The Pillsbury Company)			
Pizza, all varieties (average)	½ of 7 oz. pizza	250	26
JACK'S ORIGINAL® (Jack's Frozen Pizza Inc.)			
Cheese Pizza	¼ of 15 oz. pizza	276	20
Cheese Deluxe, super	¼ of 28.75 oz. pizza	500	30
Super Cheese, 9"	¼ of 10 oz. pizza	156	10
Super Cheese	¼ of 19 oz. pizza	258	24
Cheese and Hamburger, 9"	¼ of 9.5 oz. pizza	196	10
Cheese and Hamburger	¼ of 17 oz. pizza	334	22
Cheese and Hamburger, Super	¼ of 22.5 oz. pizza	444	24
Cheese and Pepperoni, 9"	¼ of 9 oz. pizza	188	10
Cheese and Pepperoni	¼ of 17 oz. pizza	324	24
Cheese and Pepperoni, super	¼ of 21.5 oz. pizza	414	26

† For occasional use   ** Not recommended for use

PROTEIN (gm)	FAT (gm)	SAT. FAT (gm)	CHOLES-TEROL (mg)	SODIUM (mg)	EXCHANGES
20	29	9	20	1360	3 starch, 1½ high fat meat, 3 fat
23	32	10	20	1370	3 starch, 2 high fat meat, 3 fat
24	32	11	20	1180	3½ starch, 2 high fat meat, 2½ fat
26	39	12	20	1610	4 starch, 2 high fat meat, 4 fat
9	13	—	—	600-700	2 starch, ½ high fat meat, 1 fat
14	12	—	—	742	1½ starch, 1½ meat, 1 fat
28	28	—	—	1440	2 starch, 3½ meat, 2 fat
8	6	—	—	332	1 starch, 1 meat
12	14	—	—	648	1½ starch, 1 meat, 1½ fat
8	10	—	—	386	1 starch, 1 meat, 1 fat
16	20	—	—	740	1½ starch, 1½ meat, 2 fat
26	22	—	—	1322	1½ starch, 3 meat, 2 fat
8	6	—	—	444	1 starch, 1 meat
16	16	—	—	874	1½ starch, 2 high fat meat
24	18	—	—	1382	2 starch, 2 high fat meat

* Not available ᴴ More than 2 fat exchanges 🍬 Moderate to high sugar content

Products	SERVING SIZE	CALORIES	CARBO-HYDRATE (gm)
Cheese and Sausage, 9"	¼ of 9.5 oz. pizza	196	11
Cheese and Sausage	¼ of 17 oz. pizza	334	22
Cheese and Sausage	¼ of 22 oz. pizza	414	26
Cheese and Sausage, 14"	¼ of 28 oz. pizza	560	33
Cheese and Sausage, super, 9"	¼ of 12 oz. pizza	248	12
Cheese and Sausage, super	¼ of 22.5 oz. pizza	44	24
Combination, 9"	¼ of 10.5 oz. pizza	226	11
Cheese Combination, super	¼ of 25 oz. pizza	514	26
Mexican Style, 9"	¼ of 13.5 oz. pizza	180	16
Sausage and Mushroom, 9"	¼ of 10.5 oz. pizza	202	10
Sausage and Mushroom	¼ of 20 oz. pizza	344	24
Sausage and Pepperoni Combination	¼ of 19 oz. pizza	392	22
Special Deluxe, 9"	¼ of 14.5 oz. pizza	242	16
Special Deluxe	¼ of 24 oz. pizza	392	28

PROTEIN (gm)	FAT (gm)	SAT. FAT (gm)	CHOLES- TEROL (mg)	SODIUM (mg)	EXCHANGES
9	10	—	—	386	1 starch, 1 high fat meat
16	20	—	—	742	1½ starch, 2 high fat meat, ½ fat
18	24	—	—	862	2 starch, 2 high fat meat, 1 fat
27	32	—	—	1278	2 starch, 3 high fat meat, 1½ fat
14	12	—	—	630	1 starch, 2 meat
26	22	—	—	1322	1½ starch, 3 meat, 1 fat
10	12	—	—	480	1 starch, 1 high fat meat, 1 fat
28	26	—	—	1518	2 starch, 3 high fat meat
6	14	—	—	218	1 starch, ½ meat, 1½ fat
8	10	—	—	390	1 starch, 1 high fat meat
16	22	—	—	764	1½ starch, 2 meat, 1½ fat
18	22	—	—	942	1½ starch, 2 high fat meat, 1½ fat
10	16	—	—	524	1 starch, 1½ high fat meat, ½ fat
18	26	—	—	914	2 starch, 2 high fat meat, 1½ fat

* Not available   ▤ More than 2 fat exchanges   🛒 Moderate to high sugar content

Products	SERVING SIZE	CALORIES	CARBO-HYDRATE (gm)
Vegetable Harvest	¼ of 23 oz. pizza	344	36
JENO'S® (The Pillsbury Company)			
Crisp 'n Tasty			
Canadian Style Bacon	½ of 7.7 oz. pizza	250	27
Cheese	½ of 7.4 oz. pizza	270	28
Combination Sausage and Pepperoni	½ of 7.8 oz. pizza	300	27
Hamburger	½ of 8.1 oz. pizza	290	28
Pepperoni	½ of 7.6 oz. pizza	280	27
Sausage	½ of 7.8 oz. pizza	300	28
4-Pack Pizzas			
Cheese	1 pizza	160	17
Combination	1 pizza	180	17
Hamburger	1 pizza	180	17
Pepperoni	1 pizza	170	17
Sausage	1 pizza	180	17
Microwave Pizza Rolls, all varieties (average)	6 rolls	240	23
Pizza Rolls, all varieties (average)	6 rolls	240	22

† For occasional use   ** Not recommended for use

PROTEIN (gm)	FAT (gm)	SAT. FAT (gm)	CHOLES-TEROL (mg)	SODIUM (mg)	EXCHANGES
20	14	—	—	578	2½ starch, 2 meat
11	11	—	—	880	2 starch, 1 meat, ½ fat
10	14	—	—	770	2 starch, 1 high fat meat, ½ fat
10	16	—	—	840	2 starch, 1 high fat meat, 1 fat
12	15	—	—	810	2 starch, 1 high fat meat, 1 fat
10	15	—	—	760	2 starch, 1 high fat meat, 1 fat
11	16	—	—	850	2 starch, 1 high fat meat, 1 fat
6	8	—	—	460	1 starch, ½ meat, 1 fat
7	9	—	—	470	1 starch, 1 high fat meat
8	9	—	—	500	1 starch, 1 high fat meat
6	9	—	—	460	1 starch, ½ high fat meat, 1 fat
7	9	—	—	460	1 starch, 1 high fat meat
8	13	—	—	440	1½ starch, 1 high fat meat, ½ fat
8	13	—	—	280-390	1½ starch, 1 high fat meat, ½ fat

* Not available   ▌ More than 2 fat exchanges   ☕ Moderate to high sugar content

Products	SERVING SIZE	CALORIES	CARBO-HYDRATE (gm)
MR. P'S (The Pillsbury Co.)			
Pizza, all varieties (average)	½ of 7 oz. pizza	250	26
PAPPALO'S® (The Pillsbury Co.)			
French Bread Pizzas			
Cheese	½ of 5.7 oz. pizza	180	20
Combination	½ of 6.5 oz. pizza	215	21
Pepperoni	½ of 6 oz. pizza	205	21
Sausage	½ of 6.3 oz. pizza	205	21
Pan Pizza			
Combination	⅙ of 26.5 oz. pizza	340	34
Hamburger	⅙ of 26.3 oz. pizza	310	34
Pepperoni	⅙ of 25.2 oz. pizza	330	34
Sausage	⅙ of 26.3 oz. pizza	360	34
Thin Crust			
Combination	⅙ of 22 oz. pizza	260	29
Hamburger	⅙ of 22 oz. pizza	240	28
Pepperoni	⅙ of 22 oz. pizza	270	28
Sausage	⅙ of 22 oz. pizza	250	28

† For occasional use   ** Not recommended for use

PROTEIN (gm)	FAT (gm)	SAT. FAT (gm)	CHOLES-TEROL (mg)	SODIUM (mg)	EXCHANGES
10	13	—	—	600-700	2 starch, 1 high fat meat, ½ fat
8	8	—	—	415	1 starch, 1 high fat meat
10	11	—	—	560	1½ starch, 1 high fat meat
8	10	—	—	565	1½ starch, 1 high fat meat
9	9	—	—	500	1½ starch, 1 high fat meat
17	15	—	—	700	2 starch, 1½ high fat meat, ½ fat
17	12	—	—	580	2 starch, 1½ high fat meat
16	14	—	—	710	2 starch, 1½ high fat meat, ½ fat
14	18	—	—	550	2 starch, 1½ high fat meat, 1 fat
13	10	—	—	590	2 starch, 1 high fat meat
14	8	—	—	470	2 starch, 1 meat
13	11	—	—	600	2 starch, 1 high fat meat
12	9	—	—	490	2 starch, 1 high fat meat

* Not available   ▤ More than 2 fat exchanges   ♥ Moderate to high sugar content

Products	SERVING SIZE	CALORIES	CARBO-HYDRATE (gm)
PEPPERIDGE FARM® (Campbell Soup Co.)			
Croissant Crust Pizza			
Cheese	1 pizza	490	46
Deluxe	1 pizza	520	52
Hamburger	1 pizza	510	43
Pepperoni	1 pizza	490	50
Sausage	1 pizza	540	53
PILLSBURY® (The Pillsbury Co.)			
Microwave French Bread Pizza			
Cheese	½ of 5.7 oz. pizza	185	20
Pepperoni	½ of 6 oz. pizza	215	23
Sausage	½ of 6.3 oz. pizza	205	24
Sausage and Pepperoni Combination	½ of 6.5 oz. pizza	225	24
Microwave Pizza			
Cheese	½ of 7.1 oz. pizza	240	28
Combination	½ of 9 oz. pizza	310	29
Pepperoni	½ of 8.5 oz. pizza	800	29
Sausage	½ of 8.75 oz. pizza	280	29

† For occasional use   ** Not recommended for use

PROTEIN (gm)	FAT (gm)	SAT. FAT (gm)	CHOLES-TEROL (mg)	SODIUM (mg)	EXCHANGES
17	27	—	—	730	3 starch, 1½ meat, 3½ fat
19	27	—	—	940	3½ starch, 1½ meat, 3 fat
23	27	—	—	1040	3 starch, 2 meat, 3 fat
17	25	—	—	810	3 starch, 1½ meat, 3 fat
18	29	—	—	910	3½ starch, 1½ high fat meat, 2½ fat
9	8	—	—	340	1 starch, 1 meat, ½ fat
10	10	—	—	470	1½ starch, 1 high fat meat
9	8	—	—	430	1½ starch, 1 high fat meat
10	11	—	—	950	1½ starch, 1 high fat meat
10	10	—	—	540	2 starch, 1 meat, ½ fat
14	15	—	—	780	2 starch, 1½ high fat meat
13	15	—	—	790	2 starch, 1½ high fat meat
13	13	—	—	680	2 starch, 1½ high fat meat

* Not available   ▌ More than 2 fat exchanges   🛒 Moderate to high sugar content

Products	SERVING SIZE	CALORIES	CARBO-HYDRATE (gm)
STOUFFER'S® (Stouffer Foods Corp.)			
French Bread Pizzas			
Canadian Style Bacon	½ of 11⅝ oz. pizza	360	41
Cheese	½ of 10⅜ oz. pizza	340	41
Deluxe	½ of 12⅛ oz. pizza	430	41
Double Cheese	½ of 11 ¾ oz. pizza	410	43
Hamburger	½ of 12¼ oz. pizza	410	40
Pepperoni	½ of 11¼ oz. pizza	410	41
Pepperoni and Mushroom	½ of 12¼ oz. pizza	430	40
Sausage	½ of 12 oz. pizza	420	41
Sausage and Mushroom	½ of 12½ oz. pizza	410	42
Sausage and Pepperoni	½ of 12½ oz. pizza	450	40
Vegetable Deluxe	½ of 12 ¾ oz. pizza	420	41
Traditional Pizzas			
Cheese	½ of 8½ oz. pizza	320	32
Deluxe	½ of 10 oz. pizza	370	33

PROTEIN (gm)	FAT (gm)	SAT. FAT (gm)	CHOLES-TEROL (mg)	SODIUM (mg)	EXCHANGES
18	14	—	—	960	3 starch, 1½ meat
15	13	—	—	840	3 starch, 1 meat, 1½ fat
18	21	—	—	1130	3 starch, 1½ high fat meat, 1 fat
19	18	—	—	950	3 starch, 1½ high fat meat, ½ fat
19	19	—	—	1010	2½ starch, 2 high fat meat
17	20	—	—	1120	3 starch, 1½ high fat meat, ½ fat
18	22	—	—	1340	2½ starch, 1½ high fat meat, 1½ fat
18	20	—	—	1110	3 starch, 1½ high fat meat, ½ fat
17	19	—	—	1050	3 starch, 1½ high fat meat, ½ fat
20	23	—	—	1350	2½ starch, 2 high fat meat, 1 fat
18	20	—	—	830	3 starch, 1½ high fat meat, ½ fat
14	15	—	—	640	2 starch, 1 high fat meat, 1 fat
16	19	—	—	590	2 starch, 1½ high fat meat, 1 fat

Products	SERVING SIZE	CALORIES	CARBO-HYDRATE (gm)
Extra Cheese	½ of 9¼ oz. pizza	370	33
Pepperoni	½ of 8 ¾ oz. pizza	350	34
Sausage	½ of 9⅛ oz. pizza	360	32
Sausage and Pepperoni	½ of 9⅛ oz. pizza	380	33

STOUFFER'S® LEAN CUISINE® (Stouffer Foods Corp.)
French Bread Pizzas

Cheese	5 ⅛ oz.	310	40
Deluxe	6 ⅛ oz.	350	40
Extra Cheese	5½ oz.	350	39
Pepperoni	5¼ oz.	340	40
Sausage	6 oz.	350	40

TOMBSTONE® (Tombstone® Pizza)
Light Pizza

Pepperoni	4 oz. (½ pkg.)	270	30
Sausage	4.1 oz. (½ pkg.)	250	29
Sausage & Pepperoni	4.1 oz. (½ pkg.)	260	30
Vegetable	4.4 oz. (½ pkg.)	250	29

Thin Crust Pizza

☐ Pepperoni	¼ of 12 inch pizza	526	36
☐ Singles, Pepperoni	1 single (½ pkg.)	612	42

TONY'S MICROWAVE KIDSTUFF (Tony's Pizza Service)
Pizza

☐ Cheeseburger	1 pizza (5 oz.)	560	55

PROTEIN (gm)	FAT (gm)	SAT. FAT (gm)	CHOLES- TEROL (mg)	SODIUM (mg)	EXCHANGES
17	19	—	—	720	2 starch, 1½ high fat meat, 1 fat
15	18	—	—	820	2 starch, 1 high fat meat, 2 fat
16	18	—	—	830	2 starch, 1½ high fat meat, 1 fat
16	21	—	—	860	2 starch, 1½ high fat meat, 1½ fat
16	10	3	15	750	2½ starch, 1½ meat
20	12	3	35	990	2½ starch, 2 meat
21	12	4	20	850	2½ starch, 2 meat
18	12	4	30	970	2½ starch, 2 meat
23	11	3	45	960	2½ starch, 2 meat
15	10	4	20	680	2 starch, 1½ meat
14	8	3	10	570	2 starch, 1½ lean meat
14	10	4	15	610	2 starch, 1½ meat
15	8	3	10	500	2 starch, 1½ lean meat
24	32	12	64	1256	2½ starch, 3 meat, 2½ fat
29	37	14	74	1457	3 starch, 3 meat, 3½ fat
19	29	—	55	1110	3½ starch, 2 meat, 3 fat

* Not available   ▤ More than 2 fat exchanges   🛒 Moderate to high sugar content

Products	SERVING SIZE	CALORIES	CARBO-HYDRATE (gm)
▤ Extra Cheesy	1 pizza (5 oz.)	490	53
▤ Pepperoni	1 pizza (5 oz.)	520	52
▤ Sausage	1 pizza (5 oz.)	500	53
▤ Taco Style	1 pizza (5 oz.)	490	49
TOTINO'S® (The Pillsbury Co.)			
Microwave Pizza (small)			
Cheese	3.9 oz.	250	34
Pepperoni	4 oz.	280	34
Sausage	4.2 oz.	320	33
Sausage/Pepperoni Combination	4.2 oz.	310	31
My Classic™ Deluxe Pizza			
Cheese	⅙ of 19 oz. pizza	210	23
Combination	⅙ of 22.5 oz. pizza	270	23
Pepperoni	⅙ of 21 oz. pizza	260	23
Pan Pizza			
Pepperoni	⅙ of 25 oz. pizza	330	34
Sausage	⅙ of 26 oz. pizza	320	34
Sausage and Pepperoni Combination	⅙ of 27 oz. pizza	340	34
Three Cheese	⅙ of 24 oz. pizza	290	33

† For occasional use

PROTEIN (gm)	FAT (gm)	SAT. FAT (gm)	CHOLES-TEROL (mg)	SODIUM (mg)	EXCHANGES
15	25	—	20	870	3½ starch, 1½ meat, 2½ fat
18	27	—	30	1070	3½ starch, 2 meat, 2½ fat
17	24	—	25	910	3½ starch, 1½ meat, 2½ fat
16	25	—	35	860	3 starch, 1½ meat, 3 fat
10	8	—	—	760	2 starch, 1 high fat meat
10	12	—	—	880	2 starch, 1 high fat meat, ½ fat
11	16	—	—	870	2 starch, 1 high fat meat, 1½ fat
12	15	—	—	970	2 starch, 1 high fat meat, 1 fat
10	9	—	—	420	1½ starch, 1 high fat meat
13	14	—	—	630	1½ starch, 1 high fat meat, 1 fat
12	13	—	—	630	1½ starch, 1 high fat meat, 1 fat
16	14	—	—	730	2 starch, 1½ high fat meat, ½ fat
16	13	—	—	630	2 starch, 1½ high fat meat
16	15	—	—	720	2 starch, 1½ high fat meat, ½ fat
15	10	—	—	510	2 starch, 1½ meat, ½ fat

sugar content

Products	SERVING SIZE	CALORIES	CARBO-HYDRATE (gm)
Party Pizza			
Bacon	¼ of 10 oz. pizza	185	18
Canadian Bacon	¼ of 10 oz. pizza	155	18
Cheese	¼ of 10 oz. pizza	170	17
Combination	¼ of 10 oz. pizza	190	18
Hamburger	¼ of 10 oz. pizza	185	18
Mexican Style	¼ of 10 oz. pizza	190	18
Pepperoni	¼ of 10 oz. pizza	185	18
Sausage	¼ of 10 oz. pizza	195	18
Vegetable	¼ of 10 oz. pizza	150	18
Pizza Slices			
Cheese	⅙ package	170	20
Combination	⅙ package	200	20
Pepperoni	⅙ package	190	20
Sausage	⅙ package	200	20

WEIGHT WATCHERS® (H. J. Heinz Co.)

French Bread Pizza			
Deluxe	6.12 oz.	330	27
Pepperoni	5.25 oz.	320	27

PROTEIN (gm)	FAT (gm)	SAT. FAT (gm)	CHOLES-TEROL (mg)	SODIUM (mg)	EXCHANGES
6	10	—	—	515	1 starch, ½ meat, 1½ fat
7	7	—	—	675	1 starch, ½ meat, 1 fat
7	9	—	—	500	1 starch, ½ meat, 1½ fat
7	11	—	—	615	1 starch, ½ meat, 1½ fat
8	10	—	—	530	1 starch, 1 meat, 1 fat
7	11	—	—	485	1 starch, ½ meat, 1½ fat
7	10	—	—	655	1 starch, ½ meat, 1½ fat
7	11	—	—	590	1 starch, ½ meat, 1½ fat
6	7	—	—	455	1 starch, ½ meat, 1 fat
7	7	—	—	350	1 starch, 1 meat, ½ fat
7	10	—	—	630	1 starch, 1 meat, 1 fat
7	9	—	—	530	1 starch, 1 meat, 1 fat
7	10	—	—	540	1 starch, 1 meat, 1 fat
20	12	3	30	800	2 starch, 2 meat
21	11	3	30	830	2 starch, 2 meat

* Not available   ▤ More than 2 fat exchanges   🛒 Moderate to high sugar content

Products	SERVING SIZE	CALORIES	CARBO-HYDRATE (gm)
Pizza			
Cheese	5.86 oz.	300	37
Deluxe Combination	7.15 oz.	330	35
Pepperoni	7.15 oz.	330	35
Sausage	6.25 oz.	320	35

POTATOES/POTATO SIDE DISHES

BETTY CROCKER® (General Mills Inc.)

Potato Medleys (as prepared)

Broccoli Au Gratin	½ cup	140	23
Cheddar Cheese with Mushrooms	½ cup	140	23
Scalloped with Broccoli	½ cup	140	21
Scalloped with Green Beans and Mushrooms	½ cup	140	21

Potato Mixes (as prepared)

Au Gratin	½ cup	150	21
Cheddar 'N Bacon	½ cup	140	21
Cheesy Scalloped	½ cup	140	20
Hash Browns with Onions	½ cup	160	24
Julienne	½ cup	130	18
Potato Buds®	½ cup (⅓ cup flakes)	130	17
Scalloped	½ cup	140	20
Scalloped & Ham	½ cup	160	22
Smokey Cheddar	½ cup	140	21
Sour Cream 'N Chive	½ cup	140	21

† For occasional use   ** Not recommended for use

PROTEIN (gm)	FAT (gm)	SAT. FAT (gm)	CHOLES- TEROL (mg)	SODIUM (mg)	EXCHANGES
22	7	3	35	630	2½ starch, 1½ lean meat
26	10	3	25	650	2 starch, 2 meat
26	10	3	25	650	2 starch, 3 lean meat
24	10	2	35	630	2 starch, 3 lean meat
3	4	—	—	590	1½ starch, ½ fat
3	4	—	—	530	1½ starch, ½ fat
3	5	—	—	500	1½ starch, ½ fat
3	5	—	—	500	1½ starch, ½ fat
4	5	—	—	600	1½ starch, ½ fat
3	5	—	—	520	1½ starch, ½ fat
3	5	—	—	560	1½ starch, ½ fat
2	6	—	—	460	1½ starch, ½ fat
3	5	—	—	580	1 starch, 1 fat
3	6	—	—	360	1 starch, 1 fat
3	6	—	—	580	1 starch, 1 fat
4	6	—	—	540	1½ starch, 1 fat
3	5	—	—	700	1½ starch, ½ fat
3	5	—	—	520	1½ starch, 1 fat

* Not available   **▌** More than 2 fat exchanges   🛒 Moderate to high sugar content

Products	SERVING SIZE	CALORIES	CARBO-HYDRATE (gm)
Twice Baked Potatoes (as prepared) Bacon and Cheddar	½ cup	210	21
Herbed Butter	½ serving	220	20
Mild Cheddar with Onion	½ cup	190	19
Sour Cream & Chive	½ cup	200	19
BIRDS EYE FOR ONE® (General Foods Corp.) Potatoes Au Gratin	5.5 oz.	240	24
FRENCH'S® (The Pillsbury Co.) Potato Mixes (as prepared) Au Gratin Potatoes, Tangy	½ cup	130	20
Creamy Italian Scalloped Potatoes	½ cup	120	19
Cheddar and Bacon Casserole	½ cup	130	18
Scalloped Potatoes, Crispy Top with Savory Onion	½ cup	140	20
Scalloped Potatoes, Real Cheese	½ cup	140	19
Sour Cream and Chives Potatoes	½ cup	150	19
Stroganoff Potatoes, Creamy	½ cup	130	20
Scalloped Potatoes, Real Cheese	½ cup	140	19
Sour Cream and Chives Potatoes	½ cup	150	19
Stroganoff Potatoes, Creamy	½ cup	130	20
FRENCH'S® IDAHO® (The Pillsbury Co.) Dinner Potato Pancakes (as prepared)	Three 3" cakes	90	16
Mashed Potatoes (as prepared)	½ cup	130	16

PROTEIN (gm)	FAT (gm)	SAT. FAT (gm)	CHOLES-TEROL (mg)	SODIUM (mg)	EXCHANGES
6	11	—	—	600	1½ starch, 2 fat
5	13	—	—	540	1½ starch, 2 fat
5	11	—	—	640	1 starch, 2 fat
5	11	—	—	570	1 starch, 2 fat
8	13	—	30	590	1½ starch, ½ meat, 2 fat
4	5	—	—	460	1 starch, 1 fat
4	3	—	—	430	1 starch, ½ fat
4	5	—	—	390	1 starch, 1 fat
3	5	—	—	430	1 starch, 1 fat
4	5	—	—	380	1 starch, 1 fat
3	7	—	—	550	1 starch, 1½ fat
3	4	—	—	520	1 starch, 1 fat
4	5	—	—	380	1 starch, 1 fat
3	7	—	—	550	1 starch, 1½ fat
3	4	—	—	520	1 starch, 1 fat
3	2	—	—	420	1 starch
2	6	—	—	320	1 starch, 1 fat

* Not available   ▌ More than 2 fat exchanges   🛒 Moderate to high sugar content

Products	SERVING SIZE	CALORIES	CARBO-HYDRATE (gm)
Spuds Mashed Potatoes (as prepared)	½ cup	140	17
GREEN GIANT® (The Pillsbury Co.)			
One Serving Vegetable Potatoes and Broccoli Cheese Sauce	5.5 oz.	130	19
Potatoes Au Gratin	5.5 oz.	200	20
HUNGRY JACK® (The Pillsbury Co.)			
Mashed Potato Flakes (as prepared)	½ cup	140	17
ORE-IDA® (Ore-Ida Foods, Inc.)			
Cheddar Browns™ (as purchased)	3 oz.	80	14
Cottage Fries (as purchased)	3 oz.	120	19
Country Style Dinner Fries® (as purchased)	3 oz.	110	19
Crispers!® (as purchased)	3 oz.	230	25
Crispy Crowns!® (as purchased)	3 oz.	170	20
Deep Fries, Crinkle and Regular Cut (as purchased) (average)	3 oz.	160	22
Golden Crinkles® (as purchased)	3 oz.	120	20
Golden Fries® (as purchased)	3 oz.	120	20
Golden Patties® (as purchased)	2½ oz.	140	15
Hash Browns, Shredded (as purchased)	3 oz.	70	16
Hash Browns, Southern Style (as purchased)	3 oz.	70	16
Hash Browns, Toaster (as prepared)	1.75 oz.	100	12
Home Style Potato Wedges™ (as purchased)	3 oz.	110	19

PROTEIN (gm)	FAT (gm)	SAT. FAT (gm)	CHOLES- TEROL (mg)	SODIUM (mg)	EXCHANGES
3	7	—	—	380	1 starch, 1½ fat
4	5	<1	5	720	½ starch, 2 veg., 1 fat
7	10	4	20	560	1 starch, ½ meat, 1 fat
3	7	—	—	380	1 starch, 1 fat
3	2	1	5	420	1 starch
2	5	<1	0	25	1 starch, 1 fat
2	5	<1	0	15	1 starch, ½ fat
2	15	3	0	535	1½ starch, 2½ fat
1	10	2	0	500	1 starch, 2 fat
2	7	1	0	20-30	1½ starch, 1 fat
2	4	<1	0	25	1 starch, 1 fat
2	4	<1	0	30	1 starch, 1 fat
1	8	1	0	280	1 starch, 1½ fat
1	<1	<1	0	40	1 starch
1	<1	<1	0	30	1 starch
1	6	3	5	285	1 starch, 1 fat
1	3	<1	0	25	1 starch, ½ fat

* Not available   ▉ More than 2 fat exchanges   🛒 Moderate to high sugar content

Products	SERVING SIZE	CALORIES	CARBO-HYDRATE (gm)
Lites Crinkle Cuts (as purchased)	3 oz.	90	16
Microwave (as purchased) Crinkle Cuts	3½ oz.	180	26
Hash Browns	2 oz.	120	13
Tater Tots®	4 oz.	200	29
Pixie Crinkles® (as purchased)	3 oz.	140	21
Potatoes O'Brien (as purchased)	3 oz.	60	14
Shoestrings (as purchased)	3 oz.	150	22
Tater Tots®, plain and varieties (as purchased) (average)	3 oz.	150	20
Twice Baked Potatoes (as purchased) Butter Flavor	5 oz.	210	28
Cheddar Cheese	5 oz.	230	27
Sour Cream & Chives	5 oz.	210	27
RESER'S® (Reser's Fine Foods, Inc.)			
Potato Salad Country Style	3.5 oz.	182	17
Gourmet	3.5 oz.	155	16
Mustard	3.5 oz.	140	16
Potato	3.5 oz.	180	19
STOUFFER'S (Stouffer's Foods Corp.)			
Potatoes au Gratin	⅓ of 11½ oz. pkg.	110	10
Scalloped Potatoes	⅓ of 11½ oz. pkg.	90	11

PROTEIN (gm)	FAT (gm)	SAT. FAT (gm)	CHOLES-TEROL (mg)	SODIUM (mg)	EXCHANGES
1	2	<1	0	35	1 starch
2	8	1	0	35	1½ starch, 1½ fat
1	7	1	0	180	1 starch, 1 fat
2	9	2	0	695	2 starch, 1½ fat
2	5	<1	0	45	1½ starch, 1 fat
1	<1	<1	0	25	1 starch
2	6	1	0	25	1½ starch, 1 fat
2	7	1	0	535-795	1 starch, 1½ fat
4	9	2	0	395	2 starch, 1½ fat
3	11	3	5	635	2 starch, 2 fat
3	9	2	0	370	2 starch, 1½ fat
2	12	—	40	360	1 starch, 2 fat
2	9	—	42	520	1 starch, 1½ fat
2	7	—	5	585	1 starch, 1½ fat
1	10	—	7	339	1 starch, 2 fat
4	6	—	—	510	1 starch, 1 fat
3	4	—	—	420	1 starch, ½ fat

* Not available ▊ More than 2 fat exchanges ♨ Moderate to high sugar content

Products	SERVING SIZE	CALORIES	CARBO-HYDRATE (gm)

RICE/RICE SIDE DISHES

BIRDS EYE FOR ONE® (General Foods Corp.)

Rice and Broccoli Au Gratin	5.75 oz.	180	27

CHUN KING® (ConAgra® Frozen Foods Co.)

Side Dishes

Fried Rice with Chicken	8 oz.	260	41
Fried Rice with Pork	8 oz.	270	44

FEATHERWEIGHT® (Sandoz Nutrition)

Spanish Rice, Low Sodium	7½ oz.	140	30

GOLDEN GRAIN® (Quaker Oat Company)

Rice-A-Roni® (as prepared)

Beef Flavor	½ cup	170	27
Chicken Flavor	½ cup	170	28
Chicken & Mushroom	½ cup	180	26
Chicken & Vegetables	½ cup	150	25
Fried Rice with Almonds	½ cup	140	22
Herb & Butter	½ cup	140	22
Rice Pilaf	½ cup	190	30
Risotto	½ cup	200	32
Spanish Rice	½ cup	150	25
Stroganoff	½ cup	190	27
Yellow Rice	½ cup	250	43

Rice-A-Roni Savory Classics™ (as prepared)

Broccoli Au Gratin	½ cup	180	21

† For occasional use   ** Not recommended for use

PROTEIN (gm)	FAT (gm)	SAT. FAT (gm)	CHOLES- TEROL (mg)	SODIUM (mg)	EXCHANGES
6	6	—	5	430	1 starch, 2 veg., 1 fat
14	4	—	—	1460	3 starch, 1 lean meat
10	6	—	—	1210	3 starch, ½ meat
4	0	—	0	32	2 starch
4	5	0˙	1	930	2 starch, ½ fat
4	5	0	1	780	2 starch, ½ fat
4	7	0	1	860	1 starch, 1 fat
4	4	0	—	800	1½ starch, ½ fat
3	5	0	0	710	1½ starch, ½ fat
3	4	0	1	800	1½ starch, ½ fat
5	6	0	1	1220	2 starch, 1 fat
4	6	0	2	1130	2 starch, 1 fat
4	4	0	1	1090	1½ starch, ½ fat
4	8	1	5	830	1½ starch, 1½ fat
5	7	0	1	1180	2½ starch, 1 fat
4	9	1	4	440	1½ starch, 1½ fat

* Not available   ▤ More than 2 fat exchanges   ♨ Moderate to high sugar content

Products	SERVING SIZE	CALORIES	CARBO-HYDRATE (gm)
Cauliflower Au Gratin	½ cup	170	23
Chicken Florentine	½ cup	130	22
Creamy Parmesan & Herbs	½ cup	170	22
Garden Pilaf	½ cup	140	23
Green Bean Almondine	½ cup	210	22
Spring Vegetable & Cheese	½ cup	170	23
Zesty Cheddar	½ cup	180	25

GREEN GIANT® (The Pillsbury Company)
One Serving Side Dishes

Rice 'n Broccoli in Cheese Sauce	4.5 oz.	180	25
Rice, Peas and Mushrooms with Sauce	5.5 oz.	130	27
Rice Originals® Italian Blend Rice and Spinach in Cheese Sauce	½ cup	140	22
Rice and Broccoli in Flavored Cheese Sauce	½ cup	120	18
Rice Medley	½ cup	100	19
Rice Pilaf	½ cup	110	21
White and Wild Rice	½ cup	130	24

LIPTON® (Thomas J. Lipton, Inc.)

Long Grain and Wild Rice and Sauce, all varieties (as prepared) (average)	½ cup	123	26
Rice and Sauce, all varieties (as prepared) (average)	½ cup	130	25

MINUTE® (General Foods Corporation)

Regular (as prepared without salt or butter)	½ cup	90	20

† For occasional use   ** Not recommended for use

PROTEIN (gm)	FAT (gm)	SAT. FAT (gm)	CHOLES- TEROL (mg)	SODIUM (mg)	EXCHANGES
4	7	1	5	410	1½ starch, 1 fat
4	4	0	1	910	1½ starch, ½ fat
5	7	1	7	470	1½ starch, 1½ fat
4	4	0	1	1000	1½ starch, ½ fat
5	11	1	6	490	1½ starch, 2 fat
4	7	1	6	420	1½ starch, 1 fat
5	7	1	6	580	2 starch, 1 fat
6	6	2	5	550	1 starch, 2 veg., 1 fat
4	2	<1	5	410	1½ starch
4	4	3	10	400	1½ starch, 1 fat
3	4	1	5	510	1 starch, 1 fat
3	1	<1	5	310	1 starch
2	1	<1	2	530	1½ starch
3	2	<1	0	540	1½ starch
4	0	—	0	325-530	1½ starch
3	1	—	0-4	403-596	1½ starch
2	0	—	0	0	1 starch

* Not available   ▯ More than 2 fat exchanges   🛒 Moderate to high sugar content

Products	SERVING SIZE	CALORIES	CARBO-HYDRATE (gm)
Microwave Dishes (as prepared with butter)			
Beef Flavored	½ cup	160	28
Cheddar Cheese, Broccoli and Rice	½ cup	160	26
Chicken Flavored	½ cup	150	27
French Style Rice Pilaf	½ cup	120	24
Rice Mix			
Drumstick Rice (as prepared with butter, salted)	½ cup	150	25
Fried Rice (as prepared with oil)	½ cup	160	25
Long Grain and Wild Rice (as prepared with butter, salted)	½ cup	150	25
Rib Roast Rice (as prepared with butter, salted)	½ cup	150	25
SUZI WAN™ (Uncle Ben's Foods)			
Rice Dishes (as prepared without butter)			
Chicken & Broccoli	½ cup	120	23
Chicken & Vegetables	½ cup	120	24
Sweet 'n Sour Rice	½ cup	130	28
Teriyaki Rice	½ cup	120	25
Three Flavor Rice	½ cup	120	24
UNCLE BEN'S® (Uncle Ben's Foods)			
Boil-In-Bag Rice (as packaged)	½ cup	90	20
Brown and Wild Rice (as prepared)			
Without butter	½ cup	130	27
With butter	½ cup	150	27

PROTEIN (gm)	FAT (gm)	SAT. FAT (gm)	CHOLES-TEROL (mg)	SODIUM (mg)	EXCHANGES
4	3	—	10	560	2 starch
4	4	—	10	520	2 starch
3	3	—	5	660	2 starch
2	2	—	5	410	1½ starch
3	4	—	10	690	1½ starch, ½ fat
3	5	—	0	550	1½ starch, ½ fat
3	4	—	10	570	1½ starch, ½ fat
3	4	—	10	720	1½ starch, ½/fat
4	1	—	—	500	1½ starch
3	1	—	—	550	1½ starch
3	1	—	—	460	1½ starch, ½ fruit
3	1	—	—	690	1½ starch
4	1	—	—	570	1½ starch
2	<1	—	—	10	1 starch
4	1	—	—	500	1½ starch
4	4	—	—	520	1½ starch, ½ fat

* Not available   ▌ More than 2 fat exchanges   🛒 Moderate to high sugar content

Products	SERVING SIZE	CALORIES	CARBO-HYDRATE (gm)
Chicken Stock Sauce (as prepared)			
Without butter	½ cup	140	27
With butter and salt	½ cup	160	27
Converted® Brand Rice (as prepared)			
Without butter and salt	⅓ cup	60	14
With butter and salt	⅓ cup	70	14
Natural Whole Grain Rice (as prepared)			
Without butter and salt	⅓ cup	65	14
With butter and salt	⅓ cup	75	14
Original Recipe (as prepared)			
Without butter	⅓ cup	75	17
With butter and salt	⅓ cup	90	17
Original Fast-Cooking Recipe (as prepared)			
Without butter	⅓ cup	75	16
With butter and salt	⅓ cup	98	16
Rice In An Instant™ (as prepared)			
Without butter and salt	⅓ cup	60	14
With butter and salt	⅓ cup	65	14

UNCLE BEN'S COUNTRY INN™ (Uncle Ben's Foods)

Products	SERVING SIZE	CALORIES	CARBO-HYDRATE (gm)
Rice Dishes (as packaged without butter)			
Broccoli Rice Au Gratin	½ cup	130	22
Chicken Rice Royale	½ cup	120	25
Chicken Stock Rice	½ cup	130	25
Herbed Rice Au Gratin	½ cup	140	25
Rice Alfredo	½ cup	140	24
Rice Florentine	½ cup	140	24
Vegetable Pilaf	½ cup	120	25
Vegetable Rice Medley	½ cup	140	28

PROTEIN (gm)	FAT (gm)	SAT. FAT (gm)	CHOLES-TEROL (mg)	SODIUM (mg)	EXCHANGES
4	2	—	—	650	2 starch
4	5	—	—	680	2 starch, ½ fat
1	<1	—	—	0	1 starch
1	1	—	—	205	1 starch
2	1	—	—	0	1 starch
3	2	—	—	210	1 starch
2	<1	—	—	416	1 starch
2	2	—	—	390	1 starch
2	<1	—	—	308	1 starch
2	3	—	—	338	1 starch, ½ fat
2	<1	—	—	155	1 starch
2	1	—	—	185	1 starch
4	3	—	—	300	1½ starch
4	1	—	—	560	1½ starch
4	1	—	—	560	1½ starch
4	3	—	—	450	1½ starch, ½ fat
4	4	—	—	560	1½ starch, ½ fat
4	3	—	—	480	1½ starch, ½ fat
3	1	—	—	280	1½ starch,
4	1	—	—	390	2 starch

* Not available   ▊ More than 2 fat exchanges   ☕ Moderate to high sugar content

Products	SERVING SIZE	CALORIES	CARBO-HYDRATE (gm)
10 Minute Recipes (as prepared without butter)			
Asparagus Au Gratin	½ cup	130	22
Broccoli Almondine	½ cup	130	23
Cauliflower Au Gratin	½ cup	130	23
Chicken & Cheese Risotto	½ cup	120	23
Creamy Chicken & Mushroom	½ cup	140	25
Creamy Mushroom & Wild Rice	½ cup	140	24
Green Bean & Almondine Casserole	½ cup	120	23
Homestyle Chicken & Vegetables	½ cup	140	25

SALAD DRESSINGS/ SANDWICH SPREADS

CATALINA® (Kraft, Inc.)

French Dressing	2 tsp.	47	3
Reduced Calorie Dressing	1 Tbsp.	16	3

ESTEE® (Estee Corp.)

Mayonnaise, dietetic	1 Tbsp.	50	0
Salad Dressings, dietetic, all varieties (average)	1 Tbsp.	2-8	0-2

FEATHERWEIGHT® (Sandoz Nutrition)

Mayonnaise, reduced calorie	1 Tbsp.	30	3
Soyamaise, low sodium	1 Tbsp.	100	0
Low Calorie, Low Sodium Dressings (average) Creamy Cucumber French Herb Italian New Bleu Red Wine/Vinegar	1 Tbsp.	2-18	1-3

PROTEIN (gm)	FAT (gm)	SAT. FAT (gm)	CHOLES-TEROL (mg)	SODIUM (mg)	EXCHANGES
4	3	—	—	310	1½ starch
4	2	—	—	600	1½ starch
4	3	—	—	570	1½ starch
3	2	—	—	410	1½ starch
3	3	—	—	510	1½ starch, ½ fat
3	3	—	—	310	1½ starch, ½ fat
3	2	—	—	370	1½ starch
4	3	—	—	490	1½ starch, ½ fat
0	4	1	0	121	1 fat
0	0	0	0	120	Free
0	5	1	0	80	1 fat
0	<1	<1	0-5	10-100	Free
0	2	—	10	40	½ fat
0	11	—	5	3	2 fat
0	0	—	0	5-125	Free

* Not available   ▤ More than 2 fat exchanges   ♛ Moderate to high sugar content

Products	SERVING SIZE	CALORIES	CARBO-HYDRATE (gm)
Thousand Island Zesty Tomato Garden Herb	1 Tbsp.	2-18	1-3
Creamy Dijon Italian Cheese Oriental Spice	2 tsp.	13-17	1

GOOD SEASONS® (General Foods Corp.)

Salad Dressing Mix all varieties except Lite and No Oil (as prepared) (average)	1 Tbsp.	70	1
Lite, all varieties (average)	2 tsp.	50	2
No Oil Italian (as prepared)	2 Tbsp.	12	4

HAIN® (PET, Inc.)

Mayonnaise Canola, reduced calorie	1 Tbsp.	60	2
Cold Processed	1 tsp.	37	0
Eggless, no salt added	1 tsp.	37	0
Light, low sodium	2 tsp.	40	1
Real, no salt added	1 tsp.	37	0
Safflower	1 tsp.	37	0
No Oil Dry Dressing Mixes, all varieties (as prepared) (average)	1 Tbsp.	7	1
Pourable Dressings (average) Creamy Caesar Creamy French Dijon Vinaigrette Honey & Sesame Italian Cheese Viniagrette Thousand Island	1 Tbsp.	56	0
Creamy Italian Cucumber Dill	2 tsp.	50	0

† For occasional use   ** Not recommended for use

PROTEIN (gm)	FAT (gm)	SAT. FAT (gm)	CHOLES- TEROL (mg)	SODIUM (mg)	EXCHANGES
0	0	—	0	5-125	Free
0	1	—	0	70-80	Free
0	8	—	0	110-190	1½ fat
0	6	—	0	115-135	1 fat
0	0	—	0	30	Free
0	5	0	0	160	1 fat
0	4	<1	0	23	1 fat
0	4	<1	0	5	1 fat
0	4	1	10	95	1 fat
0	4	<1	2	0	1 fat
0	4	<1	2	23	1 fat
1	0	—	—	140-340	Free
0	6	—	<5	15-220	1 fat
0	5	—	<4	17-220	1 fat

* Not available　　🗄 More than 2 fat exchanges　　🛒 Moderate to high sugar content

Products	SERVING SIZE	CALORIES	CARBO-HYDRATE (gm)
Garlic & Sour Cream			
Old Fashioned Buttermilk			
Savory Herb	2 tsp.	50	0
Swiss Cheese			
Traditional Italian			

HELLMAN'S® (Best Foods, CPC International, Inc.)

Mayonnaise, real	1 tsp.	35	0
Mayonnaise, reduced calorie	1 Tbsp.	50	1
Mayonnaise, reduced calorie, cholesterol free	1 Tbsp.	50	1
Sandwich Spread	1 Tbsp.	50	2

HENRI'S® (Henri's Food Products Co., Inc.)

Light, reduced calorie dressings, all varieties (average)	1 Tbsp.	30	4

HIDDEN VALLEY RANCH® (The Clorox Company)

Bottled Salad Dressing, all varieties (average)	1 Tbsp.	70	0
	2 tsp.	47	0
Take Heart™ Dressings, all varieties (average)	1 Tbsp.	12-20	2-5
Salad Dressing Mix, all varieties (as prepared with milk and mayonnaise) (average)	1 Tbsp.	58	1
Salad Dressing Mix, all varieties (as prepared with milk and salad dressing) (average)	1 Tbsp.	35	2
Salad Dressing Mix, reduced calorie (as prepared) (average)	1 Tbsp.	35	2

KRAFT® (Kraft, Inc.)

Free® Non-fat Mayonnaise	1 Tbsp.	12	3
Mayonnaise	1 tsp.	35	0
Mayonnaise, Light, reduced calorie	1 Tbsp.	50	1

† For occasional use   ** Not recommended for use

PROTEIN (gm)	FAT (gm)	SAT. FAT (gm)	CHOLES-TEROL (mg)	SODIUM (mg)	EXCHANGES
0	5	—	<4	17-220	1 fat
0	4	1	3	27	1 fat
0	5	1	10	120	1 fat
0	5	1	0	80	1 fat
0	5	1	5	170	1 fat
<1	2	0	0	135-230	½ fat
0	7	—	10	55-160	1½ fat
0	5	—	7	37-107	1 fat
0	0-1	0	0	115-140	Free
0	6	—	5	95-135	1 fat
0	3	—	3	99-119	½ fat
0	3	—	4	120	½ fat
0	0	0	0	190	Free
0	4	1	2	23	1 fat
0	5	1	<5	95	1 fat

* Not available   ▤ More than 2 fat exchanges   🛒 Moderate to high sugar content

Products	SERVING SIZE	CALORIES	CARBO-HYDRATE (gm)
Salad Dressing, Pourable Free® Non-fat Dressings, all varieties (average)	1 Tbsp.	15	3
Reduced Calorie Dressings, all varieties, (average)	1 Tbsp.	30	2
Salad Dressings all varieties (except Oil-Free Italian) (average)	2 tsp.	45	1
Oil-Free Italian Dressing	1 Tbsp.	4	1
Sandwich Spread	1 Tbsp.	50	3
MIRACLE WHIP® (Kraft, Inc.)			
Free® Fat Free Cholesterol Free, Non-fat Dressing	1 Tbsp.	20	5
Salad Dressing	2 tsp.	46	1
Salad Dressing, Light, reduced calorie	1 Tbsp.	45	2
NUTRADIET® (S and W Fine Foods)			
Salad Dressing, reduced calorie, all varieties (average)	2 tsp.	2-17	0-2
RANCHER'S CHOICE® (Kraft, Inc.)			
Creamy Dressing	1½ tsp.	45	1
Creamy Dressing, reduced calorie	1 Tbsp.	30	1
ROKA® (Kraft, Inc.)			
Blue Cheese Dressing	2 tsp.	40	1
Blue Cheese Dressing, reduced calorie	1 Tbsp.	16	1
SEVEN SEAS® (Seven Seas Foods, Inc.)			
Free® Non-fat Dressings, all varieties (average)	1 Tbsp.	4-6	1
WEIGHT WATCHERS® (H. J. Heinz Co.)			
Mayonnaise, reduced calorie	1 Tbsp.	50	1
Mayonnaise, reduced calorie, cholesterol free	1 Tbsp.	50	1

† For occasional use   ** Not recommended for use

PROTEIN (gm)	FAT (gm)	SAT. FAT (gm)	CHOLES-TEROL (mg)	SODIUM (mg)	EXCHANGES
0	0	0	0	120-210	Free
0	2	0	0-5	120-240	½ fat
0	5	1	0	80-180	1 fat
0	0	0	0	220	Free
0	5	1	5	95	1 fat
0	0	0	0	210	Free
0	5	1	3	57	1 fat
0	4	1	5	95	1 fat
0	0-2	—	—	70-130	Free
0	5	<1	<5	70	1 fat
0	3	0	<5	160	½ fat
1	4	1	7	114	1 fat
1	1	1	<5	280	Free
0	0	0	0	190-220	Free
—	5	1	5	100	1 fat
—	5	1	0	90	1 fat

* Not available   ᓯ More than 2 fat exchanges   ♔ Moderate to high sugar content

Products	SERVING SIZE	CALORIES	CARBO-HYDRATE (gm)
Mayonnaise, reduced calorie,	1 Tbsp.	50	1
low sodium	1 Tbsp.	50	1
Salad Dressings			
Caesar	1 Tbsp.	4	1
Creamy Cucumber	1 Tbsp.	18	4
Creamy Italian	1 Tbsp.	12	3
Creamy Peppercorn	1 Tbsp.	8	2
Creamy Ranch	2 tsp.	17	4
French Style	1 Tbsp.	10	2
Italian Style	1 Tbsp.	6	1
Thousand Island/Russian	1 Tbsp.	50	2
Tomato Vinaigrette	1 Tbsp.	8	2
Single-Serve Dressings			
Caesar	1 pouch (¾ oz.)	6	1
Creamy Ranch	1 pouch (¾ oz.)	35	8
Italian Style	1 pouch (¾ oz.)	9	2
Tartar Sauce, reduced calorie	1 Tbsp.	35	3
Whipped Salad Dressing	1 Tbsp.	45	3
WESTERN® (Western® Dressing, Inc.)			
French	1 Tbsp.	70	5
French, lite	1½ tsp.	18	3
Italian	1 Tbsp.	60	1
Italian, lite	1½ tsp.	15	1
Ranch	1½ tsp.	40	1
1000 Island	1 Tbsp.	60	3
WISHBONE® (Thomas J. Lipton, Inc.)			
Regular Dressings			
Blue Cheese, chunky	2 tsp.	49	1
Caesar	2 tsp.	51	1
French			
Deluxe	2 tsp.	40	2
Red	2 tsp.	43	3
Sweet 'n Spicy	2 tsp.	41	2

† For occasional use   ** Not recommended for use

PROTEIN (gm)	FAT (gm)	SAT. FAT (gm)	CHOLES- TEROL (mg)	SODIUM (mg)	EXCHANGES
—	5	1	0	90	1 fat
—	5	1	5	45	1 fat
—	—	—	—	200	Free
—	—	—	—	85	Free
—	—	—	—	85	Free
—	—	—	—	85	Free
—	—	—	—	65	Free
—	—	—	—	170	Free
—	—	—	—	310	Free
—	5	1	5	80	1 fat
—	—	—	—	150	Free
—	—	—	—	270	Free
—	—	—	—	140	½ fruit
—	—	—	—	430	Free
—	3	1	5	80	½ fat
—	4	1	—	100	1 fat
0	5	1	0	105	1 fat
0	<1	—	—	63	Free
0	6	1	0	150	1 fat
0	1	<1	—	65	Free
0	4	<1	<5	68	1 fat
0	5	1	—	140	1 fat
0	5	1	1	99	1 fat
0	5	1	1	165	1 fat
0	4	—	0	49	1 fat
0	4	1	0	113	1 fat
0	4	1	0	104	1 fat

* Not available   🅱 More than 2 fat exchanges   🛒 Moderate to high sugar content

Products	SERVING SIZE	CALORIES	CARBO-HYDRATE (gm)
Italian			
Blended	1 Tbsp.	36	1
Classic Olive Oil	1 Tbsp.	28	2
Creamy	1 Tbsp.	54	1
Standard	1 Tbsp.	45	1
Robusto	2 tsp.	47	1
with Cheese	1½ tsp.	43	1
Ranch	1½ tsp.	42	1
Russian	1 Tbsp.	46	6
Thousand Island	2 tsp.	40	2
Vinaigrette			
Classic Dijon	1 Tbsp.	57	1
Olive Oil	1 Tbsp.	28	2
Red Wine	1 Tbsp.	50	4
Lite Dressings			
Blue Cheese, chunky	1 Tbsp.	40	2
French			
French Style	1 Tbsp.	30	2
Red French	1 Tbsp.	17	3
Sweet 'n Spicy	1 Tbsp.	18	3
Italian			
Creamy	1 Tbsp.	26	2
Standard	1 Tbsp.	7	1
Ranch	1 Tbsp.	42	3
Russian	2 tsp.	15	3
Thousand Island	2 tsp.	24	1
Vinaigrette			
Classic Dijon	1 Tbsp.	30	1
Olive Oil	1 Tbsp.	16	2

PROTEIN (gm)	FAT (gm)	SAT. FAT (gm)	CHOLES- TEROL (mg)	SODIUM (mg)	EXCHANGES
0	4	1	0	199	1 fat
0	2	0	0	116	½ fat
0	6	1	0	149	1 fat
0	5	1	0	281	1 fat
0	5	—	0	172	1 fat
0	5	<1	0	89	1 fat
0	4	—	2	78	1 fat
0	3	0	0	147	1 fat
0	4	0	3	108	1 fat
0	6	1	0	159	1 fat
0	2	0	0	116	½ fat
0	4	1	0	216	1 fat
0	4	1	1	197	1 fat
0	3	—	0	67	½ fat
0	0	—	0	155	Free
0	1	—	0	110	Free
0	2	0	0	148	½ fat
0	0	—	0	212	Free
0	4	1	5	149	1 fat
0	0	0	0	84	Free
0	2	0	6	66	½ fat
0	3	—	0	176	½ fat
0	1	0	0	111	Free

* Not available   ▯ More than 2 fat exchanges   ♣ Moderate to high sugar content

SAUCES, SEASONINGS, GRAVIES

PASTA SAUCES, PIZZA SAUCES, AND SPAGHETTI SAUCES

Products	SERVING SIZE	CALORIES	CARBO-HYDRATE (gm)
CLASSICO® (Borden®)			
Pasta Sauces			
D'Abruzzi (Beef & Pork)	½ cup	110	<1
Di Bologna (Beef & Vegetable)	½ cup	70	5
Di Napoli (Tomato & Basil)	½ cup	70	7
Di Roma Arrabbiata (Spicy Red Pepper)	½ cup	60	5
Di Sicilia (Red Olives & Mushrooms)	½ cup	60	7
Di Veneto (Shrimp & Crab) ½ cup	60	6	2
ESTEE® (Estee Corp.)			
Spaghetti Sauce, Dietetic	½ cup	60	9
FEATHERWEIGHT® (Sandoz Nutrition)			
Spaghetti Sauce, Low Sodium, all varieties (average)	½ cup	60	11
HAIN® (PET, Inc.)			
Pasta Sauces and Mixes (as prepared)			
Creamy Parmesan	¼ pkg.	150	22
Creamy Swiss	⅕ pkg.	170	26
Fettuccini Alfredo	¼ pkg.	180	27
Italian Herb	⅕ pkg.	110	17
Marinara	¼ pkg.	120	23
Primavera	¼ pkg.	140	20
Tangy Cheddar	¼ pkg.	180	24

PROTEIN (gm)	FAT (gm)	SAT. FAT (gm)	CHOLES-TEROL (mg)	SODIUM (mg)	EXCHANGES
3	11	—	10	600	½ meat, 1½ fat
2	4	—	10	320	1 veg., 1 fat
1	4	—	<1	330	1 veg., 1 fat
1	3	—	<1	300	1 veg., ½ fat
1	2	—	<1	420	1 veg., ½ fat
3	—		20	340	1 veg., ½ fat
2	1	<1	0	30	2 veg. **or** ½ starch
2	1	—	0	310	2 veg. **or** ½ starch
8	3	—	10	400	1½ starch, ½ fat
6	4	—	—	360	2 starch, ½ fat
5	4	—	—	420	2 starch, ½ fat
4	2	—	—	160	1 starch, ½ fat
5	1	—	<5	390	1½ starch
7	4	—	10	430	1 starch, 1 lean meat
6	6	—	—	350	1½ starch, 1 fat

* Not available   ▤ More than 2 fat exchanges   🛒 Moderate to high sugar content

Products	SERVING SIZE	CALORIES	CARBO-HYDRATE (gm)
PREGO® (Campbell Soup Co.)			
Spaghetti Sauce			
Plain, Meat Flavor or with Mushrooms (average)	½ cup	150	21
No Salt Added	½ cup	100	11
Al Fresco Garden, all varieties (average)	½ cup	100	12
Extra Chunky Mushroom and Tomato Varieties (average)	½ cup	110	13
Extra Chunky Sausage and Green Pepper	½ cup	170	19
Marinara	½ cup	100	11
PRINCE® (Borden®)			
Chunky Homestyle spaghetti Sauce, all varieties (average)	½ cup	75	11
Marinara Sauce	½ cup	50	8
Traditional Spaghetti Sauce, all varieties (average)	½ cup	75	8
PROGRESSO® (PET, Inc.)			
Authentic Pasta Sauces			
Alfredo	½ cup	340	6
Bolognese	½ cup	150	12
Creamy Primavera	½ cup	190	8
Creamy Romano	½ cup	220	7
Marinara	½ cup	110	10
Seafood	½ cup	190	5
Seafood Alfredo	½ cup	220	5
Sicilian	½ cup	30	2

PROTEIN (gm)	FAT (gm)	SAT. FAT (gm)	CHOLES- TEROL (mg)	SODIUM (mg)	EXCHANGES
2	6	—	—	630	1½ starch 1 fat
2	6	—	—	35	2 veg., 1 fat
1	6	—	—	560	2 veg., 1 fat
2	6	—	—	440-540	2 veg., 1 fat **or** 1 starch, 1 fat
3	9	—	—	480	1 starch, 2 fat **or** 3 veg., 2 fat
1	5	—	—	500	2 veg., 1 fat
2	2	—	<1	480-560	1 starch **or** 2 veg., ½ fat
1	1	—	<1	500	½ starch **or** 2 veg.
2	3	—	<1	510-520	½ starch, ½ fat **or** 2 veg., ½ fat
13	30	19	95	1080	½ starch, 1½ meat, 4 fat **or** ½ skim milk, 1 meat, 5 fat
10	8	2	20	520	1 starch, 1 meat
5	17	10	54	410	½ starch, ½ meat, 2½ fat
7	19	10	64	490	½ starch, 1 meat, 2½ fat
4	6	2	4	470	2 veg., 1 fat **or** ½ starch, 1 fat
7	15	9	95	570	1 veg., 1 meat, 2 fat
8	19	12	89	360	1 veg., 1 meat, 2½ fat
0	3	0	0	660	½ fat

* Not available   ☱ More than 2 fat exchanges   🛒 Moderate to high sugar content

Products	SERVING SIZE	CALORIES	CARBO-HYDRATE (gm)
White Clam	½ cup	130	4
Marinara Sauce	½ cup	90	9
Spaghetti Sauce, all varieties (average)	½ cup	110	13
RAGU® (Chesebrough-Ponds, Inc.)			
Pizza Quick Sauce Regular, all varieties (average)	¼ cup	47	4
Spaghetti Sauces Original, all varieties (average)	½ cup	80	9
Chunky Gardenstyle, all varieties (average)	½ cup	70	10
Fresh Italian, all varieties (average)	½ cup	90	13
Homestyle, all varieties (average)	½ cup	50	6
Thick & Hearty all varieties (average)	½ cup	100	15
WEIGHT WATCHERS® (H. J. Heinz Co.) Spaghetti Sauce, all varieties (average)	⅓ cup	45	9

SAUCES, SEASONINGS, GRAVY MIXES
Estee® (Estee Corp.)

Barbecue Sauce, Dietetic	1 Tbsp.	18	3
Catsup, Dietetic	2 Tbsp.	12	2
Steak Sauce, Dietetic	½ oz.	15	3
FEATHERWEIGHT® (Sandoz Nutrition)			
Barbecue Sauce, Low Calorie, Low Sodium	1 Tbsp.	14	3

PROTEIN (gm)	FAT (gm)	SAT. FAT (gm)	CHOLES- TEROL (mg)	SODIUM (mg)	EXCHANGES
8	9	1	19	460	1 meat, 1 fat **or** ½ skim milk, ½ meat, 1 fat
4	5	1	1	520	½ starch, 1 fat **or** 2 veg., 1 fat
3	5	1	2-5	630-660	1 starch, 1 fat **or** 3 veg., 1 fat
1	3	—	0	440	1 veg., ½ fat
2	4	—	0	740	2 veg., ½ fat **or** ½ starch, ½ fat
2	3	—	—	440	2 veg., ½ fat **or** ½ starch, ½ fat
2	3	—	—	490	1 starch, ½ fat
2	2	—	0	390	1 veg., ½ fat
2	3	—	0	460	1 starch, ½ fat
1	1	—	—	430-440	½ starch **or** 2 veg.
<1	<1	<1	0	5	Free
0	0	0	0	40	Free
<1	<1	<1	0	10	Free
0	0	—	0	90	Free

* Not available   ▤ More than 2 fat exchanges   🛒 Moderate to high sugar content

Products	SERVING SIZE	CALORIES	CARBO-HYDRATE (gm)
Catsup, Low Sodium	1 Tbsp.	6	1
Chili Sauce, Low Sodium	1 Tbsp.	8	2

FRANCO-AMERICAN® (Campbell Soup Co.)
Canned Gravies

Au Jus Gravy	¼ cup (2 oz.)	10	2
Beef Gravy	2 Tbsp. (1 oz.)	13	2
Beef Gravy with Onion	2 Tbsp. (1 oz.)	13	2
Chicken Gravy	¼ cup (2 oz.)	50	3
Chicken Giblet Gravy	2 Tbsp. (1 oz.)	15	2
Mushroom Gravy	2 Tbsp. (1 oz.)	13	2
Pork Gravy	2 Tbsp. (1 oz.)	20	1
Turkey Gravy	2 Tbsp. (1 oz.)	15	2

HELLMAN'S® (Best Products, CPC International, Inc.)

Tartar Sauce	2 tsp.	47	0

K. C. MASTERPIECE® (The Clorox Company)

⬤ Barbecue Sauce, all varieties (average)	2 Tbsp.	60	14

KRAFT® (Kraft, Inc.)
All Natural Sauces

Alfredo	2 Tbsp. (1 oz.)	50	2
Bernaise Herb Butter	2 Tbsp. (1 oz.)	70	2
Cheddar Cheese	2 Tbsp. (1 oz.)	60	3
Hollandaise	2 Tbsp. (1 oz.)	80	3
Nacho Cheese	2 Tbsp. (1 oz.)	60	3
Triple Cheese	2 Tbsp. (1 oz.)	60	2

† For occasional use   ** Not recommended for use

PROTEIN (gm)	FAT (gm)	SAT. FAT (gm)	CHOLES- TEROL (mg)	SODIUM (mg)	EXCHANGES
0	0	—	0	5	Free
0	0	—	0	10	Free
0	0	—	—	330	Free
0	0	—	—	145	Free
0	0	—	—	170	Free
0	4	—	—	310	1 fat
0	1	—	—	150	Free
0	0	—	—	145	Free
0	2	—	—	175	Free
0	1	—	—	145	Free
0	5	1	3	147	1 fat
0	0	—	—	40-190	1 fruit†
2	4	—	15	170	1 fat
0	7	—	20	95	1½ fat
2	4	—	15	220	1 fat
1	7	—	20	180	1½ fat
2	4	—	15	220	1 fat
2	4	—	15	190	1 fat

* Not available   ▤ More than 2 fat exchanges   ☕ Moderate to high sugar content

Products	SERVING SIZE	CALORIES	CARBO-HYDRATE (gm)
☛ Barbecue Sauce, all varieties (except Thick 'n Spicy) (average)	2 Tbsp.	45	9
☛ Barbecue Sauce, Thick 'n Spicy, all varieties (average)	2 Tbsp.	55	12
MOLLY MC BUTTER® (Alberto-Culver USA, Inc.)			
Bacon Sprinkles	½ tsp.	4	1
Butter Sprinkles	½ tsp.	4	1
Cheese Sprinkles	½ tsp.	4	0
Sour Cream & Butter Sprinkles	½ tsp.	4	1
MRS. DASH® (Alberto-Culver USA, Inc.)			
Herb and Spice Blends			
Extra Spicy	1 tsp.	12	3
Garlic & Herb	1 tsp.	12	2
Lemon & Herb	1 tsp.	12	3
Low Pepper	1 tsp.	12	2
Original Blend	1 tsp.	12	2
Table Blend	1 tsp.	12	3
OCEAN SPRAY® (Ocean Spray Cranberries, Inc.)			
☛ Cranberry Sauce, jellied	¼ cup (2 oz.)	90	22
☛ Cranberry Sauce, whole berry	¼ cup (2 oz.)	90	22
☛ Cran-Fruit™ Sauce, all varieties (average)	¼ cup (2 oz.)	100	23
OLD EL PASO® (PET, Inc.)			
Enchilada Sauce, all varieties (average)	¼ cup	25	4
Jalapeno Relish	2 Tbsp.	16	4
Picante Salsa/Sauce, all varieties (average)	2 Tbsp.	8	2
Salsa, all varieties	2 Tbsp.	6	1
Taco Sauce, all varieties (average)	2 Tbsp.	12	3

† For occasional use   ** Not recommended for use

PROTEIN (gm)	FAT (gm)	SAT. FAT (gm)	CHOLES-TEROL (mg)	SODIUM (mg)	EXCHANGES
0	1	0	0	280-530	½ fruit†
0	1	0	0	300-510	1 fruit†
0	0	—	0	65	Free
0	0	—	0	90	Free
0	0	—	0	60	Free
0	0	—	0	65	Free
0	0	—	0	4	Free
0	0	—	0	2	Free
0	0	—	0	4	Free
0	0	—	0	4	Free
0	0	—	0	4	Free
0	0	—	0	4	Free
0	0	0	0	15	1½ fruit†
0	0	0	0	15	1½ fruit†
0	0	0	0	10-20	1½ fruit†
<1	1	—	0	250-400	1 veg.
1	0	0	0	100	Free
<1	<1	—	—	160-310	Free
<1	<1	0	0	135-270	Free
1	<1	—	0	130-300	Free

* Not available   ▌ More than 2 fat exchanges   🛒 Moderate to high sugar content

Products	SERVING SIZE	CALORIES	CARBO-HYDRATE (gm)
PILLSBURY® (The Pillsbury Co.)			
Gravy Mixes			
(as prepared)			
Brown	¼ cup	15	3
Chicken	2 Tbsp.	13	2
Home Style	¼ cup	15	3
PROGRESSO® (PET, Inc.)			
Clam Sauce, Red	½ cup	70	7
Clam Sauce, White	½ cup	110	9
Mixed Seafood Sauce	½ cup	110	12
Rock Lobster Sauce	½ cup	120	11
SAUCEWORKS® (Kraft, Inc.)			
Cocktail Sauce	1 Tbsp.	12	3
Horseradish Sauce	1 Tbsp.	50	2
Hot Mustard Sauce	1 Tbsp.	35	3
♥ Sweet 'N Sour Sauce	2 Tbsp.	50	10
Tartar Sauce, all varieties (average)	2 tsp.	50	1
WESTERN® (Western Dressings, Inc.)			
Horseradish Sauce	1 Tbsp.	50	2
♥ Ham Glaze	2 Tbsp.	50	12
WOLF'S® (Quaker Oats Company)			
Chili Hot Dog Sauce	⅓ cup	80	8

SNACK FOODS

BERRY BEARS® (General Mills, Inc.)			
All flavors (average)	1 pouch	100	22
BUGLES® (General Mills, Inc.)			
All varieties (average)	1 oz.	155	17

PROTEIN (gm)	FAT (gm)	SAT. FAT (gm)	CHOLES-TEROL (mg)	SODIUM (mg)	EXCHANGES
<1	0	—	—	300	Free
<1	1	—	—	115	Free
<1	0	—	—	300	Free
5	3	—	—	560	½ starch, ½ meat
1	8	—	—	280	½ starch, 1½ fat
5	6	<1	11	445	1 starch, 1 fat
4	8	1	10	430	2 veg., 1½ fat **or** 1 starch, 1 fat
0	0	0	0	170	Free
0	5	1	5	105	1 fat
0	2	0	5	85	½ fat
0	0	0	0	100	1 fruit†
0	5	1	3	85-160	1 fat
0	4	1	10	105	1 fat
0	0	—	—	30	1 fruit†
4	4	—	—	400	½ starch, 1 fat
<1	<1	—	—	20	1½ fruit
2	8	—	—	250-290	1 starch, 1½ fat

* Not available   ▌More than 2 fat exchanges   🛒 Moderate to high sugar content

Products	SERVING SIZE	CALORIES	CARBO-HYDRATE (gm)
CHEERIOS-TO-GO™ (General Mills, Inc.)			
Apple Cinnamon Cheerios®	1 oz. pouch	110	22
Cheerios®	¾ oz. pouch	80	15
Honey Nut Cheerios®	1 oz. pouch	110	23
CHEX® (Ralston-Purina Co.)			
Snack Mix, all varieties (average)	⅔ cup (1 oz.)	130	19
DOO DADS® (Nabisco Brands, Inc.)			
Original or Zesty Cheese (average)	½ cup (1 oz.)	140	18
ESTEE® (Estee Corp.)			
Pretzels, unsalted	15	75	15
Wheat Snax	1 oz.	100	22
FEATHERWEIGHT® (Sandoz Nutrition)			
Cheese Curls, Low Sodium	1 oz.	150	16
Corn Chips, Low Sodium	1 oz.	170	15
Microwave Popcorn, Low Sodium, all varieties (average)	3 cups	80	14
Nacho Cheese Chips, Low Sodium	1 oz.	150	18
Potato Chips, Low Sodium	1 oz.	160	14
Pretzels, Low Sodium	15	80	17
Tortilla Chips, Low Sodium	1 oz.	150	18
FI•BAR (Natural Nectar Corp.) Chewy & Nutty Snack Bar	1 bar (1.2 oz.)	130	21
Snack Bar	1 bar (1 oz.)	100	13
FLAVOR TREE® (Lawry's Foods, Inc.)			
Cheddar Sticks	¼ cup	129	12

PROTEIN (gm)	FAT (gm)	SAT. FAT (gm)	CHOLES-TEROL (mg)	SODIUM (mg)	EXCHANGES
2	2	—	0	180	1½ starch
3	2	—	0	220	1 starch
3	1	—	0	250	1½ starch
3	5	—	0	300-480	1 starch, 1 fat
3	6	—	—	360-420	1 starch, 1 fat
1-2	1-2	1-2	0	<15	1 starch
4	<1	<1	0	15	1½ starch
2	9	—	—	81	1 starch, 1½ fat
2	11	—	—	3	1 starch, 2 fat
3	1	—	—	0-70	1 starch
2	8	—	0	45	1 starch, 1½ fat
2	11	—	—	4	1 starch, 2 fat
2	1	—	—	23	1 starch
2	8	—	0	10	1 starch, 1½ fat
3	4	—	0	20	1½ starch, ½ fat
2	3	—	0	20	1 starch, ½ fat
3	8	—	—	335	1 starch, 1 fat

* Not available   ▊ More than 2 fat exchanges   🛒 Moderate to high sugar content

Products	SERVING SIZE	CALORIES	CARBO-HYDRATE (gm)
Fruit Rolls, all varieties (average)	1 roll	75	18
Party Mix	¼ cup	163	12
Party Mix, no salt added	¼ cup	163	13
Sesame Chips	¼ cup	163	11
Sesame Sticks	¼ cup	133	11
Sesame Sticks, no salt added	¼ cup	131	13
Sour Cream and Onion Sticks	¼ cup	127	13
FRITO-LAY® (Frito-Lay, Inc.)			
Baken-ets® Fried Pork Rind, all varieties (average)	1 oz.	150	1
Beef Jerky	1 (.21 oz.)	25	1
Beef Sticks	1 (.45 oz.)	80	1
Chester's™ Microwave Popcorn, all varieties (average)	3 cups (⅓ bag)	120	11
Chee•tos®, all varieties (average)	1 oz.	160	15
Chee•tos®, light	1 oz.	140	19
Delta Gold™ Potato Chips, all varieties (average)	1 oz.	160	14
Doritos® Tortilla Chips, all varieties (average)	1 oz. (15-18 chips)	140	18
Doritos® Light Tortilla Chips, all varieties (average)	1 oz.	120	21
Fritos® Corn Chips, all varieties (average)	1 oz. (≈34 chips)	160	16
Funyuns® Onion Flavored Snack	1 oz.	140	18

PROTEIN (gm)	FAT (gm)	SAT. FAT (gm)	CHOLES-TEROL (mg)	SODIUM (mg)	EXCHANGES
0	<1	—	—	11-20	1 fruit
3	11	—	—	407	1 starch, 2 fat
4	11	—	—	8	1 starch, 2 fat
3	9	—	—	380	1 starch, 2 fat
3	9	—	—	358	1 starch, 1½ fat
3	8	—	—	7	1 starch, 1½ fat
3	8	—	—	360	1 starch, 1½ fat
17	9	—	25	570-850	2 meat
3	1	—	10	200	½ lean meat
3	7	—	15	300	½ meat, 1 fat
2	8	—	9	170-230	1 starch, 1 fat
2	10	—	—	260-360	1 starch, 2 fat
2	6	—	0	360	1 starch, 1 fat
1	11	—	—	160-240	1 starch, 2 fat
2	7	—	0	170-240	1 starch, 1 fat
2	4	—	0	240-290	1 starch, 1 fat
2	10	—	0	210-310	1 starch, 2 fat
2	6	—	—	275	1 starch, 1 fat

* Not available   ▉ More than 2 fat exchanges   🛒 Moderate to high sugar content

Products	SERVING SIZE	CALORIES	CARBO-HYDRATE (gm)
Lay's® Potato Chips, all varieties (average)	1 oz.	150	14
O'Grady's® Potato Chips, all varieties (average)	1 oz.	150	16
Popcorn Cheese Flavored	½ oz.	80	7
Salted	½ oz.	70	9
Vend	½ oz.	80	6
Ruffles® Potato Chips, all varieties (average)	1 oz. (18 chips)	150	15
Ruffles® Light Potato Chips	1 oz.	130	19
Toasted Corn Nuggets	1.38 oz.	170	29
Tostitos® Tortilla Chips, all varieties (average)	1 oz. (11 chips)	150	17
FROOT BY THE FOOT™ (General Mills, Inc.)			
3 Foot Fruit Snack	1 roll	80	17
FRUIT CORNERS® (General Mills, Inc.)			
Fruit-Roll-ups®, all varieties (average)	1 roll (½ oz.)	50	12
Fruit Wrinkles®	1 pouch	100	22
GARFIELD AND FRIENDS (General Mills, Inc.)			
Fruit Snacks, all varieties (average)	1 pouch	95	21
	1 roll (½ oz.)	50	12
HAIN® (PET,Inc.)			
Carrot Chips, all varieties (average)	1 oz.	150	16
Mini Rice Cakes, all varieties (average	½ oz.	60	12
Rice Cakes, all varieties (average)	2 cakes	80	16

† For occasional use   ** Not recommended for use

PROTEIN (gm)	FAT (gm)	SAT. FAT (gm)	CHOLES- TEROL (mg)	SODIUM (mg)	EXCHANGES
2	10	—	0	10-460	1 starch, 2 fat
2	9	—	0	210-330	1 starch, 1½ fat
1	5	—	0	180	½ starch, 1 fat
1	3	—	0	200	½ starch, ½ fat
1	6	—	0	160	½ starch, 1 fat
2	9	—	—	190-320	1 starch, 1½ fat
1	6	—	0	190	1 starch, 1 fat
3	5	—	—	265	2 starch, ½ fat
2	8	—	—	160-200	1 starch, 1½ fat
<1	1	—	—	35	1 fruit
<1	<1	—	—	40	1 fruit
<1	1	—	—	55	1½ fruit
<1	2	—	—	60-70	1½ fruit
<1	<1	—	—	20-40	1 fruit
2	8	—	0	30-160	1 starch, 1½ fat
1	1	—	0	5-80	1 starch
1	1	—	0	5-20	1 starch

* Not available   ⯑ More than 2 fat exchanges   🛒 Moderate to high sugar content

Products	SERVING SIZE	CALORIES	CARBO-HYDRATE (gm)
Sesame Tortilla Chips, all varieties (average)	1 oz.	150	19
Taco Style Tortilla Chips	1 oz.	160	15

HEALTH VALLEY® (Health Valley Foods, Inc.)
Snack Bars

Fruit Bakes, all varieties (average)	1 bar	100	16
Fruit Bar, Fat Free, all varieties (average)	1 bar	140	33
Fruit & Fitness Bars®	2 bars	200	35
Oat Bran Bakes all varieties (average)	1 bar	100	16
Oat Bran Jumbo Fruit Bars, all varieties (average)	1 bar	170	29
Rice Bran Jumbo Fruit Bars	1 bar	160	27

Snack Chips

Carrot Lites™	½ oz.	75	9
Cheddar Lites™, all varieties (average)	½ oz.	80	8
Corn Chips, all varieties (average)	1 oz.	160	14
Corn Chips, no salt added	1 oz.	160	13
Potato Chips, all varieties (average)	1 oz.	160	15
Potato Chips, no salt added, all varieties (average)	1 oz.	160	15

HERSHEY'S® (Hershey Foods Corp.)
Granola Sanck Bars

☕ Chocolate Covered Chocolate Chip	1.2 oz.	170	22
☕ Chocolate Covered Cocoa Creme	1.2 oz.	180	22
☕ Chocolate Covered Cookies & Creme	1.2 oz.	170	22

PROTEIN (gm)	FAT (gm)	SAT. FAT (gm)	CHOLES-TEROL (mg)	SODIUM (mg)	EXCHANGES
2	7	—	<5	<5-270	1 starch, 1½ fat
2	11	—	<5	320	1 starch, 2 fat
2	3	—	0	20-25	1 starch, ½ fat
3	0	—	0	10	1 starch, 1 fruit
4	5	—	0	75	1 starch, 1 fruit, 1 fat
2	3	—	0	10-15	1 starch, ½ fat
4	4	—	0	10	1 starch, 1 fruit, 1 fat
3	5	—	0	5	1 starch, 1 fruit, 1 fat
1	4	—	0	5	½ starch, 1 fat
2	4	—	0	70	½ starch, 1 fat
2	11	—	0-2	90-120	1 starch, 2 fat
1	11	—	0	1	1 starch, 2 fat
2	10	—	0	60	1 starch, 1 fat
2	10	—	0	1	1 starch, 2 fat
2	8	—	—	50	1½ starch, 1 fat†
2	9	—	5	50	1½ starch, 1½ fat†
2	8	—	—	50	1½ starch, 1 fat†

* Not available   ▌ More than 2 fat exchanges   🛒 Moderate to high sugar content

Products	SERVING SIZE	CALORIES	CARBO-HYDRATE (gm)
☕ Chocolate Covered Peanut Butter	1.2 oz.	180	19
KRAFT® HANDI-SNACKS® (Kraft, Inc.)			
Cheez 'n Crackers, all varieties (average)	1 package	130	8
Peanut Butter 'n Cheez Crackers	1 package	190	11
LA CAMPANA PARADISO™ (La Campana Paradiso)			
Tortilla Chips	1 oz.	140	19
LITE MUNCHIES® (Superior Protein Products Co.)			
Lite Munchies®, all varieties (average)	½ oz.	60	6
MISTER SALTY® (Nabisco Brands, Inc.)			
Dutch Pretzels	1 oz.	110	22
Juniors® Pretzels	¾ oz.	83	16
Pretzel Rings	¾ oz.	83	15
Pretzel Sticks	¾ oz.	83	17
Pretzel Twists	0.8 oz.	88	17
NATURE VALLEY® (General Mills, Inc.)			
☕ Granola Bars, all varieties (average)	1 bar	120	17
NEW TRAIL® (Hershey Foods Corp.)			
☕ Granola Snack Bars, all varieties (average)	1.4 oz. bar	200	23
OLD EL PASO® (PET, Inc.)			
Crispy Corn Tortilla Chips	1 oz. (16 chips)	150	17
Nachips® Tortilla Chips	1 oz. (9 chips)	150	18
ORVILLE REDENBACHER® (Beatrice/Hunt-Wesson)			
Hot Air Popcorn (as prepared)	5 cups	70	18

PROTEIN (gm)	FAT (gm)	SAT. FAT (gm)	CHOLES-TEROL (mg)	SODIUM (mg)	EXCHANGES
4	10	—	5	65	1 starch, 2 fat†
4	9	4	15-20	410-440	½ starch, ½ meat, 1 fat
6	13	2	0	250	1 starch, ½ meat, 2 fat
2	6	—	—	60	1 starch, 1 fat
4	2	0	0	60-130	½ skim milk, ½ fat **or** ½ starch, ½ fat
3	1	—	—	440	1½ starch
2	1	—	—	375	1 starch
2	1	—	—	383	1 starch
2	1	—	—	465	1 starch
2	2	—	—	439	1 starch
2	5	—	0	90	1 starch, 1 fat†
4	10	—	—	100-110	1½ starch, 2 fat†
2	8	—	0	105	1 starch, 1½ fat
2	7	—	0	80	1 starch, 1½ fat
2	1	—	0	0	1 starch

* Not available   ▌ More than 2 fat exchanges   ♣ Moderate to high sugar content

Products	SERVING SIZE	CALORIES	CARBO-HYDRATE (gm)
Microwave Popcorn (as prepared)			
Butter	3 cups	80	8
Light Butter	3 cups	50	9
Salt-Free Butter	3 cups	80	8
Natural	3 cups	80	8
Light Natural	3 cups	50	9
Salt-Free Natural	3 cups	90	8
PILLSBURY (The Pillsbury Company)			
Microwave Popcorn, frozen or shelf stable, all varieties except Salt Free (average)	3 cups popped	210	20
Salt Free (frozen)	3 cups popped	170	23
POP SECRET® (General Mills, Inc.)			
Popcorn			
Butter Flavor, popped	3 cups (¼ pkg.)	100	11
Butter Flavor, salt free, popped	3 cups	140	16
Cheese Flavor, popped	2 ¾ cups (⅓ pkg.)	170	15
Natural Flavor, popped	3 cups (¼ pkg.)	100	11
Popcorn, light, all varieties, popped (average)	3 cups (¼ pkg.)	70	12
QUAKER® (Quaker Oats Company)			
Chewy® Granola Bars, all varieties (average)	1 bar (1 oz.)	130	18
Granola Dipps® Bars, all varieties (average)	1 bar (1 oz.)	150	19
Rice Cakes, all varieties (average)	1 cake	35	7

PROTEIN (gm)	FAT (gm)	SAT. FAT (gm)	CHOLES-TEROL (mg)	SODIUM (mg)	EXCHANGES
2	5	1	0	150	½ starch, 1 fat
2	1	—	—	95	½ starch
2	5	1	0	0	½ starch, 1 fat
2	5	1	0	190	½ starch, 1 fat
2	1	—	0	85	½ starch
2	6	1	0	0	½ starch, 1 fat
3	13	—	—	410-480	1 starch, 2½ fat
3	7	—	—	0	1½ starch, 1 fat
2	6	—	0	170	½ starch, 1 fat
2	9	—	0	0	1 starch, 1½ fat
3	11	—	0	260	1 starch, 2 fat
2	6	—	0	170	½ starch, 1 fat
2	3	—	0	115-160	½ starch, ½ fat
2	5	1	0	85-115	1 starch, 1 fat†
3	8	—	—	75-100	1 starch, 1½ fat†
1	0	0	0	0-53	½ starch

Products	SERVING SIZE	CALORIES	CARBO-HYDRATE (gm)
SHARK BITES™ (General Mills, Inc.)			
Fruit Snacks, all varieties (average)	1 pouch	100	22
SUNKIST® (Thomas J. Lipton, Inc.)			
Fun Fruits®, all varieties except Creme Supreme (average)	1 pkg. (.9 oz.)	100	22
Creme Supreme	1 pkg. (.9 oz.)	114	20
THUNDER JETS™ (General Mills, Inc.)			
Fruit Snacks, all varieties (average)	1 pouch	100	22
VIC'S CORN POPPER (Gourmet Popping Corn Company)			
₩ Caramel	1½ cups	330	60
Gourmet White	3 cups	180	18
Half Salt	3 cups	180	18
No Salt	3 cups	180	18
⊟ Original Cheddar	2 cups	270	12
⊟ White Chedar	2 cups	270	12
WEIGHT WATCHERS® (H. J. Heinz Co.)			
Apple Chips	1 bag (.75 oz.)	70	19
Corn Snackers™, all varieties (average)	1 bag (.5 oz.)	60	10
Fruit Snacks, all varieties (average)	1 pouch (.5 oz.)	50	13
Great Snackers™, all varieties (average)	1 bag (.5 oz.)	60	8
Popcorn Microwave	1 bag (1 oz.)	100	22
Ready to Eat, all varieties (average)	1 bag (.66 oz.)	90	11
Roasted Peanuts	1 pouch	100	4

PROTEIN (gm)	FAT (gm)	SAT. FAT (gm)	CHOLES-TEROL (mg)	SODIUM (mg)	EXCHANGES
<1	<1	—	—	20	1½ fruit
0	1	—	0	10	1½ fruit
0	4	—	—	19	1 fruit, 1 fat
<1	1	—	—	30	1½ fruit
3	9	—	0	315	**
3	12	—	0	255	1 starch, 2 fat
3	12	—	0	105	1 starch, 2 fat
3	12	—	0	0	1 starch, 2 fat
6	24	—	15	375	1 starch, 4½ fat
6	24	—	15	255	1 starch, 4½ fat
—	—	—	—	200	1 fruit
1	2	—	—	190-240	½ starch, ½ fat
<1	<1	—	—	75	1 fruit
1	3	—	—	120-170	½ starch, ½ fat
4	1	—	—	5	1½ starch
2	5	—	—	65-85	½ starch, 1 fat
8	7	—	—	50	1 high-fat meat

* Not available   ▤ More than 2 fat exchanges   ☙ Moderate to high sugar content

Products	SERVING SIZE	CALORIES	CARBO-HYDRATE (gm)

SOUPS

CAMPBELL'S® (Campbell Soup Co.)
Chunky Soups,
Individual Serving,
ready to serve

Chunky Beef	1 can (10 ¾ oz.)	190	23
Chunky Beef Stroganoff	1 can (10 ¾ oz.)	320	28
⊟ Chunky Chicken Mushroom, creamy	1 can (10½ oz.)	320	12
Chunky Chicken Noodle	1 can (10 ¾ oz.)	200	20
Chunky Chicken Nuggets with Vegetables & Noodles	1 can (10 ¾ oz.)	210	23
Chunky Chili Beef	1 can (11 oz.)	290	37
Chunky Clam Chowder, Manhattan Style	1 can (10 ¾ oz.)	160	24
⊟ Chunky Clam Chowder, New England	1 can (10 ¾ oz.)	290	25
Chunky Fisherman's Chowder	1 can (10 ¾ oz.)	260	25
Chunky Ham 'n Butter Bean	1 can (10 ¾ oz.)	280	34
⊟ Chunky Mushroom, creamy	1 can (10½ oz.)	260	13
Chunky Old Fashioned Bean with Ham	1 can (11 oz.)	290	37
Chunky Old Fashioned Chicken	1 can (10 ¾ oz.)	180	21

PROTEIN (gm)	FAT (gm)	SAT. FAT (gm)	CHOLES-TEROL (mg)	SODIUM (mg)	EXCHANGES
14	5	—	—	1090	1½ starch, 1 meat
15	16	—	—	1230	2 starch, 1 meat, 2 fat
11	25	—	—	1340	1 starch, 1 lean meat, 4 fat
13	7	—	—	1150	1 starch, 1 veg., 1 lean meat. 1 fat
10	9	—	—	1060	1½ starch, 1 lean meat, 1 fat
21	7	—	—	1120	2½ starch, 2 lean meat
7	5	—	—	1230	1½ starch, 1 fat
8	17	—	—	1180	1½ starch, ½ lean meat, 3 fat
11	14	—	—	1290	1½ starch,* 1 lean meat 2 fat
12	10	—	—	1180	2 starch, 1 lean meat 1 fat
5	21	—	—	1270	1 starch, 4 fat
14	9	—	—	1110	2½ starch, 1 meat, ½ fat
11	5	—	—	1190	1½ starch, 1 lean meat

* Not available   ▌ More than 2 fat exchanges   🛒 Moderate to high sugar content

Products	SERVING SIZE	CALORIES	CARBO-HYDRATE (gm)
Chunky Old Fashioned Vegetable Beef	1 can (10 ¾ oz.)	180	20
Chunky Pepper Steak	1 can (10 ¾ oz.)	180	24
Chunky Sirloin Burger	1 can (10 ¾ oz.)	230	24
Chunky Split Pea with Ham	1 can (10 ¾ oz.)	240	33
Chunky Steak and Potato	1 can (10 ¾ oz.)	200	24
Chunky Vegetable	1 can (10 ¾ oz.)	160	25
Chunky Soups, 19 oz. Size, ready to serve			
Chunky Beef	½ can (9½ oz.)	170	21
☷ Chunky Chicken Mushroom, creamy	½ can (9⅛ oz.)	290	10
Chunky Chicken Noodle	½ can (9½ oz.)	180	18
Chunky Chicken Nuggets with Vegetables & Noodles	½ can (9½ oz.)	190	20
Chunky Chicken Vegetable	½ can (9½ oz.)	170	19
Chunky Chicken with Rice	½ can (9½ oz.)	140	15
Chunky Chili Beef	½ can (9 ¾ oz.)	260	33
☷ Chunky Clam Chowder, Manhattan Style	½ can (9½ oz.)	150	22
☷ Chunky Clam Chowder, New England	½ can (9½ oz.)	250	22
Chunky Fisherman's Chowder	½ can (9½ oz.)	230	22

PROTEIN (gm)	FAT (gm)	SAT. FAT (gm)	CHOLES-TEROL (mg)	SODIUM (mg)	EXCHANGES
13	5	—	—	1120	1 starch, 1 veg., 1 meat
14	3	—	—	1040	1½ starch, 1½ lean meat
12	9	—	—	1240	1½ starch, 1 meat, ½ fat
12	6	—	—	1070	2 starch, 1 meat
14	5	—	—	1120	1½ starch, 1½ lean meat
4	5	—	—	1100	1½ starch, 1 fat
12	4	—	—	960	1½ starch, 1 lean meat
10	23	—	—	1200	½ starch, 1 lean meat, 4 fat
12	6	—	—	1010	1 starch, 1 lean meat, ½ fat
9	8	—	—	930	1 starch, 1 lean meat, 1 fat
10	6	—	—	1080	1 starch, 1 veg., 1 meat
10	4	—	—	1050	1 starch, 1 meat
18	6	—	—	9900	2 starch, 2 lean meat
6	4	—	—	980	1½ starch, ½ fat
7	15	—	—	1040	1½ starch, 3 fat
9	13	—	—	1140	1½ starch, 1 lean meat, 2 fat

* Not available   ▤ More than 2 fat exchanges   ♔ Moderate to high sugar content

Products	SERVING SIZE	CALORIES	CARBO-HYDRATE (gm)
Chunky Mediterranean Vegetable	½ can (9½ oz.)	160	24
Chunky Minestrone	½ can (9½ oz.)	170	25
Chunky Mushroom, creamy	½ can (9⅜ oz.)	240	12
Chunky Old Fashioned Bean wth Ham	½ can (9⅝ oz.)	250	33
Chunky Old Fashioned Chicken	½ can (9½ oz.)	150	18
Chunky Old Fashioned Vegetable Beef	½ can (9½ oz.)	160	18
Chunky Pepper Steak	½ can (9½ oz.)	160	21
Chunky Sirloin Burger	½ can (9½ oz.)	200	21
Chunky Split Pea with Ham	½ can (9½ oz.)	210	30
Chunky Steak 'n Potato	½ can (9½ oz.)	170	21
Chunky Turkey Vegetable	½ can (9⅜ oz.)	150	16
Chunky Vegetable	½ can (9½ oz.)	140	22
Condensed, canned (as prepared) Asparagus, Cream of	1 cup	90	11
Bean with Bacon	1 cup	120	22
Beef	1 cup	80	10
Beef Broth (Bouillon)	1 cup	16	1
Beef Noodle	1 cup	70	7
Beef Noodle, Homestyle	1 cup	80	8
Beefy Mushroom	1 cup	60	5
Black Bean	1 cup	110	17

† For occasional use   ** Not recommended for use

PROTEIN (gm)	FAT (gm)	SAT. FAT (gm)	CHOLES-TEROL (mg)	SODIUM (mg)	EXCHANGES
4	5	—	—	1020	1½ starch, 1 fat
6	5	—	—	890	1 starch, 1 veg., 1 fat
4	19	—	—	1130	1 starch, 3½ fat
12	8	—	—	960	2 starch, 1 lean meat, 1 fat
10	4	—	—	1050	1 starch, 1 lean meat
11	5	—	—	980	1 starch, 1 meat
12	3	—	—	920	1½ starch, 1 lean meat
10	8	—	—	1100	1½ starch, 1 meat
11	5	—	—	950	2 starch, 1 lean meat
12	4	—	—	990	1½ starch, 1 meat
9	6	—	—	1060	1 starch, 1 lean meat, ½ fat
3	4	—	—	970	1 starch, 1 veg., ½ fat
2	4	—	—	840	1 starch, ½ fat
6	4	—	—	850	1½ starch, ½ fat
5	2	—	—	840	1 starch
3	0	—	—	820	Free
4	3	—	—	830	½ starch, ½ fat
6	3	—	—	810	½ starch, ½ meat
4	3	—	—	960	½ starch, ½ fat
5	2	—	—	950	1 starch, ½ lean meat

* Not available   ▤ More than 2 fat exchanges   🛒 Moderate to high sugar content

Products	SERVING SIZE	CALORIES	CARBO-HYDRATE (gm)
Celery, Cream of	1 cup	100	8
Cheddar Cheese	1 cup	130	10
Chicken Alphabet	1 cup	70	10
Chicken Barley	1 cup	70	10
Chicken Broth	1 cup	35	3
Chicken Broth & Noodles	1 cup	60	8
Chicken Broth & Rice	1 cup	50	8
Chicken, Cream of (made with water)	1 cup	110	9
Chicken 'n Dumplings	1 cup	80	9
Chicken Gumbo	1 cup	60	8
Chicken Mushroom, creamy	1 cup	120	9
Chicken Noodle	1 cup	70	8
Chicken Noodle, Homestyle	1 cup	70	8
Chicken Noodle-O's	1 cup	70	9
Chicken with Rice	1 cup	60	7
Chicken & Stars	1 cup	60	7
Chicken Vegetable	1 cup	70	8
Chili Beef	1 cup	140	19
Clam Chowder, Manhattan Style	1 cup	70	11
Clam Chowder, New England (made with water)	1 cup	80	12
Clam Chowder, New England (made with skim milk)	1 cup	130	17
Consommé, Beef, gelatin added	1 cup	25	2

PROTEIN (gm)	FAT (gm)	SAT. FAT (gm)	CHOLES-TEROL (mg)	SODIUM (mg)	EXCHANGES
1	7	—	—	830	½ starch 1 fat
3	8	—	—	750	½ starch, 1½ fat
3	2	—	—	810	1 starch
3	2	—	—	850	1 starch
1	2	—	—	750	1 vegetable
2	2	—	—	870	½ starch, ½ fat
1	1	—	—	850	½ starch
3	7	—	—	810	½ starch, 1½ fat
4	3	—	—	980	½ starch, ½ fat
2	2	—	—	900	½ starch, ½ fat
3	8	—	—	940	½ starch, 1½ fat
3	2	—	—	910	½ starch, ½ fat
3	3	—	—	910	½ starch, ½ fat
3	2	—	—	820	½ starch, ½ fat
2	2	—	—	800	½ starch, ½ fat
3	2	—	—	870	½ starch, ½ fat
3	3	—	—	850	½ starch, ½ fat
5	5	—	—	740	1 starch, 1 fat
2	2	—	—	830	1 starch
3	3	—	—	870	1 starch, ½ fat
7	4	—	—	930	1 starch, ½ skim milk, ½ fat
4	0	—	—	760	1 vegetable

* Not available   � More than 2 fat exchanges   🛒 Moderate to high sugar content

Products	SERVING SIZE	CALORIES	CARBO-HYDRATE (gm)
Curly Noodle with Chicken	1 cup	80	9
French Onion	1 cup	60	9
Green Pea	1 cup	160	25
Meatball Alphabet	1 cup	100	11
Minestrone	1 cup	80	14
Mushroom, Cream of	1 cup	100	9
Mushroom, Golden	1 cup	80	10
Nacho Cheese (made with water)	1 cup	110	9
Nacho Cheese (made with skim milk)	1 cup	150	14
Noodles & Ground Beef	1 cup	90	10
Onion, Cream of (made with water)	1 cup	100	12
Onion Cream of (made with water & skim milk)	1 cup	120	15
Oyster Stew (made with water)	1 cup	80	5
Oyster Stew (made with skim milk)	1 cup	120	10
Pepper Pot	1 cup	90	9
Potato, Cream of (made with water)	1 cup	70	11
Potato, Cream of (made with water & skim milk)	1 cup	110	14
Scotch Broth	1 cup	80	9
Shrimp, Cream of (made with water)	1 cup	90	8

† For occasional use   ** Not recommended for use

PROTEIN (gm)	FAT (gm)	SAT. FAT (gm)	CHOLES-TEROL (mg)	SODIUM (mg)	EXCHANGES
3	3	—	—	960	½ starch, ½ fat
2	2	—	—	900	½ starch, ½ fat
8	3	—	—	830	1½ starch, ½ lean meat
4	4	—	—	910	1 starch, ½ fat
3	2	—	—	910	1 starch
1	7	—	—	820	½ starch, 1 fat
2	3	—	—	870	½ starch, ½ fat or 1 starch
3	8	—	—	750	½ starch, 1½ fat
7	9	—	—	810	½ starch, ½ skim milk 1½ fat
4	4	—	—	830	1 starch, ½ fat
2	5	—	—	830	1 starch, 1 fat
4	5	—	—	860	1 starch, 1 fat
3	5	—	—	830	½ starch, 1 fat
6	5	—	—	880	½ starch, ½ skim milk, ½ fat
5	4	—	—	960	½ starch, ½ meat
1	3	—	—	880	½ starch, ½ fat
3	3	—	—	910	1 starch, ½ fat
4	3	—	—	870	½ starch, ½ fat
2	6	—	—	800	½ starch, 1 fat

* Not available   █ More than 2 fat exchanges   ♥ Moderate to high sugar content

Products	SERVING SIZE	CALORIES	CARBO-HYDRATE (gm)
Shrimp, Cream of (made with skim milk)	1 cup	130	13
Split Pea with Ham and Bacon	1 cup	150	24
Tomato (made with water)	1 cup	90	17
Tomato (made with skim milk)	1 cup	130	22
Tomato Bisque	1 cup	120	23
Tomato, Homestyle, Cream of (made with water)	1 cup	110	20
Tomato, Homestyle, (made with skim milk)	1 cup	150	25
Tomato, Zesty	1 cup	90	19
Tomato Rice, Old Fashioned	1 cup	110	22
Turkey Noodle	1 cup	70	8
Turkey Vegetable	1 cup	70	8
Vegetable	1 cup	80	14
Vegetable Beef	1 cup	70	10
Vegetable, Homestyle	1 cup	60	10
Vegetable, Old Fashioned	1 cup	60	9
Vegetarian Vegetable	1 cup	80	14
Won Ton	1 cup	45	5
Creamy Natural Gold Label, condensed (as prepared) Asparagus (made with water)	1 cup	100	13
Asparagus (made with skim milk)	1 cup	140	18
Broccoli (made with water)	1 cup	70	10

† For occasional use   ** Not recommended for use

PROTEIN (gm)	FAT (gm)	SAT. FAT (gm)	CHOLES- TEROL (mg)	SODIUM (mg)	EXCHANGES
5	7	—	—	850	½ starch, ½ skim milk, 1 fat
8	4	—	—	800	1½ starch, ½ lean meat
1	2	—	—	670	1 starch
5	3	—	—	730	1 starch, ½ skim milk
1	3	—	—	790	1 starch, ½ fat
1	3	—	—	730	1 starch, ½ fat
5	4	—	—	880	1 starch, ½ skim milk, ½ fat
2	1	—	—	770	1 starch
1	2	—	—	730	1½ starch
3	3	—	—	870	½ starch, ½ fat
2	3	—	—	710	½ starch, ½ fat
3	2	—	—	800	1 starch
4	2	—	—	750	1 starch
2	2	—	—	880	1 starch
2	2	—	—	890	2 veg. **or** ½ starch, ½ fat
2	2	—	—	780	1 starch
3	1	—	—	870	½ starch
1	5	—	—	640	1 starch, 1 fat
5	6	—	—	690	1 starch, ½ skim milk, 1 fat
1	3	—	—	670	½ starch, ½ fat

* Not available   ▤ More than 2 fat exchanges   🛒 Moderate to high sugar content

Products	SERVING SIZE	CALORIES	CARBO-HYDRATE (gm)
Broccoli (made with skim milk)	1 cup	110	15
Cauliflower (made with water)	1 cup	130	13
Cauliflower (made with skim milk)	1 cup	170	18
Potato (made with water)	1 cup	120	12
Potato (made with skim milk)	1 cup	160	17
Spinach (made with water)	1 cup	90	9
Spinach (made with skim milk)	1 cup	130	14
Golden Classic, condensed (as prepared) Chicken Vegetable with Wild Rice	1 cup	80	11
Sirloin Beef	1 cup	70	6
Tortellini & Vegetables	1 cup	80	12
Home Cookin' Individual Size, ready to serve Chicken with Noodles	10 ¾ oz.	140	12
Country Vegetable	10 ¾ oz.	120	21
Hearty Beef	10 ¾ oz.	140	18
Hearty Lentil	10 ¾ oz.	170	29
Old Fashioned Beef	10 ¾ oz.	140	16
Old World Minestrone	10 ¾ oz.	150	23
Split Pea with Ham	10 ¾ oz.	210	30
Tomato Garden	10 ¾ oz.	150	29

† For occasional use   ** Not recommended for use

PROTEIN (gm)	FAT (gm)	SAT. FAT (gm)	CHOLES- TEROL (mg)	SODIUM (mg)	EXCHANGES
5	4	—	—	720	½ starch, ½ skim milk, ½ fat
1	9	—	—	800	1 starch, 1½ fat
5	10	—	—	850	1 starch, ½ skim milk, 1½ fat
1	7	—	—	640	1 starch, 1 fat
5	8	—	—	690	1 starch, ½ skim milk, 1 fat
1	6	—	—	680	½ starch, 1 fat
5	7	—	—	730	½ starch, ½ skim milk 1 fat
3	3	—	—	740	1 starch
5	3	—	—	870	½ starch, ½ fat
2	3	—	—	870	1 starch
13	4	—	—	1130	1 starch, 1 lean meat
4	2	—	—	1000	1½ starch
11	3	—	—	1070	1 starch 1 lean meat
10	1	—	—	940	1½ starch, 1 lean meat
13	3	—	—	1150	1 starch, 1 lean meat
4	4	—	—	1210	1½ starch, ½ fat
13	4	—	—	1230	2 starch, 1 lean meat
2	3	—	—	910	2 starch

* Not available   ▤ More than 2 fat exchanges   🛒 Moderate to high sugar content

Products	SERVING SIZE	CALORIES	CARBO-HYDRATE (gm)
Home Cookin', 19 Ounce Size, ready to serve			
Chicken with Noodles	½ can	120	10
Country Vegetable	½ can	110	18
Hearty Beef	½ can	130	16
Hearty Lentil	½ can	150	26
Old Fashioned Vegetable Beef	½ can	140	15
Old World Minestrone	½ can	130	20
Split Pea with Ham	½ can	190	26
Tomato Garden	½ can	130	26
Low Sodium, ready to serve			
Chicken Broth	10½ oz.	40	2
Chicken with Noodles	10 ¾ oz.	160	15
Chunky Chicken Vegetable	10 ¾ oz.	240	21
Mushroom, Cream of	10½ oz.	190	16
Split Pea	10 ¾ oz.	240	38
Tomato with Tomato Pieces	10½ oz.	180	29
Microwave Soup in a Bowl			
Chunky Beef with Country Vegetables	1 bowl	170	21
Chunky Chicken Noodle with Mushroom	1 bowl	180	18
Chunky New England Clam Chowder	1 bowl	250	22

† For occasional use   ** Not recommended for use

PROTEIN (gm)	FAT (gm)	SAT. FAT (gm)	CHOLES-TEROL (mg)	SODIUM (mg)	EXCHANGES
12	3	—	—	1000	½ starch, 1½ lean meat
3	2	—	—	900	1 starch, ½ fat
10	3	—	—	910	1 starch, 1 lean meat
9	1	—	—	830	1½ starch, ½ lean meat
12	3	—	—	1010	1 starch, 1 lean meat
4	3	—	—	1070	1½ starch, ½ fat
12	4	—	—	1090	2 starch, 1 lean meat
1	3	—	—	820	1½ starch
3	2	—	—	70	½ starch
13	5	—	—	85	1 starch, 1½ lean meat
15	11	—	—	95	1 starch, 1 veg., 1½ meat, ½ fat
3	13	—	—	60	1 starch 2½ fat
11	5	—	—	25	2 starch, 1 meat
3	5	—	—	40	2 starch, ½ fat
12	4	—	—	960	1 starch, 1 veg., 1 lean meat
12	7	—	—	1010	1 starch, 1 veg., 1 meat
7	15	—	—	1050	1½ starch, 3 fat **or** 1 starch, ½ skim milk, 3 fat

* Not available   ▯ More than 2 fat exchanges   🛒 Moderate to high sugar content

Products	SERVING SIZE	CALORIES	CARBO-HYDRATE (gm)
Chunky Old Fashioned Chicken with Country Vegetables	1 bowl	150	19
Chunky Sirloin Burger with Country Vegetables	1 bowl	200	21
Quality Soup and Recipe Mix, dry (as prepared)			
Chicken Noodle	8 oz.	100	16
Chicken Rice with White Meat	8 oz.	90	16
Noodle	8 oz.	110	20
Onion	8 oz.	50	10
Onion Mushroom	8 oz.	50	9
Ramen Noodle Soup, dry (as prepared)			
Cup A Ramen, all varieties (average)	1 pkg. (2.19 oz. dry)	270	38
Cup A Ramen, Low Fat, all varieties (average)	1 pkg. (2.19 oz. dry)	220	44
Low Fat, wrapper package, all varieties (as prepared)	½ pkg. (1.5 oz. dry)	160	32
Soup for One, semi-condensed (as prepared)			
Bean with Ham Old Fashioned	11 oz	220	30
Clam Chowder, New England (made with water)	11 oz.	130	19
Clam Chowder, New England (made with skim milk)	11 oz.	160	23
Golden Chicken and Noodles	11 oz.	120	14
Mushroom, Savory Cream of	11 oz.	180	14
Tomato Royale	11 oz.	180	35
Vegetable, Old World	11 oz.	130	18

PROTEIN (gm)	FAT (gm)	SAT. FAT (gm)	CHOLES-TEROL (mg)	SODIUM (mg)	EXCHANGES
10	4	—	—	1080	1 starch, 1 veg., 1 lean meat
10	8	—	—	1100	1 starch, 1 veg., 1 meat, ½ fat
5	2	—	—	810	1 starch, ½ fat
3	2	—	—	800	1 starch, ½ fat
4	2	—	—	760	1½ starch
1	0	—	—	730	½ starch
1	1	—	—	740	½ starch
6	10	—	—	1470-1530	2½ starch, 1½ fat
7	2	—	—	1500-1600	3 starch
5	1	—	—	890-940	2 starch
8	7	—	—	1340	2 starch, ½ lean meat, 1 fat
6	4	—	—	1360	1 starch, ½ meat
9	4	—	—	1410	1 starch, ½ skim milk, ½ meat
6	4	—	—	1450	1 starch, ½ meat
3	13	—	—	1500	1 starch, 2½ fat
3	3	—	—	1290	2 starch, 1 veg.
4	4	—	—	1470	1 starch, 1 fat

* Not available   ▤ More than 2 fat exchanges   🛒 Moderate to high sugar content

Products	SERVING SIZE	CALORIES	CARBO-HYDRATE (gm)
Special Request (⅓ Less Salt), condensed (as prepared)			
Bean with Bacon	1 cup	120	22
Chicken, Cream of	1 cup	110	9
Chicken Noodle	1 cup	70	8
Chicken with Rice	1 cup	60	7
Mushroom, Cream of	1 cup	100	9
Tomato	1 cup	90	17
Vegetable	1 cup	80	14
Vegetable Beef	1 cup	70	10
2 Minute Soup Mix, Cup, dry (as prepared)			
Chicken Noodle with White Meat	6 oz.	90	11
Chicken Vegetable	6 oz.	90	14
Creamy Chicken with White Meat	6 oz.	120	15
Noodle with Chicken Broth	6 oz.	100	17
Vegetable Soup with Sirloin Beef	6 oz.	110	19
FEATHERWEIGHT® (Sandoz Nutrition)			
Bouillon, Instant, Low Sodium, all varieties (average)	1 tsp.	18	2
Chicken Noodle, Low Sodium	½ can (3.75 oz.)	70	11
Mushroom, Low Sodium	½ can (3.75 oz.)	60	9
Tomato, Low Sodium	½ can (3.75 oz.)	80	14
Vegetable Beef, Low Sodium	½ can (3.75 oz.)	100	16

† For occasional use   ** Not recommended for use

PROTEIN (gm)	FAT (gm)	SAT. FAT (gm)	CHOLES- TEROL (mg)	SODIUM (mg)	EXCHANGES
6	4	—	—	540	1 starch, 1 fat
3	7	—	—	520	½ starch, 1½ fat
3	2	—	—	560	½ starch, ½ fat
2	2	—	—	520	½ starch, ½ fat
1	7	—	—	530	½ starch, 1½ fat
1	2	—	—	470	1 starch
3	2	—	—	520	1 starch
4	2	—	—	480	1 starch
6	2	—	—	720	1 starch
3	2	—	—	770	1 starch
4	5	—	—	850	1 starch, 1 fat
4	2	—	—	700	1 starch, ½ fat
3	2	—	—	900	1 starch, ½ fat
0	1	—	5	5-10	Free
5	1	—	15	390	1 starch
3	1	—	5	320	1 starch
3	1	—	5	240	1 starch
6	2	—	10	310	1 starch, ½ fat

* Not available   ▓ More than 2 fat exchanges   ♥ Moderate to high sugar content

Products	SERVING SIZE	CALORIES	CARBO-HYDRATE (gm)
HAIN® (PET, Inc.)			
*Sodium Values: Regular/No salt added			
Canned Soup			
Chicken Broth (average)	8 ¾ oz.	70	3
Chicken Noodle (average)	9½ oz.	120	11
Creamy Mushroom	9½ oz.	110	16
Italian Vege-Pasta (average)	9½ oz.	160	22
Minestrone (average)	9½ oz.	165	27
Mushroom Barley	9½ oz.	100	17
New England Clam Chowder	9¼ oz.	180	26
Split Pea (average)	9½ oz.	170	29
Turkey Rice (average)	9½ oz.	100	9
Vegetable Broth (average)	9½ oz.	45	8
Vegetable Chicken (average)	9½ oz.	120	14
Vegetarian Lentil (average)	9½ oz.	160	24
Vegetarian Vegetable (average)	9½ oz.	150	23
Dry Soup Mixes *Sodium values: Regular/ No salt added (as prepared)			
〓 Cheese & Broccoli	¾ cup	310	19
〓 Cheese Savory	¾ cup	250	20
Lentil Savory	¾ cup	130	20
Minestrone Savory	¾ cup	110	20
〓 Mushroom Savory	¾ cup	210	11
〓 Mushroom Savory, no salt added	¾ cup	250	15

† For occasional use   ** Not recommended for use

PROTEIN (gm)	FAT (gm)	SAT. FAT (gm)	CHOLES-TEROL (mg)	SODIUM (mg)	EXCHANGES
0	6	—	5	870/ 75*	1 fat
9	4	—	40-50	930/ 90*	1 starch, 1 lean meat
4	4	—	15	740	1 starch, 1 fat
4	6	—	20	910/ 90*	1½ starch, 1 fat
8	3	—	0	1060/ 35*	2 starch
4	2	—	10	600	1 starch, ½ fat
8	4	—	25	780	2 starch, ½ fat
11	1	—	0	970/ 40*	2 starch, ½ lean meat
8	3	—	40-45	1020/ 100*	½ starch, 1 lean meat
1	<1	—	0	1180/ 85*	½ starch
9	3	—	15-30	930/ 140*	1 starch, 1 lean meat
9	3	—	5	690/ 65*	1½ starch, 1 lean meat
4	5	—	0	920/ 45*	1½ starch, 1 fat
7	22	—	—	980	1 starch, ½ meat, 1 fat
6	16	—	—	890	1½ starch, 3 fat
4	2	—	—	810	1½ starch
4	1	—	—	870	1½ starch
4	15	—	—	710	1 starch, 3 fat
5	20	—	—	180	1 starch, 4 fat

* Not available   ⊟ More than 2 fat exchanges   🛒 Moderate to high sugar content

Products	SERVING SIZE	CALORIES	CARBO-HYDRATE (gm)
Onion Savory (average)	¾ cup	50	8
Potato Leek Savory	¾ cup	260	20
Split Pea Savory	¾ cup	310	16
Tomato Savory	¾ cup	220	19
Vegetable Savory (average)	¾ cup	80	13

HEALTH VALLEY® (Health Valley Foods)
*Sodium Values: Regular/No salt added

Beef Broth	7½ oz.	10	2
Black Bean	7½ oz.	150	24
Chicken Broth	7½ oz.	35	1
Chunky Five Bean Vegetable	7½ oz.	110	21
Chunky Vegetable	7½ oz.	125	20
Fat Free Soups			
Country Corn & Vegetable	7½ oz.	60	16
5 Bean Vegetable	7½ oz.	70	16
14 Garden Vegetable	7½ oz.	60	14
Real Italian Minestrone	7½ oz.	70	17
Tomato Vegetable	7½ oz.	40	10
Vegetable Barley	7½ oz.	50	14
Green Split Pea	7½ oz.	180	34
Lentil	7½ oz.	220	33
Manhattan Clam Chowder	7½ oz.	110	15
Minestrone	7½ oz.	130	19
Mushroom Barley	7½ oz.	100	16
Potato Leek	7½ oz.	130	23

† For occasional use   ** Not recommended for use

PROTEIN (gm)	FAT (gm)	SAT. FAT (gm)	CHOLES- TEROL (mg)	SODIUM (mg)	EXCHANGES
2	2	—	—	900/ 470*	½ starch
4	18	—	—	690	1½ starch, 3½ fat
4	10	—	—	940	1 starch, 2 fat
3	14	—	—	770	1 starch, 3 fat
2	1	—	—	730/ 330*	1 starch
1	0	—	1	420/ 5*	Free
7	2	—	0	280/ 20*	1½ starch, ½ lean meat
4	2	—	2	410/ 0*	½ meat
4	2	—	0	290/ 60*	1½ starch
7	2	—	12	290/ 60*	1 starch, 1 lean meat
3	0	—	0	290	1 starch
4	0	—	0	290	1 starch
4	0	—	0	290	1 starch
4	0	—	0	290	1 starch
2	0	—	0	290	½ starch **or** 2 veg.
3	0	—	0	290	½ starch **or** 2 veg.
11	0	—	0	280/ 25*	1½ starch, 1 lean meat
13	4	—	0	290/ 25*	1½ starch, 1½ lean meat
6	2	—	15	290/ 60*	1 starch, ½ lean meat
6	3	—	0	290/ 90*	1 starch, ½ meat
5	2	—	0	290/ 20*	1 starch, ½ fat
4	2	—	0	290/ 20*	1½ starch

* Not available   ▇ More than 2 fat exchanges   ♥ Moderate to high sugar content

Products	SERVING SIZE	CALORIES	CARBO-HYDRATE (gm)
Tomato	7½ oz.	130	21
Vegetable	7½ oz.	110	20

HORMEL® (George A. Hormel and Company)
Microcup® Hearty Soups

Bean and Ham Soup	7.5 oz.	190	31
Beef Vegetable Soup	7.5 oz.	80	12
Chicken Noodle Soup	7.5 oz.	110	14
Chicken with Rice and Vegetable	7.5 oz.	114	16
Country Vegetable Soup	7.5 oz.	89	13
Minestrone Soup	7.5 oz.	104	15
New England Clam Chowder	7.5 oz.	120	15

LIPTON® (Thomas J. Lipton, Inc.)
Cup-A-Soup®
(as prepared)

Chicken (Cup-A-Broth)	6 oz.	20	3
Cream of Mushroom, Cream of Chicken	6 oz.	75	9
Creamy Broccoli, Creamy Broccoli with Cheese	6 oz.	65	9
Creamy Chicken with Vegetables	6 oz.	93	14
Green Pea	6 oz.	113	14
Hearty Chicken and Noodles	6 oz.	110	20
Tomato	6 oz.	103	21
Onion	6 oz.	30	5
Chicken Noodle with Meat, Chicken 'N Rice, Chicken Vegetable, Ring Noodle, Spring Vegetable	6 oz.	45	8

† For occasional use   ** Not recommended for use

PROTEIN (gm)	FAT (gm)	SAT. FAT (gm)	CHOLES- TEROL (mg)	SODIUM (mg)	EXCHANGES
3	3	—	0	290/ 40*	1 starch, 1 veg., ½ fat
4	1	—	0	300/ 40*	1 starch, 1 veg.
10	3	—	30	670	1½ starch, 1 lean meat
5	1	—	9	810	1 starch
7	3	—	22	690	1 starch, ½ meat
5	3	—	7	890	1 starch, ½ fat
5	2	—	1	865	1 starch
7	2	—	10	903	1 starch, ½ lean meat
5	5	—	30	880	1 starch, 1 fat
0	<1	—	—	605	Free
1	4	—	—	756	½ starch, 1 fat
2	3	—	—	595- 610	½ starch, ½ fat
2	3	—	—	708	1 starch, ½ fat
4	4	—	—	553	1 starch, 1 fat
4	2	—	—	587	1½ starch
3	1	—	—	524	1½ starch
1	1	—	—	665	1 veg.
2	1	—	—	565- 746	½ starch

* Not available   ▌ More than 2 fat exchanges   ♥ Moderate to high sugar content

Products	SERVING SIZE	CALORIES	CARBO-HYDRATE (gm)
Cup-A-Soup®, Country Style (as prepared)			
Chicken Supreme	6 oz.	107	12
Harvest Vegetable	6 oz.	91	19
Hearty Chicken	6 oz.	70	11
Cup-A-Soup®, Lite (as prepared)			
Chicken Florentine, Golden Broccoli Lemon Chicken, Oriental	6 oz.	45	7
Tomato and Herb	6 oz.	66	14
Cup-A-Soup®, Lots-A-Noodles® (as prepared)			
Garden Vegetable	7 oz.	123	23
Hearty Beef and Noodles	7 oz.	107	20
Hearty Creamy Chicken	7 oz.	179	21
Dry Soup Mixes (as prepared)			
Beef Flavor Mushroom	1 cup	38	7
Beefy Onion	1 cup	29	4
Chicken Noodle with Diced White Chicken Meat	1 cup	81	12
Country Vegetable	1 cup	80	16
Giggle Noodle with Chicken Broth	1 cup	72	12
Golden Onion with Chicken Broth	1 cup	62	11
Hearty Chicken Noodle	1 cup	83	13
Hearty Noodle with Vegetables	1 cup	70	13
Noodle with Chicken Broth	1 cup	62	10
Onion	1 cup	20	4
Onion Mushroom	1 cup	41	7
Ring-O-Noodle with Chicken Broth	1 cup	67	11
Vegetable	1 cup	39	7

† For occasional use   ** Not recommended for use

PROTEIN (gm)	FAT (gm)	SAT. FAT (gm)	CHOLES-TEROL (mg)	SODIUM (mg)	EXCHANGES
2	6	—	—	757	1 starch, 1 fat
2	1	—	—	459	1 starch
4	1	—	—	687	1 starch
2	1	—	—	—	½ starch
2	0	—	—	305	1 starch
4	2	—	—	719	1½ starch
4	1	—	—	698	1½ starch
5	8	—	—	639	1½ starch, 1½ fat
2	1	—	—	763	½ starch
1	1	—	—	803	1 veg.
4	2	—	—	795	1 starch
3	1	—	0	803	1 starch
2	2	—	—	708	1 starch
1	2	—	—	716	1 starch
4	1	—	—	753	1 starch
2	1	—	—	713	1 starch
2	2	—	—	708	1 starch
1	0	—	—	632	1 veg.
2	1	—	—	684	½ starch
2	2	—	—	708	1 starch
2	1	—	—	640	½ starch

* Not available   ▤ More than 2 fat exchanges   ♔ Moderate to high sugar content

Products	SERVING SIZE	CALORIES	CARBO-HYDRATE (gm)
Oriental Noodle Soup, instant (as prepared) (average)	8 oz.	190	37
LUNCH BUCKET® (The Dial Corporation) Ready to Serve, microwave			
Beef Noodle	8.25 oz.	120	16
Chicken Noodle	8.25 oz.	110	15
Country Vegetable	8.25 oz.	90	19
Hearty Chicken	8.25 oz.	120	19
Split Pea 'n Ham	8.25 oz.	130	18
Vegetable Beef	8.25 oz.	110	15
NISSIN® (Nissin Foods)			
▤ Cup O'Noodles, all varieties (as prepared) (average)	1 container	300	32
▤ Hearty Cup O'Noodles, all varieties (as prepared) (average)	1 container	300	34
▤ Oodles of Noodles/ Top Ramen, all varieties (as prepared) (average)	1 container	390	49
PROGRESSO® (PET, Inc.) Individual Serving, ready to serve			
Beef	1 can (10½ oz.)	180	14
Beef Barley	1 can (10½ oz.)	170	17
Beef Minestrone	1 can (10½ oz.)	190	16
Beef Vegetable	1 can (10½ oz.)	160	20

† For occasional use   ** Not recommended for use

PROTEIN (gm)	FAT (gm)	SAT. FAT (gm)	CHOLES-TEROL (mg)	SODIUM (mg)	EXCHANGES
8	2	—	—	781-915	2½ starch
10	1	—	35	950	1 starch, 1 lean meat
5	3	—	25	970	1 starch, ½ lean meat
3	1	—	0	820	1 starch
5	3	—	15	1150	1 starch, ½ lean meat
8	3	—	15	740	1 starch, 1 lean meat
7	2	—	15	920	1 starch, 1 lean meat
9	16	—	10	1480-1790	2 starch, ½ meat, 2½ fat
7	15	—	8	1170-1250	2 starch, 3 fat
10	19	—	1	1660-2060	3 starch, 3 fat
15	7	—	—	1590	1 starch, 1½ meat
15	5	—	—	1300	1 starch, 2 lean meat
19	5	—	—	1140	1 starch, 2 lean meat
13	3	—	—	1260	1 starch, 1½ lean meat

* Not available   ▇ More than 2 fat exchanges   ♥ Moderate to high sugar content

Products	SERVING SIZE	CALORIES	CARBO-HYDRATE (gm)
Chicken Minestrone	1 can (10½ oz.)	140	14
Chicken Noodle	1 can (10½ oz.)	120	8
Chicken Rice	1 can (10½ oz.)	120	12
Chicken Vegetable	1 can (10½ oz.)	150	18
Green Split Pea	1 can (10½ oz.)	201	31
Hearty Chicken	1 can (10½ oz.)	130	9
Lentil	1 can (10½ oz.)	140	24
Macaroni & Bean	1 can (10½ oz.)	180	27
Minestrone	1 can (10½ oz.)	120	25
New England Style Clam Chowder	1 can (10½ oz.)	240	22
Split Pea with Ham	1 can (10½ oz.)	190	27
Vegetable	1 can (10½ oz.)	90	16
19 oz. Size, ready to serve Beef	½ can (9½ oz.)	160	12
Beef Barley	½ can (9½ oz.)	150	16

† For occasional use   ** Not recommended for use

PROTEIN (gm)	FAT (gm)	SAT. FAT (gm)	CHOLES- TEROL (mg)	SODIUM (mg)	EXCHANGES
12	4	—	—	1060	1 starch, 1½ lean meat
12	4	—	40	970	½ starch, 1½ lean meat
9	4	—	25	940	1 starch, 1 lean meat
10	4	—	25	790	1 starch, 1 veg., 1 lean meat
12	3	—	—	920	2 starch, 1 lean meat
14	4	—	30	960	½ starch, 2 lean meat
10	4	—	0	1000	1 starch, 1 lean meat
9	4	—	0	1120	2 starch, ½ meat
7	3	—	0	930	1½ starch, ½ fat
8	13	—	—	1050	1½ starch, ½ lean meat, 2 fat
12	4	—	—	1070	1½ starch, 1 meat
4	2	—	<5	1100	1 starch
14	6	—	—	1440	1 starch. 1½ lean meat
13	4	—	—	1180	1 starch, 1½ lean meat

* Not available　　🇧 More than 2 fat exchanges　　🛒 Moderate to high sugar content

Products	SERVING SIZE	CALORIES	CARBO-HYDRATE (gm)
Beef Minestrone	½ can (9½ oz.)	170	15
Beef Noodle	½ can (9½ oz.)	150	18
Chickarina	½ can (9½ oz.)	130	13
Chicken Barley	½ can (9¼ oz.)	100	12
Chicken Minestrone	½ can (9½ oz.)	130	12
Chicken Noodle	½ can (9½ oz.)	120	10
Chicken Rice	½ can (9½ oz.)	130	16
Chicken Vegetable	½ can (9½ oz.)	130	16
Corn Chowder	½ can (9¼ oz.)	200	22
Cream of Chicken	½ can (9½ oz.)	180	13
Cream of Mushroom	½ can (9¼ oz.)	160	14
Creamy Tortellini	½ can (9¼ oz.)	240	17
Escarole in Chicken Broth	½ can (9¼ oz.)	30	2
Green Split Pea	½ can (9½ oz.)	160	27

† For occasional use   ** Not recommended for use

PROTEIN (gm)	FAT (gm)	SAT. FAT (gm)	CHOLES-TEROL (mg)	SODIUM (mg)	EXCHANGES
17	4	—	—	1030	1 starch, 2 lean meat
12	3	—	—	1140	1 starch, 1½ lean meat
8	5	—	20	820	1 starch, 1 meat
12	2	—	20	710	1 starch, ½ lean meat
12	3	—	20	870	1 starch, 1 lean meat
11	4	—	35	920	1 starch, 1 lean meat
9	3	—	20	740	1 starch, ½ meat
9	3	—	25	710	1 starch, ½ meat
5	10	—	10	840	1½ starch 2 fat
8	11	—	—	760	1 starch, 1 meat, 1 fat
4	10	—	15	1120	1 starch, 2 fat
5	16	9	35	910	1 starch, 3 fat
2	1	—	<5	1100	1 veg.
11	3	—	<5	1050	1½ starch, 1 lean meat

* Not available   ▯ More than 2 fat exchanges   ♔ Moderate to high sugar content

Products	SERVING SIZE	CALORIES	CARBO-HYDRATE (gm)
Ham & Bean	½ can (9½ oz.)	180	30
Hearty Beef	½ can (9½ oz.)	160	15
Hearty Chicken	½ can (9½ oz.)	130	11
Hearty Minestrone	½ can (9¼ oz.)	110	16
Homestyle Chicken	½ can (9½ oz.)	110	12
Lentil	½ can (9½ oz.)	140	25
Lentil with Sausage	½ can (9½ oz.)	180	20
Macaroni & Bean	½ can (9½ oz.)	170	25
Manhattan Clam Chowder	½ can (9½ oz.)	120	17
Minestrone	½ can (9½ oz.)	130	22
New England Style Clam Chowder	½ can (9¼ oz.)	220	20
Split Pea with Ham	½ can (9½ oz.)	170	24
Tomato	½ can (9½ oz.)	120	20
Tomato Beef with Rotini	½ can (9½ oz.)	170	19

† For occasional use   ** Not recommended for use

PROTEIN (gm)	FAT (gm)	SAT. FAT (gm)	CHOLES-TEROL (mg)	SODIUM (mg)	EXCHANGES
12	2	—	—	1130	2 starch, 1 lean meat
15	4	2	35	1210	1 starch, 1½ lean meat
13	4	—	25	900	1 starch, 1½ lean meat
7	2	—	<5	740	1 starch, 1 lean meat
11	3	—	20	740	1 starch, 1 lean meat
10	4	—	0	840	1½ starch, 1 lean meat
9	7	—	—	940	1 starch, 1 high-fat meat
8	5	—	0	1070	1½ starch, 1 fat
8	2	—	—	1050	1 starch, 1 lean meat
7	4	—	0	1010	1½ starch, ½ fat
8	12	—	—	950	1 starch, 1 lean meat, 2 fat
11	4	—	—	970	1½ starch 1 lean meat
4	3	—	0	1100	1 starch, ½ fat
11	6	—	—	1250	1 starch, 1 meat

* Not available   ▤ More than 2 fat exchanges   ♨ Moderate to high sugar content

Products	SERVING SIZE	CALORIES	CARBO-HYDRATE (gm)
Tomato Tortellini	½ can (9¼ oz.)	130	16
Tortellini	½ can (9½ oz.)	190	12
Vegetable	½ can (9½ oz.)	80	15
Zesty Minestrone	½ can (9½ oz.)	150	19
STOUFFER'S® (Stouffer Foods Corp.)			
Cream of Spinach	8 oz.	210	12
New England Clam Chowder	8 oz.	180	16
SWANSON® (Campbell Soup Company)			
Beef Broth	7¼ oz.	13	0
Chicken Broth	7¼ oz.	30	2
WEIGHT WATCHERS® (H. J. Heinz Co.)			
Broth Mix, all varieties (average)	1 packet	8	1
Ready to Serve, individual Chicken Noodle	10.5 oz.	80	9
Chunky Vegetarian	10.5 oz.	100	18
Cream of Mushroom	10.5 oz.	90	14
Turkey Vegetable	10.5 oz.	70	10
Vegetable with Beef Stock	10.5 oz.	90	13

† For occasional use   ** Not recommended for use

PROTEIN (gm)	FAT (gm)	SAT. FAT (gm)	CHOLES-TEROL (mg)	SODIUM (mg)	EXCHANGES
5	5	—	10	1040	1 starch, 1 fat
16	3	—	10	840	1 starch, 2 lean meat
4	2	—	<5	1190	1 starch
7	8	—	10	1130	1 starch, ½ meat, 1 fat
7	15	—	—	1020	1 veg., ½ skim milk, 3 fat
8	9	—	—	790	½ starch, ½ skim milk, 2 fat
2	1	—	—	750	Free
2	2	—	—	910	½ fat
1	0	—	—	930-990	Free
6	2	—	—	1230	½ starch, ½ lean meat
3	2	—	—	1250	1 starch, ½ fat
3	2	—	—	1250	1 starch
4	2	—	—	1020	1 starch
4	2	—	—	1370	1 starch

* Not available   ▊ More than 2 fat exchanges   🛒 Moderate to high sugar content

Products	SERVING SIZE	CALORIES	CARBO-HYDRATE (gm)

STUFFING, STUFFING MIXES

BETTY CROCKER® (General Mills, Inc.)
Stuffing Mix (as prepared)

Chicken	½ cup	180	21
Herb, Traditional	½ cup	190	22

GOLDEN GRAIN® (Quaker Oats Company)

Bread Stuffing Mix, all varieties (as prepared) (average)	½ cup	180	21

PEPPERIDGE FARMS® (Campbell Soup Company)

Distinctive Stuffing, all varieties (as prepared) (average)	1 oz.	110	18
Stuffing, all varieties (as prepared) (average)	1 oz.	110	22

STOVETOP® (General Foods Corp.)

Stuffing Mix, all varieties, (as prepared (with butter, salted) (average)	½ cup	180	21
Stuffing Mix, Microwave all varieties, (as prepared with butter, salted) (average)	½ cup	165	20

VEGETABLES

BIRDS EYE FOR ONE® (General Foods Corp.)

Broccoli, Cauliflower, and Carrots in Cheese Sauce	5 oz.	110	11

BIRDS EYE® (General Foods Corp.)
Combination Vegetables

Creamed Spinach	3 oz.	50	5
French Green Beans with Almonds	3 oz.	50	8
Grean Peas with Cream Sauce	5 oz.	180	16
Small Onions with Cream Sauce	5 oz.	140	12

† For occasional use   ** Not recommended for use

PROTEIN (gm)	FAT (gm)	SAT. FAT (gm)	CHOLES- TEROL (mg)	SODIUM (mg)	EXCHANGES
4	9	—	—	620	1½ starch 1½ fat
4	9	—	—	640	1½ starch, 1½ fat
4	9	0	0	710-870	1½ starch, 1½ fat
4	3	—	—	210-330	1 starch, ½ fat
3	1	—	—	320-430	1½ starch
4	9	—	20	490-650	1½ starch, 1½ fat
4	7	—	10-15	450-580	1½ starch, 1 fat
6	5	—	5	410	2 veg., 1 fat
2	4	—	0	310	1 veg., 1 fat
3	2	—	0	310	1 veg., ½ fat
5	11	—	0	480	1 starch, 2 fat
2	10	—	0	400	2 veg., 2 fat

* Not available   More than 2 fat exchanges   Moderate to high sugar content

Products	SERVING SIZE	CALORIES	CARBO-HYDRATE (gm)
Combination Vegetables in Butter Sauce			
Broccoli, Cauliflower, and Carrots in Butter Sauce	3.3 oz.	45	6
Broccoli Spears in Butter sauce	3.3 oz.	45	5
Tender Sweet Corn in Butter Sauce	3.3 oz.	90	17
Combination Vegetables with Cheese Sauce			
Baby Brussels Sprouts with Cheese Sauce	4.5 oz.	130	12
Broccoli, Cauliflower, and Carrots with Cheese Sauce	4.5 oz.	110	11
Broccoli with Cheese Sauce	5 oz.	130	12
Cauliflower with Cheese Sauce	5 oz.	130	12
Peas and Pearl Onions with Cheese Sauce	5 oz.	140	17
Custom Cuisine (*Values do not include other ingredients added in preparation.)			
Chow Mein Vegetables in Oriental Sauce	4.6 oz.	80	14
Pasta and Vegetables in Creamy Stroganoff Sauce	4.6. oz.	120	15
Pasta and Vegetables with White Cheese Sauce	4.6 oz.	150	19
Vegetables with Authentic Oriental Sauce for Beef	4.6 oz.	90	11
Vegetables with Creamy Mushroom Sauce for Beef	4.6 oz.	90	8
Vegetables with Delicate Herb Sauce for Chicken or Shrimp	4.6 oz.	90	8
Vegetables with Dijon Mustard Sauce for Chicken or Fish	4.6 oz.	70	9
Vegetables with Savory Tomato Basil Sauce for Chicken	4.6 oz.	110	17

† For occasional use   ** Not recommended for use

PROTEIN (gm)	FAT (gm)	SAT. FAT (gm)	CHOLES-TEROL (mg)	SODIUM (mg)	EXCHANGES
2	2	—	5	290	1 veg., ½ fat
2	2	—	5	320	1 veg., ½ fat
2	2	—	5	250	1 starch, ½ fat
6	7	—	5	500	2 veg., 1½ fat
5	5	—	5	410	2 veg., 1 fat
6	7	—	10	560	2 veg., 1½ fat
5	7	—	10	560	2 veg., 1½ fat
6	5	—	5	470	1 starch, 1 fat
3	2	—	0	570	½ starch, 1 veg., 1 fat
5	5	—	30	700	½ starch, 1 veg., 1 fat
7	6	—	15	440	1 starch, 1 veg., 1 fat
6	4	—	0	350	1 starch, 1 veg., ½ fat
3	5	—	0	460	2 veg., 1 fat
3	5	—	0	460	2 veg., 1 fat
4	3	—	5	310	2 veg., ½ fat
5	3	—	0	360	½ starch, 2 veg., ½ fat

* Not available   ▤ More than 2 fat exchanges   ⛟ Moderate to high sugar content

Products	SERVING SIZE	CALORIES	CARBO-HYDRATE (gm)
Vegetables with Wild Rice in White Wine Sauce for Chicken	4.6 oz.	100	19
International Rice Recipes			
Country Style	3.3 oz.	90	19
French Style	3.3 oz.	110	23
Spanish Style	3.3 oz.	110	24
International Recipes - Vegetables with Seasoned Sauces			
Bavarian Style Recipe with Green Beans and Spaetzle	3.3 oz.	100	11
Italian Style	3.3 oz.	100	11
Japanese Style	3.3 oz.	90	10
New England Style	3.3 oz.	130	14
Oriental Style	3.3 oz.	70	8
Pasta Primavera	3.3 oz.	120	14
San Francisco Style	3.3 oz.	100	11
GREEN GIANT® (The Pillsbury Company)			
Cream and Cheese Sauce Vegetables			
Broccoli, Cauliflower, Carrots in Cheese Flavored Sauce	½ cup	60	9
Broccoli in Cheese Flavored Sauce	½ cup	60	9
Cauliflower in Cheese Flavored Sauce	½ cup	60	8
Creamed Spinach	½ cup	60	9
Cream Style Corn	½ cup	110	25
Microwave Garden Gourmet			
Asparagus Pilaf	1 pkg.	190	37
Creamy Mushroom	1 pkg.	220	29
Fettucine Primavera	1 pkg.	230	26
Pasta Dijon	1 pkg.	260	21

PROTEIN (gm)	FAT (gm)	SAT. FAT (gm)	CHOLES- TEROL (mg)	SODIUM (mg)	EXCHANGES
3	0	—	0	510	1 starch, 1 veg.
2	0	—	0	380	1 starch, 2 veg.
3	0	—	0	610	1 starch, 1 veg.
3	0	—	0	540	1 starch, 1 veg.
2	5	—	10	350	2 veg., 1 fat
2	5	—	0	490	2 veg., 1 fat
2	5	—	0	420	2 veg., 1 fat
3	7	—	0	430	1 starch, 1 fat
2	4	—	0	300	1 veg., 1 fat
5	5	—	5	340	3 veg., 1 fat **or** 1 starch, 1 fat
2	5	—	0	400	2 veg., 1 fat
3	2	<1	2	490	2 veg.
3	2	<1	2	530	2 veg.
2	2	<1	2	500	2 veg.
4	2	1	2	510	2 veg.
3	1	0	0	370	1½ starch
5	4	2	10	610	1½ starch, 2 veg., ½ fat
6	11	6	25	860	1 starch, 2 veg., 2 fat
13	8	3	25	610	1½ starch, 1 veg., 1 meat
7	17	9	55	630	1 starch, 1 veg., 3 fat

* Not available   ▊ More than 2 fat exchanges   🛒 Moderate to high sugar content

Products	SERVING SIZE	CALORIES	CARBO-HYDRATE (gm)
Pasta Florentine	1 pkg.	230	27
Rotini Cheddar	1 pkg.	230	32
Sherry Wild Rice	1 pkg.	210	40
Tortellini Provencale	1 pkg.	210	36
One Serving Vegetables			
Broccoli, Carrots, Rotini in Cheese Sauce	5.5 oz.	120	20
Broccoli, Cauliflower, Carrots (no sauce)	4 oz.	25	7
Broccoli, Cauliflower, Carrots in Cheese Sauce	5 oz.	70	12
Broccoli Cuts in Carrots in Cheese Sauce	5 oz.	70	11
Broccoli in Butter sauce	4.5 oz.	45	7
Cauliflower in Cheese Sauce	5.5 oz.	80	14
Corn on the Cob	2 half ears	120	26
Early Peas in Butter Sauce	4.5 oz.	90	16
Green Beans in Butter Sauce	5.5 oz.	60	10
Niblets® Corn in Butter Sauce	4.5 oz.	120	24
MRS. PAUL'S® (Campbell Soup Company)			
Candied Sweet Potatoes	4 oz.	190	97
Candied Sweets 'n Apples	4 oz.	160	39
Crispy Onion Rings	2½ oz.	180	20
Eggplant Parmagiana	5 oz.	260	19
Fried Eggplant Sticks	3½ oz.	240	29

PROTEIN (gm)	FAT (gm)	SAT. FAT (gm)	CHOLES-TEROL (mg)	SODIUM (mg)	EXCHANGES
14	9	5	25	840	1½ starch, 1 veg., 1 meat
9	10	6	20	570	1½ starch, 1 veg., ½ meat, 1 fat
6	4	2	10	580	2 starch, 1 veg., ½ fat
7	5	1	15	720	2 starch, 1 veg., ½ fat
4	3	<1	2	550	1 starch, 1 veg., ½ fat
2	0	0	0	45	1 veg.
3	3	<1	5	610	2 veg., ½ fat
4	3	<1	2	660	2 veg., ½ fat
3	2	<1	5	420	1 veg., ½ fat
3	2	<1	5	690	2 veg., ½ fat
4	1	0	0	10	1½ starch
6	2	<1	5	500	1 starch
2	2	1	5	360	2 veg.
3	2	<1	5	350	1½ starch
1	0	—	—	60	**
0	0	—	—	70	1 starch, 1½ fruit†
2	10	—	—	270	1 starch, 1 veg., 2 fat
6	17	—	—	600	1 starch, 1 veg., ½ meat, 3 fat
4	12	—	—	610	2 starch, 2 fat

* Not available   ▤ More than 2 fat exchanges   🛒 Moderate to high sugar content

Products	SERVING SIZE	CALORIES	CARBO-HYDRATE (gm)
Light Batter Zucchini Sticks	3 oz.	200	21
ORE-IDA® (Ore-Ida Foods, Inc.)			
Breaded Vegetables (as purchased) Medley	3 oz.	160	17
Mushrooms	2⅔ oz.	140	14
Onion Ringers®	2 oz.	140	18
Okra	3 oz.	170	17
Zucchini	3 oz.	150	15
S & W® (S & W Fine Foods, Inc.)			
Artichoke Hearts, marinated in oil	3 oz.	225	6
Beets, pickled	½ cup	70	16
Onions, in brine	½ cup	35	9
Tomato Paste	½ cup	100	23
Tomato Puree	½ cup	60	14
Tomato Sauce	½ cup	40	9
Yams, candied	½ cup	180	44
STOUFFER'S (Stouffer Foods Corp.)			
Corn Souffle	⅓ of 12 oz. package	160	18
Creamed Spinach	½ of 9 oz. package	170	7
Green Bean Mushroom Casserole	½ of 9½ oz. package	160	13

† For occasional use   ** Not recommended for use

PROTEIN (gm)	FAT (gm)	SAT. FAT (gm)	CHOLES- TEROL (mg)	SODIUM (mg)	EXCHANGES
2	12	—	—	440	1 starch, 1 veg., 2 fat
3	9	2	5	500	1 starch, 1 veg., 1½ fat
4	8	1	5	515	½ starch, 1 veg., 1½ fat
2	7	1	0	180	1 starch, 1½ fat
3	10	2	5	665	1 starch, 1 veg., 1½ fat
3	9	2	5	445	1 starch, 1 veg., 1½ fat
2	26	—	—	15	1 veg., 5 fat
1	0	—	—	215	1 veg., ½ fruit†
1	0	—	—	345	1 veg.
4	0	—	—	67	4 veg. **or** 1 starch
2	0	—	—	35	3 veg. **or** 1 starch
2	0	—	—	620	2 veg. **or** ½ starch
1	0	—		355	**
5	7	—	—	560	1 starch, 1½ fat
4	14	—	—	380	2 veg., 2½ fat
3	11	—	—	680	2 veg., 2 fat

* Not available   ▤ More than 2 fat exchanges   ♥ Moderate to high sugar content

Products	SERVING SIZE	CALORIES	CARBO-HYDRATE (gm)
Spinach Souffle	⅓ of 12 oz. package	140	8

VEGETARIAN

LOMA LINDA® (Worthington Foods, Inc.)

Big Franks	1 frank	110	2
Chik-Nuggets	5 pieces (3 oz.)	270	8
Corn Dogs	1 dog	190	15
Dinner Cuts	3½ oz.	110	2
Fried Chicken	1 piece (2 oz.)	180	2
Fried Chicken with Gravy	2 pieces (2.75 oz.)	230	4
Griddle Stak	1 steak (2 oz.)	140	4
Little Links	2 links	90	2
Linketts	2 links	140	2
Nutreena	½" slice	160	6
Proteena	½" slice	140	5
Redi-Burger	½" slice	130	5
Sandwich Spread	3 Tbsp.	70	4
Savory Meatballs	7 meatballs	190	7
Sizzle Burger	1 pattie	220	10
Sizzle Franks	2 franks	170	3
Swiss Steak	3½ oz.	170	7
Tender Bits	2 oz.	80	5
Tender Rounds	6 meatballs	120	7

† For occasional use   ** Not recommended for use

PROTEIN (gm)	FAT (gm)	SAT. FAT (gm)	CHOLES-TEROL (mg)	SODIUM (mg)	EXCHANGES
6	9	—	—	500	2 veg., 2 fat
11	6	—	—	—	2 lean meat
15	20	—	—	—	½ starch, 2 meat, 2 fat
13	8	—	—	—	1 starch, 1½ meat
22	1	—	—	—	2 lean meat
11	14	—	—	—	1½ meat, 1½ fat
15	17	—	—	—	1 veg., 2 meat, 1½ fat
14	7	—	—	—	1 veg., 2 lean meat
9	5	—	—	—	1½ lean meat
15	8	—	—	—	2 lean meat, ½ fat
8	12	—	—	—	1 veg., 1 meat, 1½ fat
17	6	—	—	—	1 veg., 2 lean meat
14	6	—	—	—	1 veg., 2 lean meat
4	4	—	—	—	1 veg., 1 fat
22	8	—	—	—	1 veg., 3 lean meat
17	12	—	—	—	½ starch, 2 meat, ½ fat
10	13	—	—	—	1½ meat, 1 fat
14	10	—	—	—	1 veg., 2 meat
9	3	—	—	—	1 veg., 1 lean meat
15	4	—	—	—	1 veg., 2 lean meat

* Not available   ▯ More than 2 fat exchanges   🛒 Moderate to high sugar content

Products	SERVING SIZE	CALORIES	CARBO-HYDRATE (gm)
Vege-Burger	½ cup	110	3
Vegelona	½" slice	100	6

MORNINGSTAR FARMS® (Worthington Foods, Inc.)
Frozen Products

Breakfast Links	2 links	127	2
Breakfast Pattie	1 pattie	95	4
Breakfast Strips	3 strips (1 oz.)	80	4
Country Crisp Patties	1 pattie (¼ pkg.)	220	13
Grillers®	1 pattie (¼ pkg.)	180	5
Homestyle Country Crisps™	3 oz. (¼ pkg.)	250	18

NATURAL TOUCH® (Worthington Foods, Inc.)
Canned Products

Vegetarian Chili	⅔ cup (⅕ can)	230	19

Dry Products

Loaf Mix (as packaged)	4 oz. (¼ pkg.)	180	7
Stroganoff Mix (as prepared)	4 oz. (¼ pkg.)	90	10
Taco Mix (as packaged)	2 Tbsp.	90	6

Frozen Products

Dinner Entree	1 pattie (3 oz.)	230	6
Harvest Bake™ Lentil Rice Loaf	2 slices (4 oz.)	190	18
Okara® Patties	1 pattie (¼ pkg.)	160	7
Tofu Garden Patties	1 pattie (¼ pkg.)	90	3

† For occasional use   ** Not recommended for use

PROTEIN (gm)	FAT (gm)	SAT. FAT (gm)	CHOLES- TEROL (mg)	SODIUM (mg)	EXCHANGES
21	2	—	—	—	2 lean meat
18	1	—	—	—	1 veg., 1½ lean meat
8	9	1	0	335	1 lean meat, 1½ fat
8	6	1	0	355	1 veg., 1 meat
3	6	1	0	350	1 veg., 1 fat
8	15	2	0	620	1 starch, 1 meat, 1½ fat
13	12	2	0	350	1 veg., 1½ meat 1 fat
8	16	—	0	480	1 starch, 1 meat, 2 fat
12	12	1	0	890	1 starch, 1½ meat, 1 fat
21	7	—	0	25	1 veg., 3 lean meat
4	3	—	—	—	½ starch, ½ meat
10	2	—	—	—	1 veg., 1 lean meat
20	14	2	0	300	1 veg., 3 meat
8	9	1	0	620	1 starch, 1 meat, 1 fat
11	10	1	0	420	1 veg., 1½ meat ½ fat
10	4	1	0	260	1½ lean meat

* Not available   ▤ More than 2 fat exchanges   🛒 Moderate to high sugar content

Products	SERVING SIZE	CALORIES	CARBO-HYDRATE (gm)
WORTHINGTON® (Worthington Foods, Inc.)			
Canned Products			
Chili	⅔ cup	190	15
Choplets®	¼ can (2 slices)	100	5
Country Stew	½ can (9½ oz.)	220	23
Chik, diced	¼ cup (2 oz.)	90	2
Chik, sliced	2 slices (¼ can)	90	2
Fri Chik®	2 pieces (3 oz.)	180	4
Multigrain Cutlets	2 slices (¼ can)	90	5
Non-Meat Balls™	3 meat-balls	100	4
Numete®	½" slice (⅛ can)	160	6
Prime Stakes™	1 piece (3 oz.)	160	7
Protose®	½" slice	180	9
Saucettes®	2 links	140	5
Savory Slices	2 slices (2 oz.)	100	4
Super Links™	1 link	100	3
Turkee Slices	2 slices (¼ can)	130	3
Vegetable Skallops®	½ cup (3 oz.)	90	4
Vegetable Skallops®, no salt added	½ cup (3 oz.)	80	4
Vegetable Steaks™	2½ pieces (3 oz.)	110	5
Vegetarian Burger™	½ cup	150	9

PROTEIN (gm)	FAT (gm)	SAT. FAT (gm)	CHOLES-TEROL (mg)	SODIUM (mg)	EXCHANGES
10	10	1	0	550	1 starch, 1 meat, 1 fat
17	2	—	0	350	1 veg., 2 lean meat
10	10	1	0	760	1 starch, 1 veg., 1 meat, 1 fat
4	8	—	0	330	½ meat, 1 fat
4	8	—	0	330	½ meat, 1 fat
11	13	—	0	610	1½ meat, 1½ fat
14	2	—	0	550	1 veg., 1½ lean meat
7	6	1	0	220	1 veg., 1 meat
8	11	2	0	570	1 veg., 1 meat, 1 fat
10	10	—	0	410	½ starch, 1 meat, 1 fat
17	8	1	0	470	½ starch, 2 meat
10	9	1	0	350	1 veg., 1 meat, 1 fat
8	6	—	0	340	1 veg., 1 meat
7	7	1	0	440	1 high fat meat
9	9	—	0	430	1 meat, 1 fat
15	2	—	0	430	2 lean meat
13	1	—	0	80	1½ lean meat
17	2	—	0	400	1 veg., 2 lean meat
19	4	1	0	780	½ starch, 2 lean meat

* Not available   ▊ More than 2 fat exchanges   🛒 Moderate to high sugar content

Products	SERVING SIZE	CALORIES	CARBO-HYDRATE (gm)
Vegetarian Burger™, no salt added	½ cup	160	9
Vegetarian Cutlets	1½ slices (3 oz.)	100	4
Veja-Links®	2 links	140	4
Dry Products Granburger®	6 Tbsp.	110	7
Soyamel®, powdered soy milk	1 oz. dry (8 oz. prepared)	130	10
Frozen Products Bolono™	2 slices	60	2
Chic-ketts®	½ cup (3 oz.)	160	6
Chik Stiks™	1 piece	110	4
Crispy Chik	3 oz. (¼ pkg.)	280	17
Crispy Chik Patties	1 pattie (¼ pkg.)	220	13
Dinner Roast	2 oz.	120	5
Dixie Dogs	1 dixie dog (¼ pkg.)	200	21
FriPats®	1 piece (¼ pkg.)	180	5
Golden Croquettes	3 ¾ oz. (¼ pkg.)	280	20
Leanies®	1 link	100	2
Meatless Beef Style	4 slices (2.5 oz.)	130	7
Meatless Chicken	2 slices (2 oz.)	130	3
Meatless Chicken, diced	½ cup (3 oz.)	190	5
Meatless Corned Beef	4 slices (2 oz.)	120	8

† For occasional use   ** Not recommended for use

PROTEIN (gm)	FAT (gm)	SAT. FAT (gm)	CHOLES-TEROL (mg)	SODIUM (mg)	EXCHANGES
17	5	—	0	500	½ starch, 2 lean meat
16	2	—	0	270	2 lean meat
8	10	—	0	330	1 veg., 1 meat, 1 fat
19	1	—	0	700	1 veg., 2 lean meat
7	7	1	0	210	1 skim milk, 1 fat
7	2	0	0	390	1 lean meat
19	7	1	0	640	1 veg., 2½ lean meat
9	7	1	0	390	1 veg., 1 meat
10	19	—	0	500	1 starch, 1 meat, 3 fat
8	15	2	0	620	1 starch, 1 meat 1½ fat
7	8	1	0	440	1 veg., 1 meat, ½ fat
8	10	—	0	640	1 starch, 1 meat, 1 fat
13	12	2	0	350	1 veg., 1½ meat, 1 fat
19	14	2	0	890	1 starch, 2½ meat
8	6	1	0	440	1 meat
12	6	—	0	750	1 veg., 1½ meat
9	9	1	0	460	1 veg., 1 meat ½ fat
13	13	2	0	680	1 veg., 1½ meat, 1 fat
9	6	1	0	740	½ starch, 1 meat

* Not available   ░ More than 2 fat exchanges   ♥ Moderate to high sugar content

Products	SERVING SIZE	CALORIES	CARBO-HYDRATE (gm)
Meatless Salami	2 slices (2 oz.)	90	2
Meatless Smoked Beef	3 slices (2 oz.)	120	7
Meatless Smoked Turkey	4 slices (⅓ pkg.)	180	5
Prosage®	2⅜" slices (2½ oz.)	180	4
Prosage® Links	3 links	190	4
Prosage® Patties	2 patties	210	4
Stakelets®	1 piece	150	7
Stripples	4 strips	120	6
Tuno®	2 oz.	100	3
Veelets™	2½ oz. (¼ pkg.)	230	12
Vegetarian Egg Rolls	1 roll (3 oz.)	160	20
Vegetarian Fillets™	2 fillets (3 oz.)	180	9
Vegetarian Pie Beef	8 oz.	360	44
Chicken	8 oz.	380	43
Wham™	3 slices (2½ oz.)	120	3

PROTEIN (gm)	FAT (gm)	SAT. FAT (gm)	CHOLES-TEROL (mg)	SODIUM (mg)	EXCHANGES
8	5	1	0	460	1 meat
10	6	—	0	790	½ starch, 1 meat
13	12	—	0	820	1 veg., 1½ meat, 1 fat
13	12	2	0	570	1 veg., 1½ meat 1 fat
13	14	2	0	570	1 veg., 1½ meat, 1 fat
18	14	3	0	780	1 veg., 2 meat, 1 fat
13	8	1	0	460	½ starch, 2 lean meat
4	9	1	0	460	½ starch, ½ meat, 1 fat
5	7	1	0	310	1 meat, ½ fat
14	14	3	0	390	1 starch, 2 meat
6	6	1	0	530	1 starch, 1 veg., 1 fat
15	9	2	0	910	½ starch, 2 meat
9	16	—	0	1940	2½ starch, 1 veg., 3 fat
7	20	3	0	1200	2½ starch, 1 veg., 3½ fat
11	7	1	0	940	1½ meat

* Not available   ▉ More than 2 fat exchanges   ♥ Moderate to high sugar content

Products	SERVING SIZE	CALORIES	CARBO-HYDRATE (gm)

YOGURT

Author's Note: Many of these products contain large amounts of refined sugars. We recommend that these products be use in moderation, if at all. If you decide to use them, work the specific product into your meal plan, using the nutrition information supplied here. And if you have diabetes, remember that when you to eat a high-sugar yogurt, do so with a meal, when it will be more slowly absorbed; or before exercise, so that it will be readily used for energy.

DANNON® (The Dannon Co., Inc.)

Products	SERVING SIZE	CALORIES	CARBO-HYDRATE (gm)
☰ Fruit-on-the-Bottom Yogurt, all varieties (average)	4.4 oz.	120	23
	8 oz.	240	43
Lowfat Yogurt Plain	8 oz.	140	15
☰ Blended with Fruit, all varieties (average)	4.4 oz.	130	24
☰ Flavored: Coffee, Lemon, Vanilla (average)	8 oz.	200	34
Nonfat Yogurt Plain	8 oz.	110	15
☰ Blended	6 oz.	140	27
Light (with aspartame)	4.4 oz.	60	8
	8 oz.	100	17
KEMPS® (Marigold Foods, Inc.)			
Lite Yogurt, all varieties (average)	6 oz.	80	13

PROTEIN (gm)	FAT (gm)	SAT. FAT (gm)	CHOLES-TEROL (mg)	SODIUM (mg)	EXCHANGES
5	1	—	5	65	½ skim milk, 1 fruit†
9	3	—	10	120	1 skim milk, 2 fruit, ½ fat **or** 1 starch, 1 lean meat, 2 fruit†
11	4	—	15	125	1¼ skim milk, ½ fat **or** 1 starch, 1 meat
5	2	—	5	80	½ skim milk, 1 fruit, ½ fat†
10	3	—	10	120	1¼ skim milk, 1 fruit, ½ fat **or** 1 starch, 1 lean meat, 1 fruit†
12	0	—	5	140	1¼ skim milk **or** 1 starch, 1 lean meat
8	0	—	<5	105	1 skim milk, 1 fruit†
6	0	—	<5	70	¾ skim milk
9	0	—	<5	130	1 skim milk
6	0	—	—	—	1 skim milk

* Not available   ▤ More than 2 fat exchanges   🛒 Moderate to high sugar content

Products	SERVING SIZE	CALORIES	CARBO-HYDRATE (gm)
☕ Yogurt Jr.'s	4 oz.	130	24
LIGHT N' LIVELY® (Kraft, Inc.) Free™ Nonfat Yogurt with Aspartame, all varieties (average)	4.4 oz.	50	8
WEIGHT WATCHERS® (H. J. Heinz Co.) Yogurt			
☕ Nonfat Fruited	1 cup	150	27
Plain	1 cup	90	13
Ultimate 90™	1 cup	90	13
YOPLAIT® (General Mills, Inc.)			
☕ Breakfast Yogurt™, all varieties (average)	6 oz.	210	39
☕ Custard Style™, all varieties (average)	4 oz.	130	20
	6 oz.	190	31
☕ Fat Free, all varieties (average)	6 oz.	150	30
Light, all varieties (average)	4 oz.	60	9
	6 oz.	90	14
Nonfat Plain	8 oz.	120	18
☕ Vanilla	8 oz	180	35
Original Fruit Flavors (average)	4 oz.	120	21
	6 oz.	190	32
Plain	6 oz.	130	15
☕ Vanilla	6 oz.	180	29

PROTEIN (gm)	FAT (gm)	SAT. FAT (gm)	CHOLES-TEROL (mg)	SODIUM (mg)	EXCHANGES
6	1	—	—	—	1 fruit, 1 skim milk†
4	0	0	0	60	½ skim milk
9	<1	—	5	120	1 skim milk, 1 fruit†
10	<1	—	5	135	1 skim milk
10	0	—	5	120	1 skim milk
8	3	2	10	90-95	2 fruit, 1 skim milk **or** 1 starch, 1 lean meat, 1½ fruit†
5	3	—	15	60-70	1 fruit, ½ skim milk, ½ fat†
7	4	—	20	95-110	1 fruit, 1 skim milk, ½ fat†
8	0	—	<5	95-110	1 skim milk, 1 fruit†
5	0	—	<5	65	¾ skim milk
7	0	—	<5	100	1 skim milk
13	0	—	5	160	1½ skim milk
11	0	—	5	140	1½ skim milk, 1 fruit†
5	2	—	10	75	½ skim milk, 1 fruit†
8	3	—	10	110	1 skim milk, 1 fruit, ½ fat†
10	3	—	15	140	1¼ skim milk, ½ fat
9	3	—	15	120	1¼ skim milk, 1 fruit, ½ fat†

* Not available   ▉ More than 2 fat exchanges   ♥ Moderate to high sugar content

Index

A

Y

DCI Publishing Books of Related Interest

Fast Food Facts *by Marion Franz, RD, MS.* This revised and up-to-date best-seller shows how to make smart nutritional choices at fast food restaurants—and tells what to avoid. Includes complete nutrition information on more than 1,000 menu offerings from the 32 largest fast food chains.

- ☐ Standard-size edition   004068, ISBN 0-937721-67-0 $6.95
- ☐ Pocket edition   004073, ISBN 0-937721-69-7 $4.95

All-American Low-Fat Meals in Minutes *by M.J. Smith, RD, LD, MA.* Filled with tantalizing recipes and valuable tips, this cookbook makes great-tasting low-fat foods a snap for holidays, special occasions, or everyday. Most recipes take only minutes to prepare.

- ☐   004079, ISBN 0-937721-73-5 $12.95

The Guiltless Gourmet *by Judy Gilliard and Joy Kirkpatrick, RD.* A perfect fusion of sound nutrition and creative cooking, this book is loaded with delicious recipes high in flavor and low in fat, sugar, cholesterol, and salt.

- ☐   004021, ISBN 0-937721-23-9 $9.95

The Guiltless Gourmet Goes Ethnic *by Judy Gilliard and Joy Kirkpatrick, RD.* More than a cookbook, this sequel to The Guiltless Gourmet shows how easy it is to lower the sugar, calories, sodium, and fat in your favorite ethnic dishes—without sacrificing taste.

- ☐   004072, ISBN 0-937721-68-9 $11.95

European Cuisine from the Guiltless Gourmet *by Judy Gilliard and Joy Kirkpatrick, RD.* This innovative book makes it possible to create enticing Greek, English, German, Russian, and Scandinavian dishes without all of the salt, sugar, cholesterol, fat, and calories.

☐ 004085, ISBN 0-937721-81-6 $11.95

Convenience Food Facts *by Marion Franz, RD, MS, and Arlene Monk, RD.* Includes complete nutrition information, tips, and exchange values on over 1,500 popular name-brand processed foods commonly found in grocery store freezers and shelves. It helps you plan easy-to-prepare, nutritious meals.

☐ 004081, ISBN 0-937721-77-8 $9.95

Exchanges for All Occasions *by Marion Franz, RD, MS.* Exchanges and meal planning suggestions for just about any occasion, sample meal plans, special tips for people with diabetes, and more.

☐ 004003, ISBN 0-937721-22-0 $8.95

Fight Fat & Win *by Elaine Moquette-Magee, RD, MPH.* This breakthrough book explains how to easily incorporate low-fat dietary guidelines into every modern eating experience, from fast food and common restaurants to quick meals at home, simply by making smarter choices.

☐ 004070, ISBN 0-937721-65-4 $9.95

Joy of Snacks *by Nancy Cooper, RD.* Offers over 200 delicious recipes and nutritional information for hearty snacks including sandwiches, appetizers, soups, spreads, cookies, muffins, and treats especially for kids. The book also suggests guidelines for selecting convenience snacks and interpreting information on food labels.

☐ 004086, ISBN 0-937721-82-4 $12.95

Opening the Door to Good Nutrition *by Marion Franz, RD, MS.* This book is for all of us who want to have healthy eating habits but don't know where to start. It not only provides nutrition facts, but also a step-by-step process for improving eating behavior.

☐ 004013, ISBN 0-937721-15-8 $7.95

Pass the Pepper Please by Diane Reader, RD, and Marion Franz, RD, MS. This imaginative book is loaded with fresh and clear suggestions for cutting back on salt to lower blood pressure and maintain good health.

☐ 004020, ISBN 0-937721-17-4 $3.95

The Expresslane Diet by Audrey Fran Blumenfeld, RD. This 21-day weight-management plan meets U.S. recommended daily allowances using brand name convenience and frozen foods and even some fast foods. With this nutritious diet you'll lose weight quickly—up to seven pounds a week.

☐ 004055, ISBN 0-937721-61-1 $7.95

Buy them at you local bookstore or use this convenient coupon for ordering.

DCI Publishing
P.O. Box 47945
Minneapolis, MN 55447-9727

Please send me the books I have checked above. I am enclosing $_____. (Please add $2.50 to this order to cover postage and handling. Minnesota residents add 6% sales tax.) Send Check or money order, no cash or C.O.D.'s. Prices are subject to change without notice.

Name _____

Address _____

City _____ State _____ Zip Code _____

Allow 4 to 6 weeks for delivery.
Quantity discounts available upon request.

Or order by phone: 1-800-848-2793,
1-800-444-5951 (non-metro area of Minnesota)
612-541-0239 (Minneapolis/St. Paul metro area).

Please have your credit card number ready.

Notes

Notes

Notes

Notes